Alessa Johns is an Assistant Professor of English at the University of California, Davis.

Dreadful Visitations

CONFRONTING NATURAL CATASTROPHE
IN THE AGE OF ENLIGHTENMENT

Edited by

Alessa Johns

ROUTLEDGE

NEW YORK AND LONDON

Published in 1999 by
Routledge
29 West 35th Street
New York, NY 10001

Published in Great Britain by
Routledge
11 New Fetter Lane
London EC4P 4EE

LIBRARY OF CONGRESS CATALOGING-IN-PUBLICATION DATA

Dreadful visitations : confronting natural catastrophe in the age of enlightenment / edited by Alessa Johns.
    p. cm.
    Includes bibliographical references and index.
    ISBN 0-415-92175-9. — ISBN 0-415-92176-7 (pbk.)
       1. Natural disasters—History—18th century. I. Johns, Alessa.
    GB5014.D74 1999
    363.34' 09' 033—dc21   98-45499
                                      CIP

Interior designed by Cynthia Dunne

Contents

List of Illustrations

FIGURE 1. Plan of Avola (V. Amico, *Lexicon Topographicum Siculum*, vol. II, Palermo and Catania: P. Bentivenga, 1757–60)

FIGURE 2. Air View of Noto, 1972 (Author)

FIGURE 3. Modern Model of *Gaiola* Construction (J.-A. França, *A Reconstrução de Lisboa e a aquitectura pombalina*, 2d ed., Biblioteca Breve, vol. 12, Lisbon: Instituto de Cultura e Língua, Portuguesa Ministério da Educação e Ciência, 1981)

FIGURE 4. The *Casa Baraccata* (G. Vivenzio, *Istoria de' Tremuoti avvenuti nella provincia di Calabria Ulteriore e nella città di Messina nell'anno 1783, e di quanto nella Calabrie fu fatto per lo suo risorgimento fino al 1787. Preceduta da una teoria, ed istoria generale de' tremuoti*, Naples: Stamperia Regale, 1788)

FIGURE 5. Project for the City of Filadelfia (E. Serrao, *De' tremuoti e della nuova Filadelfia in Calabria*, Naples: Raimondi, 1785)

FIGURE 6. The Veduta of Noto Drawn by Paolo Labisi in the 1760s and Redated 1783 (Formerly in the Biblioteca Comunale di Noto, Now Lost [Author])

Acknowledgments

This volume grew out of a conference I organized at the University of California, Berkeley, held in February 1995 and entitled *Disaster in the Eighteenth Century: Cultural Responses to Natural Catastrophe*. I would like to thank all those who made the meeting such a success and thereby inspired this book: the conference participants; the members of the Bay Area Eighteenth-Century Studies Group; and Eric Chandler, for whose energetic and capable leadership I am especially grateful. My assistant Sharon O'Toole Dubois assiduously researched material for my introductory essay. I am also indebted to Brendan O'Malley, of Routledge, for his fine editorial work and his unflagging interest in the project, and to Daniel Gordon, George Starr, and Alan Taylor for their helpful suggestions and much appreciated support. My parents, Jorun and Donald Johns, and my mother-in-law, Mary Lee Reynolds, helped me through a period of challenges and changes: one of these, my son Gabriel, arrived right in the middle of the project. He and my husband, Christopher Reynolds, have sustained me with their humor, their patience, and their loving companionship.

Introduction

ALESSA JOHNS

An ugly report creeps about that Mr. Hervey and another English gentleman are lost by their curiosity leading them to Mont Vesuvius just as the Eruption broke out . . . (29 April 1766)

You give us no account of Mont Vesuvius, tho' this Erruption is often seen at Naples . . . pray give us news of this extraordinary matter. (30 May 1766)

You never mention Mont Vesuvius no more than if you were not there. (25 December 1767)

—Sarah Byng Osborn to her grandson Jack in Naples,
*Political and Social Letters of a Lady of the
Eighteenth Century 1721–1771,* 1890

From the comfort and security of Chicksands Priory, seventy-three-year-old Sarah Byng Osborn grows impatient with her grandson Jack for news of Vesuvius's eruption. Just how terrifying was it? Did it tragically answer the English gentlemen's questions about the dangers of such a natural phenomenon? How can we account for grandson Jack's uncooperative and persistent silence on a subject so interesting to his grandmother and his countrymen in Italy?

Indeed, it might well have seemed a particularly calamitous period to the people of the eighteenth century. The Bengal famine of 1770 is estimated to have killed ten million; earthquakes in Portugal, Peru, Calabria, and Japan leveled cities, killing tens of thousands of inhabitants, igniting volcanoes, and setting in motion destructive tidal waves that smashed ports and swallowed up entire islands; cyclones in India in 1737 and 1789 claimed hundreds of thousands of lives; avalanches in Switzerland buried whole towns and their populations, among them the faithful of Leukerbad, who gathered for vespers in January 1718 and were crushed under tons of snow; hurricanes made their way through the Caribbean and the Atlantic coast of North America, sweeping away people and property in every decade of the century; and volcanic eruptions killed thousands, witness Vesuvius in Italy, Laki in Iceland—where one-third of the population died in 1783—and Papandayan in Java, where in 1772 three thousand people in mountainside villages were sucked into a lake of lava.[1] Increased trade and traffic made information about disasters widely available, especially in Europe and North America, where newspapers as well as published letters and journals offered vivid accounts that excited the imaginations of writers, politicians, and divines, all of whom chimed in with interpretations about the meanings of these calamitous events. Daniel Defoe is perhaps the best-known European commentator; George Starr analyzes Defoe's work in this volume, offering suggestive reasons why the vivid images from Defoe's writings, many of which were fictional, have so often appeared in general histories of the period: they have provided more evocative representations of eighteenth-century disaster than mere tables and lists could furnish, transporting readers effectively into a scene of devastation by eliciting the sights, smells, and tormenting moral calculations of catastrophe.

Despite the staggering number of disasters and casualties in the eighteenth century and the interest they spawned, however, twentieth-century historians and literary scholars, like Sarah Osborn's grandson Jack, have for the most part ignored the subject of natural disasters, focusing instead on eighteenth-century political and social matters or on the evolution of literary genres and styles. And yet, "viewing human institutions under the stress of a natural disaster provides a test of those institutions that otherwise would be unobtainable from the past," as one scholar has noted.[2] Therefore, this book seeks to redirect historical attention to a topic that once fascinated people of the eighteenth century, a subject that provides new perspectives not only on ways of life and systems of belief in that period but also on those of our own. These essays take a global look at the interpretations of and the reactions to natural disaster that increasing trade, territorial expansion, and changing economic arrangements of the eighteenth century elicited. Since this was an era of colonial relations between European states and much of the rest of the world, studies of catastrophes in North and South America, Asia, and Europe show how natural disaster research helps to trace both the interdependence and the independence of cultures and economies in ways fundamental to the shaping of our own "globalized" world.

Above all, the historical and literary study of natural disasters focuses attention forcefully on the human contributions to catastrophe. As Anthony Oliver-Smith argues, "human groups and institutions play a far more active role in the creation of destructive agents and circumstances than is usually imagined or portrayed."[3] If a disaster is defined as a physical phenomenon—an earthquake, a hurricane, or a flood, for example—affecting a human group adversely, then surely the activities of that human community, both before and after the event, require investigation. The social, political, and economic activities of eighteenth-century societies must therefore be examined to determine the extent to which they delayed or exacerbated disaster.

For example, several essays in this volume demonstrate how the eighteenth-century European expansion of commerce and colonial activity actually increased the susceptibility of non-European trade partners to catastrophe. By having their kinship ties loosened, their health compromised by new diseases, their savings decimated through taxation, and their labor exacted by European governors and trade companies, indigenous people were ill-equipped to grow and store surplus food for themselves, to build or rebuild safely, and to collect the supplies and establish the networks necessary to combat the effects of disasters. David Arnold takes up the Bengal famine of 1770, responsible for the deaths of ten million people, or one-third of the population at the time.[4] While native responses to that catastrophe are scarce, the disaster offers a window on British attitudes: since it was the first major calamity to face the British as rulers of the region, it significantly shaped their view of India as a subject and disaster-prone area better served by extending an ideology of paternalism than by importing emerging European laissez-faire ideas. Charles Walker's examination of the Lima, Quito, and Arequipa earthquakes suggests that ideologies buttressing European control over the indigenous population were actually unsettled in the aftermath of the tremors; ruling elites squabbled as the Indians were forced to pay for the paltry relief extended and to support rebuilding efforts on behalf of the dominant classes. In all these cases, European governors and trade partners looked first to their own profits and largely ignored the vulnerability of native peoples. This is true too of the people of Sicily, as Stephen Tobriner argues; they were ruled by foreign governments more concerned with "economic exploitation and maintaining order" than with legislating measures for mitigating hazards.

An important contrast emerges with regard to Canada. As Alan Taylor reveals, British ambitions there led them to aid rather than exploit or neglect the people in time of dearth: the British sent grain to relieve Canadians' hunger. (That hunger might have been assuaged in the first place had the Canadians diversified their crop rather than focus on wheat, which fetched high prices in the European market.) As it happens, however, across the border in America entrepreneurs sought profit by selling grain to Europeans and flour to Canadians rather than help their own starving compatriots on the frontier. Consequently American grain actually ended up feeding British Loyalists while frontier Americans themselves resorted to boiling bark and foraging for wild leeks.

It was not only through pursuing their economic advantage that individuals and nations aggravated calamity; pride, fear, and a flair for the aesthetic played a part as well. Tobriner points out how the people of Noto, Italy, eventually returned to erecting unsafe structures despite their experience of repeated earthquakes and a knowledge of architectural theories explaining safer building methods. Like the people of Lisbon after them, they at first built squat structures following the earthquake of 1693, only to succumb over the years to constructing edifices higher and closer together, ornamenting facades, and erecting domes and towers. This tendency to weigh risk against the benefit of aesthetic satisfaction and displays of public power reveals that disasters were not solely interpreted as monitory messages from a displeased Deity, despite the plethora of sermons preached to bring the populace to its knees.[5] Tobriner's study also reinforces a conclusion apt to sound familiar to those watching today's television news: that even though they know better, people will be optimistic about their prospects for survival despite building costly homes on earthquake faults and precipitous beachfront cliffs.

Within Europe itself, therefore, some of the most interesting questions raised by eighteenth-century natural disasters center on the limits of optimism in societies technologically advanced but still uncertain that whatever is, is necessarily right. Daniel Gordon discusses how Enlightenment thinkers theorized that fear itself intensified the effects of the plague in Marseilles. While writers of Marseilles developed a story about the unprecedented nature of the disaster and the limits of human knowledge and capacity to deal with the epidemic, the *philosophes* were relying on outmoded theories of plague causation to bolster their idea of rationality, to promote the concept of universal knowledge, and to shore up a project like the *Encyclopédie*. George Starr explains how Daniel Defoe dispassionately calculated the extent to which fear and loss for some meant gain and profit for others. A salient example of the progressive-minded, enlightened individual, Defoe, however, consistently offered religious explanations of calamitous events.

Eighteenth-century European responses to catastrophe thus raise a number of significant issues. First, if the European Enlightenment forms the basis of today's "technocratic" culture, as one commentator has argued,[6] then its views nonetheless continuously reinforced or reacted to notions of divine intervention and supernatural agency. Current discussions of the European Enlightenment tend to emphasize its Baconian method, valorizing a questionable scientific progress: commentators often echo Theodor W. Adorno and Max Horkheimer's dismal appraisal of the Enlightenment celebration of progress, of scientific and industrial innovation.[7] Yet a study of disasters shows that the West was not as unidimensionally rational or technologically adept as the epithet "the Age of Reason" would suggest. This period only shifts the balance between physical and metaphysical explanations of catastrophe.

Indeed, scientific explanations of catastrophe have vied with religious ones throughout Western history, and sometimes the two have been used in tandem; a rational or interventionist approach to catastrophe cannot be said to characterize one era more than another. As early as the sixth-century B.C.E., the Milesian school countered the apocalyptic thinking of its time with theories of the *kosmos*, ascribing such phenomena as thunder, lightning, and earthquakes to the arrangement of the inhabited world and the heavenly bodies surrounding it.[8] Thales, for one, posited that Earth was a vessel floating on water, and that earthquakes resulted from movements of the water.[9] Anaximenes hypothesized that masses of eroding rock would fall and strike other blocks violently. Anaximander is said to have saved Spartan lives by warning the people of an upcoming temblor, which he may have predicted by watching the nervous behavior of animals.[10] Anaxagoras, a later follower of Anaximenes, theorized that air, trapped in underground cavities because of rain blocking the earth's pores, caused rumbling as it sought escape. Aristotle largely concurred with this hypothesis, though he felt the underground winds resulted from the heating and drying of the earth.[11] Later Lucretius, in *De Rerum Natura*, ascribes the cause of earthquakes to underground rivers and wind, and Seneca looks to air in his *Quaestiones Naturales*, where, inspired by the Campaia earthquake of 5 February 63, he surveys the known theories, weighs their merits, and concludes:

> The principal cause of an earthquake is air, swift by nature and changing from place to place. As long as it is not shoved and it lurks in a vacant space, it lies harmless and is no trouble to surrounding areas. When a cause coming from outside stirs it up and pushes it together and drives it into a narrow space, it merely gives way and shifts about if it is still permitted to do so. When the chance of getting away is cut off and it is beset on all sides then "With a mighty

rumbling of the mountain, Around the barriers" it rages, and after beating against these barriers a long time the air pulls them apart and hurls them aside, becoming more violent the stronger the obstacles with which it has struggled.[12]

If such theories fail to resemble "science" as we know it, they nonetheless were rational, systematic interpretations based on observation to counter what were perceived as superstitious explanations of calamities.

Further, in response to these theories the ancients suggested technological solutions: geological trepanning was the commonest form of earthquake prevention. Pliny—who died in the Vesuvius eruption of 79—implies that this might be effective in his *Natural History,* where he points to the ways wells and caves allow "an outlet for the confined breath" within the earth.[13] The applied solution thus involved drilling holes to allow vapors accumulated underground to disperse. This approach was recommended throughout the Renaissance and into the eighteenth century; Tobriner suggests that caves found hollowed out under major structures of the new city of Noto might represent eighteenth-century evidence of this kind of antiseismic architecture.[14] If such a technological expedient was indeed rejected by some medievals—who admonished thinkers for seeking to penetrate God's mysteries[15]—the scientific views of the ancients were nonetheless known and debated at the time. A commentator such as Konrad von Megenberg (who died in 1374) scoffs at the "ridiculous fable" believed by many to explain earthquakes, wherein "the earth rests on a great fish called Celebrant, which grasps its tail in its mouth. When this fish moves or turns, the earth trembles." Instead, he also advocates the theory that vapors collect in subterranean caverns and that "these sometimes gather in such enormous volumes that the caverns can no longer hold them." If the vapors rest for too long underground they can in fact become poisonous and when they escape they bring about pestilence; as Gordon points out, this view of the plague remained viable even into the seventeenth century.[16]

Therefore, while the Enlightenment certainly embraced ideas of progress, of technological innovation and economic expansion, a study of disaster underscores the need for a more nuanced reading of the period's ideological orientations, since a scientific approach to catastrophe can in fact be traced to ancient times and was constantly vying with a religious one. Furthermore, individual predilections, market enticements, political ambitions, and social pressures led communities in the Enlightenment to create institutions that not only served to remedy but also intensified the effects of catastrophes. Since these societies, with all their institutional know-how, did not manage to immunize themselves against the effects of calamity more successfully than non-Western ones, they can effectively be compared with other cultures in this regard. And if documentation for non-Western societies is sometimes scarce and to be found in European rather than Asian or South American archives—with the attendant risk of skewed data and inaccurate interpretations—what we can glean from the evidence of non-Western cultures reinforces the possibility of defining continuities. The study of disaster therefore offers a way of comparing global cultures otherwise perceived as incommensurably different.

The ways these essays emphasize human participation in aggravating hazards suggest that disaster research helps to deconstruct the persistent Western nature-culture dualism; even this short summary demonstrates how the one term depends upon the other. Moreover, that conceptual dichotomy has undergirded other questionable oppositions that these essays expose as well, especially concerning categories of gender and race. For example, Arnold's analysis of the Bengal famine shows how "othering" the non-European by means of a gendered opposition proved especially useful to Europeans seeking justification for colonial enterprises. Indians were portrayed as passive, effeminate victims of the 1770 famine; their alleged inertia in the face of hunger led the British to conclude that Indians were to some extent responsible for their own misery and in need of subjection. Such racial othering served the same colonial purpose in South America, as Walker's analysis of Andean earthquakes makes clear. He argues that the Spanish identified South American Indians and blacks, who proved industrious looters following the Lima earthquake, with a savage nature needing to be tamed. Both these views thus reinforced a picture of the Other as requiring the discipline of "masculine" Europeans.

Current gender debates clarify how persistent such categories have remained in Western, and especially American, culture. Preconceptions about what constitutes a "masculine" response to crisis, for instance, recall the discussions between Lawrence Kohlberg and Carol Gilligan on measuring moral maturity. Kohlberg interpreted boys' responses to crisis situations as mature because they placed greater value on life than on property and accepted the inadequacy of human laws under certain circumstances. This attitude describes the British response to the Indians, whose alleged unwillingness to steal during a famine (Arnold points out that this perception was itself false) rendered them feminine, deficient in moral maturity, because they valued life too little. Carol Gilligan, by contrast, questioned Kohlberg's definition of masculinity and, admittedly remaining within an essentialist gender paradigm, asked how girls' speaking "in a different voice"—one calling for communication and compromise—might not represent the more just reaction to crisis.[17] European responses to Asian and South American sufferers of natural catastrophe in the eighteenth century thus reinforced a conceptual gender and race dichotomy that has been carried into debates in our own time, and they offer occasions for calling such dichotomies into question.

In addition, the sufferers' responses point to the ways natural disasters allow us to trace not only conceptual categories and lines of power but also the consolidation of national identities. Taylor concludes that the 1789 dearth established a Canadian identity based to some extent on direct political intervention, one quite intentionally contrasting with American entrepreneurial and individualist notions across the border. Arnold, as I have suggested, shows how the Europeans identified their trade partners as weak in order to justify imperial dominion. Even within Western Europe, however, international disasters served to demarcate national identities. For instance, Walker points out how the British decried the responses of Spanish colonizers to South American earthquakes in order to pave the way for their own hoped-for control of the region. And

Gordon argues that chroniclers of Marseilles, seeking to establish an identity separate from that of the absolutist French regime, developed a plague rhetoric contrasting with discourses of centralization inscribed by both court and Enlightenment *philosophes.*[18]

To what extent, then, do discourses of catastrophe today reinforce or counter the received perceptions of both disaster and its victims? The dominant perspective, according to geographer Kenneth Hewitt, sees natural disasters as unique, cataclysmic environmental events, unpredictable and severely damaging to the social, physical, and economic life of human communities.[19] In order to return societies to a predisaster status quo, one viewed as "normal," they require development, modernization, technology, and an accompanying technical expertise. This current conventional approach, Hewitt argues, traces its beginning precisely to the development of scientific method in the seventeenth and eighteenth centuries. In this period economies came to favor the development of cities and, as Hewitt claims, the greater the historical or geographic distance a society has "from urban-industrialism, the surer studies of disaster are to find its people to be 'fatalistic,' 'subjective,' and in the thrall of 'mystical,' 'arational' or at least 'pre-scientific' notions." What has emerged is an array of scientific institutions and a "citadel of expertise" that ignores local practices and grassroots ideas.[20]

Hewitt and anthropologist Oliver-Smith proffer an alternative to the conventional approach. From their perspective disasters, rather than being freak events caused by unexpected forces, are ongoing natural agents in an ever-changing world.[21] Seen from this perspective, natural disasters, which have always occurred everywhere in some form or another, elucidate societies' views of the "normal" and the ideological work they will undertake as well as the material conditions they will sustain to reinforce that condition of normalcy. Their alternative view suggests in particular that maintaining a Western standard of living in the first world and then exporting it elsewhere breeds economic forces and market pressures that ultimately work to destroy the global environment, with the implication that natural disaster can appear innocent, even innocuous, in the face of human-made destructive agents such as nuclear accidents, deforestation, and industrial pollution.

Yet while it may naively, even destructively, applaud technological development and the formation of technocratic institutions, the dominant perspective does theoretically provide a foundation for developing a rational, sustainable relationship between human societies and their natural locales. If human beings have brought themselves to the point where human-made disasters can rival natural ones in their destructive power, then, it is hoped, they can also challenge the consequences and reverse some of the damage. Technocracy, while it has indeed led to extremes of specialization—and not merely of scientists and social scientists—need not in every instance represent the deadening force Hewitt and Oliver-Smith suggest. The "experts" as well as local inhabitants can offer crucial knowledge and efficient methods for solving problems associated with natural catastrophes. While warnings about annihilation are surely warranted and necessary in an era of atomic bombs and nuclear accidents, current discussions of catastrophe must convey solid information and accessible ideas for restructuring institutions if we are to avoid simply echoing the apocalyptic predictions of the ages.

Consequently, the essays here seek to offer specialists and nonspecialists alike a historical, culturally embedded perspective on responses to disasters from a period critical to forming the technological outlook of our time. They incline to doubt about whether human beings are in fact capable of viewing calamity not as a freak event but as a necessary geophysical or meteorological adjustment in the cycles of a larger universe. They suggest that historically, people have focused locally and desired above all a community's return to at least a modified form of the preimpact state of affairs. Indeed, those individuals or communities thinking beyond their borders in the eighteenth century most often sought to further hegemonic aims; they offered aid paternalistically in order to strengthen their grip on a devastated region and its people. And perhaps one practical result of a historical view of eighteenth-century calamities is that it urges us to consider whether aid to disaster-stricken areas today occurs more out of altruism or self-interest. Can we argue that nations and relief agencies operate selflessly or even largely in the interests of disaster victims? This question is less a cynical interrogation of psychological and economic motivation or of national ambition than it is a logical first step in defining the most useful and fair responses to unpredictable catastrophes around the world in our own time.

While "globalization" has been touted in the press as the new concept of the late twentieth century, a study of eighteenth-century disaster underscores the profound global interrelationships already in place two to three hundred years ago. Different peoples contended locally with various calamities—famines, earthquakes, and plagues—but the chapters in this volume show that the structure of institutions and psychological responses revealed by the crises point not only to cultural distinctions but also to telling patterns of interdependency and similarity. They raise the question whether the science and commerce intended to avert vulnerability for Europeans actually increased the susceptibility of their trade partners on other continents, in turn generating a Western view of these regions as prone to threatening forces, incapable of securing themselves, and suffering from divine disapprobation. Conversely, non-Europeans sometimes gained a sense of their group interest when disaster struck, and devised methods of resisting further subordination or vulnerability. If globalization finally gains general visibility in the twentieth century via economic ties between nations and continents, it can be traced meaningfully to the eighteenth century by way of cultural responses to ubiquitous natural catastrophes. By looking broadly at disaster in the eighteenth century we are in a better position to interpret "globalization" and to recognize the impact of catastrophe on the world as a whole rather than to view it partially with an isolated focus only on its wealthiest or its worst-hit regions.

NOTES

I would like to thank Daniel Gordon, Brendan O'Malley, Sharon O'Toole Dubois, Christopher Reynolds, and George Starr, all of whom provided helpful suggestions for this introduction.

1 See Lee Davis, *Natural Disasters: From the Black Plague to the Eruption of Mt. Pinatubo* (New York & Oxford: Facts on File, 1992).

2 John C. Burnham, "A Neglected Field: The History of Natural Disasters," *Perspectives: The American Historical Association Newsletter* 26, no. 4 (April 1988): 22–24, quotation 23. Charles Walker's chapter in this collection offers examples: "accounts [of disasters] describe . . . the domestic sphere, discussing sleeping arrangements or spatial divisions, topics rarely mentioned in archival sources. They also open up cloistered areas such as monasteries, providing details on nuns' material and even spiritual life. Natural disasters do not just take us, however, into usually prohibited or obscure physical locations. They also expose belief systems."

3 Anthony Oliver-Smith, "Introduction: Disaster Context and Causation: An Overview of Changing Perspectives in Disaster Research," in *Natural Disasters and Cultural Responses*, ed. Anthony Oliver-Smith, Publication 36 of *Studies in Third World Societies* (1986): 1–34, quotation 8.

4 India suffered severe droughts and famines also in the nineteenth century, as David Arnold discusses in *Colonizing the Body: State Medicine and Epidemic Disease in Nineteenth-Century India* (Berkeley and Los Angeles: University of California Press, 1993).

5 The best-known English example of this type of sermonizing is Thomas Sherlock's *Letter from the Lord Bishop of London, to the Clergy and People of London and Westminster; On Occasion of the Late Earthquakes* (London: John Whiston, 1750), in which he decries the "Wickedness and Corruption" (3) of the city manifested in antireligious publications, popery, homosexuality, and lewd diversions. "Let every Man reform himself, and others as far as his Influence goes," he urges. "This is *our* only proper Remedy; for the dissolute Wickedness of the Age, is a more dreadful Sign and Prognostication of Divine Anger, than even the Trembling of the Earth under us" (17). Other divines seconded Sherlock in preaching repentance and reform; see T. D. Kendrick, *The Lisbon Earthquake* (Philadelphia: J. B. Lippincott, 1955), chap. 1, for a survey of English attitudes.

6 Kenneth Hewitt, "The Idea of Calamity in a Technocratic Age," in *Interpretations of Calamity*, ed. K. Hewitt (Boston: Allen & Unwin, 1983), 3–32, pp. 7, 13, and passim.

7 Max Horkheimer and Theodor W. Adorno, *Dialektik der Aufklärung* (Frankfurt: Fischer, 1969).

8 The Milesian school included Thales, Anaximander, and Anaximenes of Miletos;

Xenophanes of nearby Colophon is often included. See William Mullen, "The Agenda of the Milesian School: The Post-Catastrophic Paradigm Shift in Ancient Greece," in *Natural Catastrophes During Bronze Age Civilisations: Archaeological, Geological, Astronomical and Cultural Perspectives* [British Archaeological Reports], ed. M. E. Bailey, T. Palmer, and B. J. Peiser (Oxford: Archaeopress, 1998). Mullen argues in favor of the "catastrophist" view, suggesting that the Milesian agenda—"1) systematically surveying the cosmos, 2) theorizing about its fundamental elements and processes, and 3) redefining traditional understandings of life and divinity"—itself constituted a response to recent disasters, and that historians holding to the traditional "uniformitarian" theory of the development of Western thought are overlooking the significance of world destructions and the desire to explain destructive phenomena as motivations for such a research agenda. I am grateful to Professors Peiser and Mullen for allowing me to see the article before its publication. In my discussion of ancient theories I have also consulted W. K. C. Guthrie, *A History of Greek Philosophy*, 6 vols. (Cambridge: Cambridge University Press, 1962–1981); G. S. Kirk, J. E. Raven, and M. Schofield, *The Presocratic Philosophers*, 2d ed. (Cambridge: Cambridge University Press, 1983); Richard D. McKirahan, Jr., *Philosophy Before Socrates* (Indianapolis: Hackett, 1994); Charles H. Kahn, *Anaximander and the Origins of Greek Cosmology* (New York: Columbia University Press, 1960); and Frank Dawson Adams, *The Birth and Development of the Geological Sciences* (New York: Dover, 1954). The book by Adams unfortunately contains errors; proceed with caution in using it.

9   According to McKirahan, "in hypothesizing an unobserved natural state of affairs (no one had seen the earth resting on water) to explain an observed phenomenon, Thales was making an intellectual move which has remained a principal part of scientific thinking to this day" (29).

10   For Anaximander's prediction, see Cicero, *De Divinatione* I: 50, 112. Discussed in McKirahan, 33.

11   See Aristotle's *Meteorologica* II: vii–viii, 365a14–369a.

12   Seneca, *Naturales Quaestiones* VI: 18, 1–2, trans. Thomas Corcoran; Lucretius, *De Rerum Natura* VI: 535–600. The theories are cited in Adams, 400 ff.

13   Pliny, *Natural History* II: 82, 192 ff.; trans. H. Rackham.

14   According to Adams, Arnolfo di Cambio (whom he misidentifies as Arnolfo di Lapo, confusing him with the later builder Giovanni di Lapo Ghini), apparently called on this method of earthquake prevention as he constructed the Cathedral of Santa Maria del Fiore in medieval Florence, ordering holes dug around the emerging church to allow air to escape from beneath (413). Adams cites the chronicle of Giovanni Villani— who died in the Black Plague of 1348—but I have not located this description of earthquake prevention in Villani's work or other sources. Adams (405–13) is more specific in his discussion of Renaissance texts, esp. Galesius (Bologna, 1571) and Isnard (Paris, 1758).

15   See for example Alain Ducellier, "Les tremblements de terre balkanique au Moyen Age: aspects matériels et mentaux," in *Les catastrophes naturelles dans l'Europe médiévale et moderne,* ed. Bartolome Benassar (Toulouse: Presses Universitaires du Mirail, 1996), 61–76, who, looking at the Balkans, cites the sixth-century *Christian Cosmography* of Kosmas Indikopleutes and the work of Michel Attaleiates in the eleventh century.

16   Konrad von Megenberg, *Das Buch der Natur,* ed. Franz Pfeiffer (Hildesheim: George Olms, 1962), 107 ff. This book, written in 1349–1350, is called "the first natural history in the German language." Translated passage in Adams, 404–05.

17   Carol Gilligan, *In a Different Voice: Psychological Theory and Women's Development* (Cambridge: Harvard University Press, 1982), 25 ff.; see also Seyla Benhabib's analysis of the debate in "The Generalized and the Concrete Other: The Kohlberg-Gilligan Controversy and Feminist Theory," in Seyla Benhabib and Drucilla Cornell, eds., *Feminism as Critique: On the Politics of Gender* (Minneapolis: University of Minnesota Press, 1987), 77–95.

18   See also Daniel Gordon, "The City and the Plague in the Age of Enlightenment," *Yale French Studies* 92 (1997): 67–87, esp. 80 ff.

19   Hewitt, "The Idea of Calamity in a Technocratic Age," 16.

20   Hewitt 17–18, 20. See also Michael Watts, who draws on the work of W. Leiss and C. Merchant to argue that in the seventeenth century "'nature' became materially and ideologically commoditised, an object of control and domination"; in "On the Poverty of Theory: Natural Hazards Research in Context," in Hewitt, ed., *Interpretations of Calamity,* 231–62, 233.

21   Oliver-Smith, "Disaster Context and Causation," 2.

PART I

European Responses
to Catastrophe

1

Confrontations with the Plague in Eighteenth-Century France

Daniel Gordon

"Cancer": why does it frighten us with its name, as if thereby the unnameable were designated? . . . Here is a cell that doesn't hear the command, that develops lawlessly, in a way that could be called anarchic. It does still more: it destroys the very idea of a program, blurring the exchange and the message. It wrecks the possibility of reducing everything to the equivalent of signs. Cancer, from this perspective, is a political phenomenon, one of the rare ways to dislocate the system, to disarticulate, through proliferation and disorder, the universal programming and signifying power. This task was accomplished in other times by leprosy, then by the plague.

—Maurice Blanchot, *The Writing of the Disaster,* 1986

In the history of modern Europe, certain periods are evocative of progress, while others symbolize the backward condition from which progress supposedly has been made. We are all familiar with the concept of the eighteenth century as an age of "Enlightenment," a period in which the prejudices of the traditional "Old Regime" began to yield to rationality and humanity. But we have also learned to be skeptical of historical schemes that separate ages of light from ages of darkness. Scholarship shows that the relationship between two apparently opposed historical moments is dialectical, not purely adversarial. Every critical movement owes something to the culture against which it stands; it absorbs the energy of its opponent as part of its strategy of combat. From this perspective, one can observe that Voltaire's hatred of the clergy had a messianic tone, or that Rousseau's *Social Contract* expresses absolutism in a democratic form.

Dialectic, however, is not the only technique for questioning the relationship of the Enlightenment to the traditions that it challenged. Another method is inversion—a thought experiment in which one swaps the conventional definitions of a movement and its context, proceeding then to verify, as far as possible, this ironic exchange of meanings. Perhaps the Enlightenment articulated rudimentary ideas about some phenomena that had been conceptualized with great sophistication under the Old Regime. The following discussion aims to show that disaster, specifically the bubonic plague, is a case in point.

The articles on "Plague" in the *Encyclopédie* of Diderot and d'Alembert (the central work of the French Enlightenment) provide good material for an analysis of Enlightenment attitudes toward natural disaster. These articles are complex, but overall they reveal the tendency of thinkers in the French Enlightenment to turn a blind eye toward the ravages of disaster and to insist in a doctrinaire manner that all events are subject to human control. It was not merely the belief in "progress" that produced this tendency to underrate disasters; it was also the specific way in which Enlightenment thinkers construed the locus and mechanics of progress. Progress, in the minds of a broad range of Enlightenment thinkers, occurred in "civil society" understood as a network of exchanges—conversations, commercial transactions—that enriched and civilized humankind.[1] Contagious epidemic diseases were especially difficult to acknowledge in this framework, for contagion represented the perversion of social exchange, the transmission not of wealth, knowledge, or refinement, but of death. As critics of traditional hierarchies, Enlightenment thinkers forged a positive vision of horizontal human action—of all socioeconomic processes in which the goal was not to reproduce the eternal Chain of Being but to create new relationships of mutual service. The phenomenon of contagion, however, imposed a limit upon the benefits of exchange. In the *Encyclopédie*, we can see some representatives of the Enlightenment confronting this limit and struggling to avoid giving it full recognition.

While a refusal to recognize the limits of civil society was a feature of the Enlightenment, a fascination with these limits was common both before the Enlightenment and in other fields of discourse throughout the eighteenth century. A suggestive counterpoint to the *Encyclopédie* is the plague literature—a large corpus of poems, novels, histories, and medical treatises—published in Marseilles in the eighteenth century. As the center of trade between France and the Levant (in which European plague epidemics frequently originated), Marseilles was repeatedly devastated by the dreaded illness. This city was a site of intensive reflection on the causes of the plague and on the relationship of epidemic disease to commercialization. In Marseilles, one can see the formation of an attitude toward disaster that is clearly distinct from Enlightenment thought but that is difficult to classify as either traditional or modern. On the one hand, the Marseilles plague literature is traditional on account of its emphasis on the terrible and uncontrollable nature of natural disasters. On the other hand, this literature is modern because it often portrays the plague as a product of commercial, not divine, agency. The plague literature is thus a form of social analysis, though a more tragic form than what we usually find in the writings of the Enlightenment. The plague literature was also in itself a type of commerce, a set of texts for sale, though the content of these texts did not contribute to the idealization of commerce that was a recurrent theme in the Enlightenment. A fuller comparison of the concept of plague in the *Encyclopédie* and in the Marseilles literature can reveal the nuances of different early-modern attitudes toward disaster as well as the competition among them to fix the meaning of commercial society.

THE WORD *PESTE* BEFORE THE ENLIGHTENMENT

In the first edition of the *Dictionnaire de l'Académie Française* (1694), the word *peste* is defined as: "A contagious illness, a kind of epidemic malady, which is usually caused by a general corruption of the air and which causes a great mortality."[2] It was common in the seventeenth century to attribute epidemic diseases to bad air stemming from either the decomposition of organic matter or from what were called "exhalations" of the earth—putrid gases released from underground by earthquakes. The definition in the *Dictionnaire* also indicates that the plague is contagious. Doctors hotly debated the precise nature of contagion, but on certain points they generally agreed. From the fifteenth century onward, it was accepted that some diseases were transmitted from person to person through physical contact.[3] The contagious nature of *la peste* (which around the middle of the sixteenth century ceased to refer to epidemics in general and came to refer specifically to one disease, the bubonic plague) was rarely questioned. What remained unsolved was the relationship between atmospheric corruption and interhuman contagion. The miasmatic conception of the disease's source did not square easily with observations of its direct transmission from person to person. This incongruity between the disease's imagined causes, on the one hand, and its path of transmission, on the other, opened a space for a broad range of debate about the ultimate nature of the plague and how to prevent and cure it.

However, nearly everyone in late-seventeenth-century Europe—the lay public as well as doctors—recognized that the disease was indeed contagious and highly destructive. The *Dictionnaire* registers the widespread perception of the plague as uncontrollable and devastating when it notes that it "causes a great mortality." In addition, a set of figurative meanings itemized in the *Dictionnaire* shows that the plague was not just a concrete evil but one of the great symbols of misfortune in general. *Plague* signified a specific illness, but the illness was so devastating that the word also functioned more generally as a shorthand for everything that was excessive and irremediable. Thus, one could say of a person whom one hated, "He is a plague." In a severe frost, one could say, "Plague, it's cold!"[4]

Furetière's *Dictionnaire Universel* (1690) offers essentially the same image of the plague: the plague is contagious, dangerous, and symbolic of all suffering that is not susceptible to human control. "Plague: A contagious and generally fatal malady." Furetière adds: "Galen calls the plague a wild beast, the mortal enemy of humankind." He repeats the conventional thesis that the cause of the disease is corruption of the air. He also notes that no remedy is reliable; the best measure is simply to flee. His examples of proper usage of the term refer to plague, war, and famine as the most severe "scourges" of God. Figuratively, he observes, one can describe as plagues the most profound forms of immorality: heresy and libertinage, which corrupt the minds of men.[5] Here the figurative usages are clearly more religious and moral in tone than those in the Académie's dictionary, but the use of the word *plague* to establish the extremity of an evil is evident in both dictionaries.

Let us pass from these two French dictionaries, the most comprehensive and authoritative in the late seventeenth century, to the *Encyclopédie* of Diderot and d'Alembert, which was an attempt to create an alternative and more authoritative dictionary based on principles of reason. That the *Encyclopédie* (which began to appear in 1751) was nothing other than an effort to propagate a rational lexicon is evident from its subtitle: *Dictionnaire raisonné des sciences, des arts et des métiers, par une société de gens de lettres* (A Systematic Dictionary of the Sciences, Arts, and Professions by a Society of Men of Letters). Older French dictionaries were based on the standard of "usage." They registered the meaning of the term in a Wittgensteinian sense: the meaning must be derived from the examples already established by a community of speakers in France. That is why the abstract definitions are followed by complete sentences in which the term is commonly employed. It is true that the usages of the court and of other areas of "polite" society counted more than the usages of the poor. Yet popular proverbs and everyday expressions of ordinary people are not entirely absent, even in the dictionary of the elitist Académie Française.

In the older dictionaries, to define a term meant to reveal the rules of its usage; in contrast, for the *Encyclopédie*, to define a term was to systematize it, to assign it a permanent denotation consistent with the definitions of other things, not merely to collect its actual usages. The *Encyclopédie* imposes definitions; it does not distill them from preexisting conventions. According to Diderot, the purpose of the *Encyclopédie* was to form a "universal vocabulary" in which terms would designate "the essential attributes of things" through "exact, clear, and precise" definitions.[6] Authority thus inheres not in a community of speakers external to the text but in the definitions themselves and the men of letters whose function was, in the words of d'Alembert, "to fix the use of language" and to "legislate for the rest of the nation in matters of philosophy and taste."[7] Another way of stating the same thing is to say that while the older dictionaries tended to collect meanings from the social environment, the *Encyclopédie* tended to exclude them. It sought to improve reality by reducing the sense of each word to a single clear denotation.

At this point, it would seem appropriate to compare the definitions of *plague* in the *Encyclopédie* with those examined above. But there is a more nuanced way to reveal the process by which the *Encyclopédie* attempted to limit the sense of terms. This approach is to compare the way the word *plague* is discussed in the articles devoted to it in the *Encyclopédie* to the way the word is used incidentally in all other articles of the *Encyclopédie*. In this manner, one can detect a tension not merely between the *Encyclopédie* and previous dictionaries but within the language of the *Encyclopédie* itself: a tension between the rationalization of attitudes toward disaster in the main articles and the persistent use of older usages elsewhere in the text.

In more formal terms, while author A might define word X in a certain fashion, there was no way to coordinate all the other contributors to the *Encyclopédie* so that those who uttered X in their respective articles would stick to A's definition. From a logical viewpoint, the goal of the *Encyclopédie*, to create a new and self-consistent lexicon, could have reached fruition only by having every author write his article after all the other ones were written—a logical impossibility that the older dictionaries were not subject to!

Systematic attention to all occurrences of the word *peste* and its variants (*pestiféré, pestilentiel,* etc.) bears out this hypothesis of a discrepancy between the primary definitions of plague and the incidental usages of the word throughout the text. The word *peste* and its variants occur 581 times in the *Encyclopédie*. Of these, 137 occur in the main articles on "Peste." The rest, or more than three-quarters of the occurrences, are incidental usages in other articles that are not primarily devoted to the subject of plague.[8] Needless to say, many of the contexts hold little interest, such as when an author states that a certain person died of the plague in a certain year. But if one pays close attention to occurrences that are not merely statements of historical fact, occurrences in which *plague* refers not to one incidence of the disease but to the malady in general, then it is evident that many contributors to the *Encyclopédie* continued to envision the plague as it had been envisioned earlier: as a highly contagious, destructive, and terrifying disease, a symbol of everything that creates chaos and sorrow. Before turning to the main entries on plague, we will consider some of these incidental usages.

Concerning the extremely lethal nature of the plague itself, we are told, in one article, that the plague is so swift and deadly that people often collapse and expire suddenly on the streets.[9] Another author refers to famine and the plague as the two most "cruel" calamities.[10] In an article on monasteries and convents, we learn that these institutions have corporate identities that are perpetual and that continue even when all the members suddenly die—as sometimes happens in wars and in plague epidemics.[11] The pairing of war and plague in this context shows that the two are assumed to be recognizable to readers as extreme disasters, events that are capable of erasing the entire membership of a religious community.

In other articles, the authors refer to the plague as the ultimate disaster, only to suggest that some underrated problem is equally harmful to the human race. One author, for example, affirms that smallpox "creates as much destruction as the plague."[12] Another states that angina "makes more people perish than the plague."[13] Here again it is clear that the authors assume that readers already regard the plague as extraordinarily lethal. When they liken other afflictions to the plague, they are trying to confer upon these afflictions the mortal mystique of the plague.

Several articles dealing with medicines and other techniques for warding off diseases refer to the plague. Often the point is to suggest how potent the antidisease agent is, or how powerful people's faith in the agent is. To show that something was effective against plague, or that some people considered it to be so, was a way to stress the importance of the antidote in question. The author of "Amulet" observes that some people believe the charms to be so effective that they protect even against the plague.[14] In "Litanies" (meaning here "religious processions"), the author highlights the enormous confidence that some people placed in these rituals by noting that they considered it a proper way to soften God's wrath in times of plague.[15] In the article "Music, Effects of," the author notes that the ancients attributed so much power to music that they believed it could cure the plague.[16]

In these articles the authors do not mock or reject popular belief in charms and processions. But in other articles the authors do question the credulity of the populace—notably in the article "Flagellants," in which the author ridicules the "insane zeal" and "fanaticism" of those who think that flagellation is a way to end the plague.[17] It might be interesting to study systematically the attitudes expressed in the *Encyclopédie* toward popular pagan and Christian practices. For the purposes of this analysis, however, it does not matter whether the authors criticize popular beliefs, approve of them, or report on them neutrally. What matters is that plague is constantly evoked as the limit-case of disaster, as the worst imaginable affliction. An author wishing to stress the potency of a cure would refer to plague as the ultimate challenge in the field of medicine, just as an author wishing to stress the superstitions of the populace would refer to the plague to show the vastness of popular credulity.

Figurative usages of the word *plague* further illustrate that the plague appears in the *Encyclopédie* as a symbol of evil. "Plague" was the instinctively employed shorthand for everything pernicious: the very paradigm of disaster. The author of "Christianity" states: "Fanaticism is a plague that periodically spreads germs capable of infecting the earth."[18] And the author of "Poland" affirms that slavery is a "civil plague."[19]

Two features of such usage are worth noting. The first is that an inversion of values is taking place in the *Encyclopédie*. Furetière used *plague* to designate heresy as evil. The author just cited on fanaticism, in contrast, used it to portray excessive religious passion as evil. The second is that the figurative usage of *plague* to portray unequal social relations (e.g., slavery) as disasters appears to be unprecedented before the *Encyclopédie*. Both points verify the typical conception of the Enlightenment as a secularizing movement that called hierarchical institutions into question. But throughout this change, reference to the plague as the ultimate metaphor for evil remains constant. The discourse of plague-as-disaster was thus a sort of fixed spot around which an ideological arc could be described. *Plague* was indeterminate in its referents, but it was stable as the epitome of mass suffering.

Now, if we turn to the articles in the *Encyclopédie* wholly devoted to plague, and especially to the way the last great plague epidemic in French history (that of Marseilles in 1720) is represented in these articles, we can detect an impulse to eliminate plague as the master symbol of evil. At times, it is true, the plague is presented as a paradigm of disaster, but it is also evoked as a model of humankind's irrational fear of disaster. Overall, one can detect a tension between the optimism and rationalism of the *Encyclopédie*, on the one hand, and the classically morbid associations of plague, on the other.

There are three articles on "Peste." One of these, "Peste d'Orient," is a brief entry about a specific epidemic in the sixth century. In a gruesome account of the epidemic that draws directly on the contemporary narrative by Procopius, the author states that the disease annihilated entire towns; it was unstoppable and attacked everyone, regardless of sex, age, and temperament.[20] Another article, "Peste (Médecine)," also stresses the lack of human mastery over the disease. "Indeed, it is the cruelest of all evils. Everyone shudders at the mere name of this illness."[21] The author traces the gruesome symptoms of fever, convulsions, vomiting, and dementia. As for the source of the malady, the author notes that the plague stems from bad air but confesses that its exact nature remains a mystery:

> One must conclude from everything that has been said about the plague that this malady is totally unknown in its causes and treatment, and that experience has only too well instructed us in its fatal effects.[22]

The plague thus appears to be a lesson about the limits of human knowledge.

"However," the same article also affirms, "the plague is not always so dangerous as one commonly imagines." The author seems to shift the grounds of interpretation. "The essential thing is not to panic in times of plague; death spares those who show it disdain and pursues those who are afraid of it." And now occurs the first reference to the Marseilles epidemic of 1720:

> Not all the inhabitants of Marseilles perished from the plague, and fear killed more of them than the illness. The plague does not produce such great losses among the Turks and the other peoples of the Orient who are accustomed to it as epidemics produce here, even though they take few or no precautions—and this is because they are not afraid.[23]

It was commonly believed among educated Europeans in the eighteenth century that Muslims and other peoples of the East fatalistically accepted all events as part of a divine plan. Hence, according to the author of this article in the *Encyclopédie*, these peoples did not panic in the face of disasters. His point, then, is that most of those who died in Marseilles died of fear, not the plague per se.

Whether this section occurred to the anonymous author as an afterthought or was inserted by an editor is unclear. In either case, it throws the article into strange contradiction with itself and with the whole image that appears elsewhere in the *Encyclopédie* of the plague as a disaster of the highest order. When the author first notes, "Everyone shudders at the mere name of this malady," it is clear that people shudder on account of the horrifying and uncontrollable nature of the illness. For he adds, "This fear is only too well founded; a thousand times more fatal than war, it [the plague] kills more people than fire and sword."[24] Yet when commenting on the Marseilles plague in particular, the text reverses the logic: it is not death that makes the word *plague* fearful but only fear of plague that makes death on a large scale.

How to explain this curious inversion of the whole relationship between consciousness and disaster? It seems that something about Marseilles and its devastating epidemic[25] did not fit well into the *Encyclopédie*. A clue to where the problem came from is embedded in the third article on plague, entitled "Peste (Histoire ancienne & moderne)." While the other articles are unsigned, this one is signed by the Chevalier de Jaucourt. Jaucourt was one of the most prolific contributors to the *Encyclopédie*. Among his articles are those on "Society" and "Sociability"—articles that are excellent illustrations of the Enlightenment tendency, noted above, to idealize commerce and exchange.[26] "The last plague we have seen in Europe," he writes, "was that of Marseilles in 1720 and 1721. It carried off in this one city about fifty thousand people; the memory of it is still fresh."[27]

"The memory of it is still fresh": But what was the nature of this memory? It seems that the author himself knew, but did not wish to give weight to the local memory of disaster:

> There is no shortage of books on the plague. The amount of writing on it is so vast that a collection of authors who have written treatises about it would form a little library. The Marseilles plague alone has produced more than two hundred volumes which have already fallen into oblivion. In a word, of so many works on this horrible malady, one can scarcely count a dozen that are worth consulting.[28]

Jaucourt's assertion that we can ignore the hundreds of works on the Marseilles plague is a sign that the subject held interest for others but that he himself regarded it as antithetical to the purposes of the *Encyclopédie*.

In fact, a closer look at the plague discourse that arose in Marseilles reveals a disaster-centered outlook that had to be repudiated in order for the *Encyclopédie* to implement one of its fundamental goals: to create an equivalence between signs and the things signified such that the sharpening of language within the *Encyclopédie* would be tantamount to the improvement of the world. While references in the *Encyclopédie* to the Marseilles epidemic tamed the word *plague*, depriving it of deadly power among humans who dare to treat disease with disdain, the authors from Marseilles, in contrast, intensified the deadly meaning of plague by creating a corpus of tragic narratives—a set of stories in which modern society cowered before the superior being of disaster. This literature thwarted all conceptions of progress and even suggested that it was precisely those places at the forefront of commercial advancement that were most vulnerable to devastation by an uncontrollable force.

Conceptualizing Plague in Marseilles

When Antonin Artaud, in 1934, described the plague as "a superior disease" that "reveals the dark powers to men," he was speaking as an avant-garde critic who wanted to see disaster reenacted on the theatrical stage.[29] But he was also reiterating a traditional fascination with the metaphysics of disaster that he had imbibed as a native son of Marseilles. When a student at the College of the Sacred Heart in Marseilles, Artaud must have been exposed to stories of the plague of 1720, for the devotion of the Sacred Heart in Marseilles owed its origins to this epidemic when Bishop Belsunce, on 1 November 1720, dedicated the city to this cult in atonement for its sins.[30]

Artaud, in fact, began his famous manifesto, "The Theater and the Plague," with an account of the 1720 epidemic. He then offered the plague as a model for the experience of theater, arguing that like the plague, the theater ought to break down static conventions and "return the mind to the origins of its inner struggles."[31] For Artaud, theater ought to be like the plague—an "absolute crisis" that destroys all normal relationships and moral rules and that refuses to conform to the rational calculations that usually allow humans to make the world into whatever they want it to be.[32]

The notion of plague as crisis is one of the legacies of the Marseilles epidemic of 1720, but for that reason it is still a suggestive starting point for examining the epidemic in historical terms. Scholars have often refused to treat the plague as a crisis and have instead reduced it to the statics of the method known as "social history." For example, Paul Slack, the leading historian of the plague in early-modern England, states in the theoretical introduction to his *The Impact of Plague*, "Sudden disastrous events such as epidemics illuminate many facets of the societies with which they collide."[33] By implication, the epidemic does not modify society but merely highlights its stable structures, such as class antagonisms and professional boundaries.[34] Indeed, Slack also notes, "Extreme reactions tell us something about normality. The divisions [that arise during an epidemic] occur along preexisting fissures in the social fabric, and the social norms which are broken or exaggerated leave people's most fundamental loyalties and assumptions exposed to view."[35]

For historians like Slack, working with a method that presupposes an inertia in the social structure, the plague is catastrophic only in the sense of bringing about the deaths of many people, not in the sense of forcing people to confront realities that shock and disorient them. That is why it is so intriguing when Artaud insists that the plague breaks out of the mold of social normality. A "frenzied pointlessness" emerges and the behavior of people loses its predictability. "The lewd become chaste. The miser chucks handfuls of gold out of the windows."[36] And finally, Artaud points to the possibility of a moral transformation that is excluded in normal times. The plague "shakes off stifling material dullness" and reveals "a hidden strength to men, urging them to take a nobler, more heroic stand in the face of destiny than they would have assumed without it."[37]

We are now able to articulate a dilemma as to how to approach the 1720 epidemic: as a case study in social history, or as crisis? It is true that any complete history would have to begin with an account of the social conditions of Marseilles prior to 1720. It would also not have to rule out in advance the possibility of structural continuities during the epidemic. But it would certainly be more interesting to focus on the reversal of normal conditions. The flight of doctors and midwives; the emptying out of the poorhouses and asylums to make way for the sick; the liberation of galley slaves in exchange for their services in removing corpses from the streets; the shutting down of criminal courts and the transfer of judicial power to a special commander of the city; the emergence of novel religious practices such as the Sacred Heart—these were extraordinary events and procedures, not old structures.[38]

In *The Normal and the Pathological*, Georges Canguilhem drew attention to the idea, prevalent in nineteenth- and early-twentieth-century biology, that pathology is significant primarily for what it reveals about normality. In this view, disease assists the study of normal conditions and does not fundamentally alter the framework of existence.[39] According to Canguilhem, this medical approach stemmed from the influence of classical physics on biology. A system that regards all movement in nature as governed by constant laws has no place for the older Aristotelian conception of a distinct pathological mechanics. The assumption made by social historians of disease, that epidemics are of interest on account of the normal social structures that they bring into relief, appears to rest on the same epistemology—a conception of knowledge as a set of propositions about permanent facts. Canguilhem, however, argues for more attention to disease as something sui generis, and historians would do well to follow this suggestion.

For the purposes of this chapter, which makes no claim to sketching a complete history of the Marseilles epidemic, it is not necessary to resolve the problem of how to balance structural readings of an epidemic with readings that portray epidemics as crises. Since our purpose is to identify a counterpoint to the articles on plague in the *Encyclopédie*, it is enough to note that in eighteenth-century Marseilles a literature arose, for the first time in France, that formulated the meaning of the plague as a crisis in commercial society. These were the hundreds of works that the author in the *Encyclopédie* referred to with derision.

Authors from Marseilles took a morbid pride in the devastation of their city by the plague. In spite of its terrible toll, the disaster offered a blessing: it restored civic consciousness to a city that had been violently stripped of its autonomy in the previous century. Up to the mid-seventeenth century, Marseilles was a highly independent city, electing its own officials and maintaining its own militia. In 1660 Louis XIV opened a breach in the city's walls and symbolically rode in as conqueror. The city's constitution was rewritten and drained of its republican features. To appease the notables, Louis XIV turned the city into the only duty-free port in southern France, thus ensuring its career as the leading center of seaborne trade in the country. Marseilles rapidly achieved commercial greatness, but a nostalgia for independence still lingered.[40]

In 1720, Marseilles recovered its lost autonomy, though only in an ephemeral way. The city was thrown upon its own resources during a period when it was cordoned off from the rest of the country. The municipal officials came to exercise their old powers. In addition, the plague provided the city with an emblem of distinction, albeit a negative and gruesome one. The plague, in other words, represented a crisis that pointed to the limits of the absolutist state and the commercial system imposed on the city. Louis XIV had destroyed the old walls that marked Marseilles as a separate community. He had tried to make Marseilles into a nodal point in the national economy. But the plague once again demarcated Marseilles as a locality whose separateness had to be respected.

Modern history shows that when a community is in the process of being integrated into a larger entity, when the boundaries of its existence are no longer clear, it may claim a disaster as its title of distinction, as a sign of its differences in relation to those whom it is in fact coming more and more to resemble. The example of the Jews, who have created a Holocaust literature at the same time that they have become assimilated more than ever before into non-Jewish communities, is a clear case of this use of disaster in recent times. The creation of a plague literature in Marseilles may well be the first case of this kind—the first instance in which disaster was used as an emblem of pride to counteract the homogenizing tendencies of modernity.

Beginning in 1720, writers in Marseilles dwelled on the plague to a degree that French writers had never done before. Previously, accounts of the plague had figured episodically in French literature—a chapter in a chronicle, a scene in an epic poem. Now the plague became the framework for the entire action of novels, histories, and other genres. The disaster, in short, became the plot. Contemporaries were conscious of the surge in plague literature and commented upon it. Jean-Baptiste Bertrand, a physician and author of the *Relation historique de la peste de Marseille* (1721), devoted a chapter of his book to what he called "the literary history of our plague"—a summary of the odes, pastoral letters, epistles, and histories that had already been printed since 1720.[41] The writing of plague literature did not cease when the epidemic came to an end but instead institutionalized itself and continues even to this day. A new novel on the 1720 epidemic appears in Provence about every five years. The nuances vary but the lessons are the same. The story has never escaped from its original mode of commemoration in which Marseilles, having been subjugated by the absolutist state, emerges once again through disaster.

One of the most interesting of these founding texts is Bertrand's *Relation historique* itself. When the plague struck Marseilles, Bertrand was one of the twelve doctors in the city's College of Physicians. (The college was not an educational institution but the guild of physicians licensed to practice in the city. Marseilles had twelve doctors for a population of about 85,000.) Bertrand had studied medicine in Avignon and entered the Marseilles college in 1708. The next year, during the great frost of 1709, he was one of four doctors working in the Hôtel-Dieu, or royal hospital in Marseilles, and the only one who remained at his post at the peak of the disaster. He served again during the plague of 1720, though he lost his wife and two daughters to the epidemic.[42]

Bertrand's *Relation historique* has a few features that distinguish it from the corpus of plague literature in Marseilles as a whole. It is longer than most works. Its five hundred pages narrate in great detail not only the unfolding of the plague and the town government's responses to it but also controversies among doctors over the nature of the illness and popular reactions to events. The work was clearly a commercial success, judging by the fact that it went through several editions both in French and English in the 1720s and that it was reprinted later in the century too.[43] But while its comprehensiveness and success mark Bertrand's *Relation historique* as a special book, its manner of representing the epidemic, or what we might call its plague rhetoric, is largely identical to other accounts of the Marseilles plague.

One feature of this rhetoric is the theme of uniqueness—the supposedly unprecedented nature of the disaster in Marseilles. According to Bertrand, the plague is the worst kind of catastrophe, and the Marseilles plague is the worst of all known instances of this special illness. He begins by emphasizing that his story will be a tale of "ravages" and "disorders," for "of all public calamities, the plague is consistently the most cruel and terrible. War and famine present nothing so horrible as what one sees in a city afflicted with this misfortune."[44] Bertrand reviews the entire history of the plague in Europe, including the great European-wide epidemic of the mid-fourteenth century. Yet, he concludes that the Marseilles plague is the most destructive of all time. "Indeed, no matter how horrible may seem the picture I have just given of the plague's dire results, it is just a feeble sketch of those which have afflicted this city."[45] Elsewhere he calls the Marseilles epidemic "the most cruel massacre that has ever been seen." And near the end of the book he concludes: "All we have to say about the nature of the malady is that there had never been one so malign, more contagious, or more fatal; and I dare to affirm that of all cases that historians report, that medical writers describe, and that our merchants and seamen have seen in different countries of the Levant— none has ever progressed so rapidly or produced such violent effects as this one."[46]

A second feature of the plague rhetoric is the theme of social stoppage and breakdown. As Bertrand portrays it, the plague is a spectacular cessation of activity in an otherwise mobile metropolis. The plague changes a vibrant and productive community into a solitary and frozen one: "In just a few days, it can turn the most populous and opulent city into a horrifying desert." At the economic level, "the contagion brings a halt to commerce in a city; it seems to dissolve society."[47] Describing the high point reached by the epidemic in August 1720, Bertrand affirms:

> One no longer found any shops open, all projects, public and private, ceased; commerce had long since been prohibited; the churches, the schools, the business exchange, and all public places were closed, religious ceremonies were suspended, the courts of justice shut down. There was no longer communication among relatives and friends, no more society.[48]

Images like these show that "commerce" and "society" are not absolute. The plague, as represented by Bertrand, reveals the contingent aspects of civil society's existence and the superiority of nature over the economy.

Another way of characterizing Bertrand's plague rhetoric is to say that it is, essentially, a discourse about human limits. This is particularly clear in his analysis of the causes of the disease. Bertrand's understanding of the etiology of the plague was remarkably prescient. In another work, *Observations faites sur la peste qui règnent à présent à Marseille* (1722), he delineated a theory that plague is caused by tiny organisms, which he called "insects."[49] This theory was novel at the time and contradicted the prevailing theories attributing the plague to bad air. Bertrand, who did not use a microscope, deduced the existence of organisms too tiny to see from two observations. The first observation was that when the plague attacks someone, it stays with the person for many days or weeks. The second observation was that the plague passes rapidly from one victim to another. Bertrand reasoned that the only way to explain this paradox is to assume that the cause of the plague is a living entity that reproduces.[50] Thus, it can simultaneously infest one person and spread to another.

It is possible to imagine a book on the history of disease in which Bertrand figures as a pioneering scientist, a man who was ahead of his time with his understanding of pathogenic microorganisms. But that is not the book Bertrand himself wrote. Although he did reiterate his insect theory in the *Relation historique*, he did not claim to have a deep understanding of the disease. Instead, he emphasizes the limits of humankind's knowledge of the plague. The exact nature of the insects, he notes, is a mystery. Hence there is no cure: "Modern ideas are of no use against the plague."[51] The disease even frustrates detection, for the variety of symptoms frequently makes it impossible to identify the plague in individuals before an epidemic breaks out on a large scale.[52] Bertrand also dwells on the fact that humans unwittingly spread the disease through innocent activities. There is no way to sort out safe situations from dangerous ones.[53] Like other authors from Marseilles,[54] he notes that commerce, the very source of the city's prosperity, can turn into a vehicle of destruction at any time.[55]

Thus, while Bertrand may have been one of the most subtle plague doctors of his age, he was also epistemologically the most modest. "This malady eludes every science and the capacity of the finest minds."[56] Both his medical and historical writings portrayed the plague as a disaster that overwhelmed the human intellect and the institutions of commercial society. It is interesting to consider that Bertrand's works belong to the set of writings that Jaucourt had in mind when he referred with disdain to the "two hundred volumes" on the Marseilles plague that had fallen into oblivion. The *Encyclopédie*, of course, was not yet under way when Bertrand wrote, so we have no reaction from him to that work. The ideas in the *Encyclopédie*, however, did not appear out of nowhere. And it seems that an important doctor who influenced the plague discourse of the *Encyclopédie* was precisely the person with whom Bertrand did carry on extensive polemics.

The figure in question was François de Chicoyneau, dean of the renowned Montpellier Medical Faculty at the time of the Marseilles plague and later a physician at the court of Versailles. Chicoyneau was the head of a group of doctors at Montpellier who insisted that the plague was not contagious at all. This theory attracted much attention and criticism, for, as noted earlier, nearly all doctors in France perceived the plague to be contagious, regardless of other differences of interpretation concerning the exact nature of the disease. According to Chicoyneau, the source of the plague was nothing other than fear of the plague. Other doctors had noted that fear could compound the sufferings of plague victims, but Chicoyneau's theory was more radical because it reduced the plague entirely to psychosomatic dimensions.

In a ceremonious lecture delivered at the beginning of the 1722 academic year at Montpellier, Chicoyneau explained:

> Briefly, gentlemen, the concept of contagion gives birth to fear, or a conviction that one will be attacked; from this fear, a perpetual imbalance of the mind; from this imbalance, a quivering of the brain; from this quivering a vertigo and a strong belief that illness and death are not far off; from this belief a growth of terror; from this a stoppage of the blood and lymph or the blockage of fluids and solids; from this blockage, inflammations and gangrene; and finally the plague and death, which arrive sooner or later in accordance with the degree of terror.[57]

Chicoyneau had expounded these ideas even during the plague of 1720, and that is why Bertrand, whose work is free of polemics in general, singled out Chicoyneau and the Montpellier faculty for "contradicting the most natural conceptions of the malady" and "finding terror to be the only cause of the illness."[58]

It will require more research to determine how Chicoyneau arrived at his conceptions and why he maintained them so imperiously during the 1720s. While much work has been done on the history of medicine in France during the period shortly before and during the Revolution of 1789, there is little scholarship for the early decades of the eighteenth century. It seems that the debate about contagion played into urban rivalries between Marseilles and Montpellier. In this contest, doctors from Marseilles aggrandized the significance of their city's experience by turning the history of the plague into a field where an absolute force revealed its power to humankind. The Montpellier doctors blamed the people of Marseilles for their own suffering and seem to have taken pride in the absolute power of medicine to explain and solve the most dreaded of diseases.

By the middle of the eighteenth century, the ideas of the Montpellier doctors on the relationship between terror and plague were clearly out of favor. This is evident from the fact that after the 1740s no medical treatises on the plague took Chicoyneau's position. (Chicoyneau himself also stopped defending the position, at least in writing, after the 1720s.) For this reason, it is peculiar to find in the *Encyclopédie* an account of the Marseilles epidemic that is an only slightly attenuated version of Chicoyneau's account ("The essential thing is not to panic . . . fear killed more of them than the illness").

We have thus reached a point where we can see that the conception of plague in the *Encyclopédie* was not more scientifically advanced than conceptions of the plague outside of the Enlightenment. Moreover, the *Encyclopédie* seems to echo Chicoyneau's views not on account of their scientific merits but on account of their ideological affinity with the project of the *Encyclopédie* itself. For Chicoyneau's theory upheld the constitutive role of discourse in the making of the plague. It offered the possibility of ameliorating the world by modifying humankind's linguistic habits. His theory also emphasized human will and reason and minimized the uncontrollable nature of disaster—a perspective that fit well into the voluntaristic program of the *Encyclopédie*. Finally, the theory that the plague had more to do with fear than with contagious organisms preserved the ideal image of economic growth that both absolutist and Enlightenment thinkers articulated in the eighteenth century. Bertrand and other authors from Marseilles had stigmatized commerce as a vector of disease, but Chicoyneau's theory left the blessings of capitalist development intact.

CONCLUSION

Before criticizing the Enlightenment as a whole for denying the significance of disaster, we should note that the *Encyclopédie* is not a register of all Enlightenment thought. The most sophisticated thinkers of the Enlightenment often defy generalizations about the movement, generalizations based on collective projects such as the *Encyclopédie*, or the works of influential but less complex authors. Voltaire, for example, emphasized the uncontrollable nature of disasters, including the plague. "You have seen earthquakes, but tell me, young lady, have you ever had the plague?"[59] These words of the old woman in *Candide* suggest that no disaster compares to the plague. References to the horrors of plague, in fact, occur in many of Voltaire's other writings as well.[60]

But if the articles on plague in the *Encyclopédie*, with their tendency to belittle disaster, do not offer a measure of the most sophisticated thinkers in the Enlightenment, they do suggest a definition for what that intellectual sophistication is. The greatest figures of the Enlightenment were those few who upheld liberal theories of progress but who also questioned the limits of these theories in extreme situations. Voltaire, then, is a great thinker because he dared to dwell on events that contradicted his own liberal reformism.

But Voltaire, like Defoe in England, was an exception—a rare case of a champion of commercial development who also had an obsession with disaster. Overall, it is fair to speak of a tendency in the Enlightenment to deny the significance of disaster, and it is worth reflecting on the legacy of this tendency today, for in the late twentieth century, we have been living through a kind of second Enlightenment. The fall of communist regimes in Russia and Eastern Europe has revitalized the image of capitalism as the last happy stage of universal history. The increasing emphasis given to the values of health and longevity has created seemingly objective reference points (average income, average lifespan, and so forth) with which Western societies can repeatedly measure and proclaim their own supposed progress. But while the curves on charts measuring prosperity and health may continue to rise, the lives of individuals will always be embedded to some degree in misfortunes whose meaning cannot be registered by statistics. If we define the literature of disaster as the art of portraying those painful events that do not fit into the positive self-images of modernity, than it is clear that this literature arose in the eighteenth century, when the idea of progress first appeared, and that it has been struggling ever since to counterbalance the tendency to idealize commercial and technological change. In the case of Marseilles, the literature of disaster had some parochial and self-serving features, but perhaps we ought to value it nonetheless. For by reminding us that the Age of Enlightenment had its dark side, it forces us to consider the fact that our age does too. Indeed, once the eighteenth century is critically conceptualized in relationship to disaster, our own time, which owes many of its most optimistic values to this period, begins to look different. The study of past disasters and the philosophical responses to them can help us to see the present with more detachment and to think about the limits of our own social objectives with more humility.

NOTES

1   On the concepts of civil society, commerce, and exchange, see Daniel Gordon, *Citizens Without Sovereignty: Equality and Sociability in French Thought, 1670–1789* (Princeton: Princeton University Press, 1994); Dena Goodman, *The Republic of Letters: A Cultural History of the French Enlightenment* (Ithaca, NY: Cornell University Press, 1994); Albert Hirschman, *The Passions and the Interests: Political Arguments for Capitalism Before Its Triumph* (Princeton: Princeton University Press, 1977); Keith Michael Baker, "Enlightenment and the Institution of Society: Notes for a Conceptual History," in *Main Trends in Cultural History*, ed. W. Melching and W. Velema (Amsterdam, 1994), 95–120.

2   *Dictionnaire de l'Académie Française* (Paris, 1694), "Peste."

3   Charles-Edward Amory Winslow, *The Conquest of Epidemic Disease* (Princeton: Princeton University Press, 1944), 117–60.

4   *Dictionnaire de l'Académie Française*, "Peste."

5   Antoine de Furetière, *Dictionnaire Universel* (The Hague, 1690), "Peste."

6   Denis Diderot, "Encyclopédie," in *Encyclopédie*, vol. 4 (1754), 635.

7   Jean le Rond d'Alembert, *Essai sur la société des gens de lettres et de grands*, cited by Keith Baker, *Inventing the French Revolution* (Cambridge: Cambridge University Press, 1990), 116.

8   I am grateful to the Project for American Research on the Treasure of the French Language (ARTFL) at the University of Chicago for allowing me to use its computer-readable version of the *Encyclopédie*. The research was done with ARTFL's word search program, which tracks the occurrences of specific words, or words with a common root. In this case, the search was for all words beginning with the letters *pest*—and all occurrences were checked afterward to ensure that no extraneous terms were included.

9   *Encyclopédie,* "Acre" [Acrid], vol. 1 (1751), 113.

10   "Leyde" [Leiden], vol. 9 (1765), 451.

11   "Communauté" [Ecclesiastical Communities], vol. 3 (1753), 717.

12   "Inoculation" [Inoculation], vol. 8 (1765), 771.

13   "Esquinancie" [Angina], vol. 5 (1755), 978.

14   "Amulette" [Amulet], vol. 1 (1751), 383.

15   "Litanies" (Litanies), vol. 9 (1765), 586.

16   "Musique, effets de la" [Music, effects of], vol. 10 (1765), 906.

17   "Flagellants" [Flagellants], vol. 6 (1756), 833.

18   "Christianisme" [Christiananity], vol. 3 (1753), p. 384.

19   "Pologne" [Poland], vol. 12 (1765), 934.

20   "Peste d'Orient" [Oriental Plague], vol. 12 (1765), 457.

21   "Peste (Médecine)" [Plague (Medicine)], vol. 12 (1765), 454.

22   Ibid., 455.

23   Ibid., 454.

24   Ibid., 454.

25   The most recent book-length study of the Marseilles plague of 1720 is C. Carrière, M. Courdurié, and F. Rebuffat, *Marseilles: Ville morte, la peste de 1720* (Marseille, first published in 1968 and reprinted in 1988). The number of deaths in Marseilles during the plague is usually numbered at fiftythousand, but I have moderated the figure in light of my own recent research in the Marseilles archives, which suggests that the figures have been inflated. Writers (including scholars) from Provence have tended to exaggerate the destruction of the 1720 epidemic, just as those from Paris have tended to exaggerate its insignificance. I hope to realize a fuller study of the actual course of the epidemic and the various attitudes toward it in modern French intellectual history.

26.   Gordon, *Citizens Without Sovereignty,* 64–65.

27   "Peste (Histoire ancienne & moderne)" [Plague, ancient and modern history], vol. 12 (1765), 457.

28   Ibid., 457.

29   Antonin Artaud, "The Theater and the Plague," in *The Theater and its Double,* trans. Victor Corti (London, 1993), 18.

30   For a fascinating account of the ceremonies in which Belsunce dedicated the city to the Sacred Heart, see the contemporary chronicle of Pichatty de Croissainte, *Journal abrégé de ce qui s'est passé en la ville de Marseille depuis qu'elle est affligée de la contagion* (Marseilles, 1721), 45–47.

31   Ibid., 20.

32   Ibid., 22.

33   Paul Slack, *The Impact of Plague in Tudor and Stuart England* (Oxford, 1990), 4.

34   Other examples of this "social history" approach are Richard J. Evans, *Death in Hamburg: Society and Politics in the Cholera Years, 1830–1910* (London, 1990); and Colin Jones, "Plague and Its Metaphors in Early-Modern France," *Representations* (winter 1966): 97–127. Evans uses cholera to map the perennial social and political divisions of an industrial society. Jones tries to correlate representations of the plague to entrenched professional divisions.

35   Slack, *The Impact of Plague in Tudor and Stuart England,* 5.

36   Artaud, "The Theater,"15.

37   Ibid., 22.

38   Most of these events receive some treatment in Carrière et al., *Marseille: Ville morte.* They are also described in the contemporary chronicles. Finally, there is rich documentary evidence in the Municipal Library of Marseilles, the Departmental Archives of the Bouches-du-Rhône, and the Archives of the Marseilles Chamber of Commerce.

39   Georges Canguilhem, *Le Normal et le pathologique* (Paris, 1966).

40   The simple facts of this paragraph are not new and can be found in any history of Marseilles, such as the standard work by Raoul Busquet, *Histoire de Marseille* (Paris, 1945), 231–35. What is harder to demonstrate is the pervasiveness of the "nostalgia" I refer to. I hope to document this in more detail in a later study, but see my "The City and the Plague in the Age of Enlightenment," *Yale French Studies* no. 92 (1997): 126–48, for further reflections.

41   Jean-Baptiste Bertrand, *Relation historique de la peste de Marseille* (Cologne, 1721), 369 ff.

42   Sources for this biographical information: Lucien Montel, *Jean-Baptiste Bertrand* (Marseille, 1976); Claude Bollet, "A Propos du traitement de la peste en 1720 à Marseilles," Thèse, Docteur en Pharmacie, 1983, Université d'Aix-Marseille; Gilles Ammar, "Le Collège des Agrégés en 1720 à Marseilles," Thèse, Faculté de Médecine, 1986, Université d'Aix-Marseille.

43   French editions appeared in 1721, 1723, and 1779; English editions in 1721, 1722, and 1805. There may have been others that are not catalogued, for the editor of a set of documents pertaining to the Marseilles plague stated in 1820 that copies of the *Relation historique* were so available that he did not need to include an extract from the text in his collection. Louis-François Jauffret, *Pièces historiques sur la peste de Marseille* (Marseilles, 1820), 1:230.

44   Bertrand, *Relation historique*, preface (n.p.) and p. 1.

45   Ibid., 8.

46   Ibid., 438, 483.

47   Ibid., 34.

48   Ibid., 93.

49   Jean-Baptiste Bertrand, *Observations faites sur la peste qui règnent à présent à Marseille* (Marseilles, 1722), 10. This work is not to be confused with the "Observations sur la maladie contagieuse de Marseille," which appears as an appendix to the *Relation historique*.

50   Ibid., 11, 14, 16–17, 20, 36.

51   Bertrand, *Relation historique*, 511.

52   Ibid., 498.

53   Ibid., 438.

54   On the backfiring of commerce, consider also the anonymous *La Contagion de la peste expliquée* (Marseilles, 1722), 55: "Since commerce brings into a kingdom abundance and wealth, it ought to be sustained and favored as much as possible. But sometimes it is also accompanied by the most distressing reversals, for people thereby communicate to each other their most pernicious diseases. Europe was infected with leprosy by Asia and with venereal disease by America. She communicated smallpox to America and Africa, and even more common is the plague, which nations often communicate to each other by means of commerce."

55   Bertrand, *Relation historique*, 27.

56   Bertrand, *Observations*, 4.

57   François de Chicoyneau, *Discours prononcé . . . le 26 octobre de l'année 1722* (Montpellier, 1723), 59.

58   Bertrand, *Relation historique*, preface (n.p.) and 382. See 376 ff. for extended criticism of Chicoyneau.

59   Voltaire, *Candide*, trans. Daniel Gordon (New York: St. Martin's, 1999), 64.

60   Here again the ARTFL database is useful and reveals the richness of Voltaire's references to plague—including the 1720 epidemic in Marseilles—in a variety of works, such as *Essai sur l'histoire générale* (1756) and the *Traité sur la tolérance* (1763). His response to the Lisbon earthquake of 1755 in "Poème sur le désastre de Lisbon" is also important in this context.

2

Defoe and Disasters

G. A. STARR

*The English Tradesman is a kind of Phoenix, who often rises out
of his own Ashes, and makes the Ruin of his Fortunes be a firm
Foundation to build his Recovery . . . . A Tradesman is the best
fitted to struggle with Disasters of any Part of Mankind: The
Soldier, indeed, takes up a Musket, or gets a Commission, and
having a hundred thousand to one Odds against him, is knock'd
on the Head, or rises to something: The Scholar, got into
Misfortune, is good for just nothing, but to scribble for Bread . . . .
But the Tradesman can live in any Part of the World; give him but
Liberty, and something to begin with, he will not fail to engage in
something or other that may turn to Account. . . . In all other
Disasters of Life, once unhappy, ever unfortunate. . . . A
Tradesman is never out of Hope to rise, till he is nail'd up in his
Coffin, and six Foot under Ground.*[1]

This is the voice of the complete English tradesman, brash, irre-
pressible, flexing the ideological muscle of his increasingly confident class, not to be turned aside or kept down long by bankrupt-
cies or natural catastrophes. This is the voice of modernity, with no time for
brooding or mourning over disasters, keen instead on seeing if they can be
"turn[ed] to Account," transformed into new business opportunities. The

price of this phoenixlike resilience would appear to be a kind of callous philistinism, alert to profit and loss but insensible to natural sublimity or human tragedy. Defoe's thinking about disasters runs these risks, and sometimes succumbs to them, but the chamber of commerce mode is only one of his ways of looking at the world, or at disasters. Defoe considers disasters under four distinct rubrics: in addition to the commercial one, there is the religious, the scientific, and what might be called the "subtractive"—namely, the way that disasters reveal something about the essential nature of human beings, by showing what is left when all the familiar customs and institutions of civilization are taken away.

Various kinds of disasters find their way into Defoe's writings, and two provide the subject of entire books: an outbreak of bubonic plague that afflicted London in 1665, and a hurricane that swept over southern England in 1703. *The Storm* appeared in 1704 and dealt with an episode that had occurred only months before, whereas *A Journal of the Plague Year* and *Due Preparations for the Plague, as well for Soul as Body,* published nearly two decades later when Defoe was a man of sixty-two, concern events that took place when he was only five years old. There is a third disaster, the supposed explosion and submergence of the West Indian island of Saint Vincent in June 1718, to which he devoted space in *Mist's Journal* (XV: 241–50). Defoe the amateur scientist thought the likeliest explanation was that an earthquake had caused the sea to "come pouring into the vast body of . . . subterranean fires, which, having kindled themselves in the body of the earth, do, in several places, extend themselves to a prodigious space" (XV: 248–49). But subsequent dispatches from the Caribbean spoiled everything, with news that the event he was accounting for had not happened: there had been a minor volcanic eruption, but the island itself was still there, quite intact. The other two disasters did take place, but my concern will be less with what actually went on than with the different ways of thinking about and representing disasters to be found in Defoe's writings.

In his day, if one were able to think at all in the midst of a disaster, one would still be apt to ask some version of the questions posed in the last act of *King Lear*: "Is this the promis'd end? Or image of that horror?" In other words, "Is this the apocalypse, the beginning of the end as spelled out in *Revelations*?" Because the answer has hitherto been no, every disaster has been something of a disappointment to believers: a foretaste or warning of the approaching millennium, but never quite the real thing. If no disaster has yet fulfilled the eschatological predictions of John the Divine, however, this does not mean that disasters have defied or eluded theological interpretation. After all, there are numerous other catastrophes to be drawn upon in the Old as well as the New Testament. The religious reading of a garden-variety disaster could be either retrospective or prospective: as a divine punishment of evildoers, or as a divine call to repentance on the part of survivors. By the eighteenth century some otherwise pious people were balking at both doctrines. If God's primary objective is punitive, his methods seem rather crude and indiscriminate, since they strike down the innocent along with the guilty. But if his emphasis is monitory, then his solicitude for the spiritual welfare of survivors seems hard to reconcile with his apparent indifference toward those he kills *pour encourager les autres*. As responses to the Lisbon earthquake of 1755 indicate, such misgivings about the providential function of disasters by no means put an end to religious interpretations of them, which continued to be preached and published throughout the century.[2]

Defoe himself finds in disasters overwhelming evidence of God's existence and power, but he does not try to vindicate them as exercises of divine justice or mercy. He accepts the doctrine of particular Providence, and therefore believes that God not only uses disasters as warnings, but sometimes contrives an entire cataclysm for the edification of a single individual. To most modern readers, Robinson Crusoe is guilty of hubris in supposing that a storm at sea had been designed specifically as an admonition to him to repent. The resulting shipwreck claims the lives of everyone else aboard, and his eventual conviction that the whole thing is a message from on high, directed to him alone, is evidently shared by the author. Indeed, there can be little question that Defoe's advocacy of the doctrine of Providence in works like the *Serious Reflections . . . of Robinson*

Crusoe (1720), is as sincere as it is emphatic. Alongside it, however, is a more agnostic attitude, ready to acknowledge how little we understand about the origin or the mechanism of disasters, or for that matter any events out of the ordinary. In this more secular mode, Defoe does not challenge the providential interpretation, but treats it as a way of cutting short the difficult attempt to account for things according to natural laws. Thus he argues in *The Storm* that to give up the laborious tracing of second causes, and invoke God as first cause, is "to end the rational Enquiry, and resolve it into Speculation" (2). If you take this leap prematurely, Defoe suggests, you may be a good Christian but you are no scientist. On the other hand, in the same book Defoe groups various puzzling phenomena, including winds, among "those Inscrutables of Nature, in which humane Search has not yet been able to arrive" at firm "Knowledge." These "Secrets in Nature," Defoe believes, are "expressive" of God's infinite might; so in the face of scientific bafflement, an eventual leap of faith is legitimate.

But one must distinguish between those at a sufficient distance to be able to contemplate disasters as edifying texts, and the poor people who got "used up," as Mark Twain would say, by the plague of 1665 or the hurricane of 1703. Whatever the disaster, if you are squarely in its path, too bad for you, doomed not merely to die, but to point a moral, adorn a tale, or become a statistic. If you were a resident of Sodom or Gomorrah you might enjoy a kind of immortality as the subject of pulpit rhetoric, but you might prefer to be spared such immortality, especially at such a price. The position of survivor has distinct advantages over that of victim, not least of which is being able to tell your own story, rather than being a *memento mori* in somebody else's. At the same time, it is best not to be too far from the scene of action, either. Greater detachment may give one more perspective, a fuller sense of the meaning and implications of a disaster; but this kind of understanding, which depends on temporal or spatial distance, is liable to lose more in dramatic immediacy than it gains in scope and balance. A jury may have a fuller, more judicious view than a witness, but the vivid if fragmentary testimony of someone who was there is irreplaceable and what we most prize as readers. A jury may be ideally situated to comprehend, but a witness is better placed to apprehend—to form sharp, detailed impressions.[3] *A Journal of the Plague Year* certainly owes some of its force to the fact that it combines both perspectives; and it does so in the interest not only of vividness but also of exhaustiveness, as it anatomizes the impact of a disaster on individuals and the city itself. The concerns of the book are largely mimetic, seeking to convey what it was like to live through the plague, but they are also interpretative, trying to define and assess the nature and significance of this "dreadful visitation." In any case, a key factor in the relative success of Defoe's treatments of disasters is the different point of view adopted in each—as crucial to the representation of an extraordinary English hurricane in 1703 as of an ordinary Irish day in 1903.

The impact of a disaster narrative is not as dependent on the magnitude of the event itself, or on its casualty or damage toll, as on the voice reporting and interpreting what has occurred. More than any other single factor, this determines whether readers can sympathize with the narrator or (through the narrator) with the victims. In *The Storm* the litany of losses has limited emotional impact because they are seldom adequately individualized. From the inventories of drowned livestock, toppled steeples, uprooted trees, collapsed buildings, and foundered ships we do get a sense of enormous damage, but not of human pain or grief. Perhaps the same bookkeeping mentality is at work here as in Defoe's other fiction. Many readers have shared Robinson Crusoe's or Moll Flanders's satisfaction in tallying up their worldly gains, but it seems unlikely that the lists of losses in *The Storm* have ever caused readers to participate imaginatively. Cataloguing can be an effective rhetorical device, as Defoe, Swift, and many other eighteenth-century writers demonstrate, and the sheer piling up of data can generate emotional as well as evidentiary weight. All the same, the tabulations of tribulations in *The Storm* tend to be rather inert; the number of victims and the magnitude of their losses are both impressive, but little is done to translate quantitative suffering into personalized, individualized woe. There is no moment in this book comparable to the passage early in *Colonel Jack*, at

once bizarre and moving, in which the hero thinks he has lost forever a bag
of money that he has dropped into a hole in a hollow tree. Although minus-
cule in its intrinsic scope and gravity, Colonel Jack's youthful mishap is nevertheless momentous for him, and the keenness of his distress is dramatized
vividly. Despite the vast destruction that it painstakingly chronicles, *The
Storm* fails to enlist any such sympathetic readerly involvement: its victims
tend to remain items in balance sheets rather than recognizable human
beings, as is necessary for their plight to affect us.

Some features of Defoe's undertaking are nevertheless quite interesting
and original. Here I have in mind not his catalogues and inventories,
which represent an innovative and modern-spirited technique even
though they do not, in my opinion, achieve the emotional resonance that
they often take on elsewhere in Defoe's writings. I am referring to a different device, his enlistment of public participation in the project. Within
a week or two of the hurricane, advertisements like this one ran in *The
Gazette*, a semiofficial journal sent all over the country, inviting readers to
send in accounts of what the storm had done in their own localities:

> To preserve the Remembrance of the late Dreadful Tempest, an exact
> and faithful Collection is preparing of the most remarkable Disasters
> which happened on that Occasion, with the Places where, and
> Persons concern'd, whether at Sea or on Shore. For the perfecting so
> good a Work, 'tis humbly recommended by the Author to all
> Gentlemen of the Clergy, or others, who have made any
> Observations of this Calamity, that they would transmit as distinct
> an Account as possible, of what they have observed, to the
> Undertakers, directed to John Nutt, near Stationers hall, London. All
> Gentlemen that are pleas'd to send any such Accounts, are desired to
> write no Particulars but what they are well satisfied to be true, and to
> set their Names to the Observations they send, which the
> Undertakers of this Work promise shall be faithfully Recorded, and
> the Favour publickly acknowledged. (2–6 Dec. 1703)

The greater part of the eventually published book consists of what appear to be genuine submissions, many bearing the signatures of identifiable people. The majority are from country vicars, reporting on what happened in their own and nearby parishes; a few are from well-known provincial naturalists, like Ralph Thoresby of Leeds; and a number are from simpler folk, writing in a vernacular that the editor ostentatiously leaves alone, as evidence that the letters are authentic and that their contents are therefore reliable.

A decade earlier, John Dunton's *Athenian Mercury* had been (or purported to be) based on letters submitted by readers. So Defoe did not originate such a scheme, but he must have been among the first to recognize that involving the public as contributors would help to attract readers. In itself this device had great promise—for instance, the potential of conferring on material drawn from a large geographical area an eyewitness immediacy it might otherwise lack. Perhaps if correspondents had confined themselves to recounting what happened in their own families and neighborhoods, this would have been the result; indeed, in brief fragments, the method does work and the enterprise comes to life. But most of the letter writers, especially the clerical ones, approach their task with a sense of its dignity, and of their own, that is artistically fatal. Lofty moralizing often threatens to crowd out mere narrative, and much of the local material, besides being on tiptoes stylistically, is secondhand reportage rather than firsthand observation. As a consequence, the epistolary apparatus increases the scope of the book but lessens its vigor. Most of the letter writers do not sound deeply affected by the storm, and a directly implicated, personal note is also missing in the editorial voice. In contrast, much of the power of *Due Preparations for the Plague,* and particularly of *A Journal of the Plague Year,* is owing to the sustained presence of an authorial or narrative voice that is not merely astounded but moved by the events described. In *The Storm,* epistolarity makes for a collage, not a linear narrative. One could regard the resulting randomness and diffuseness as very modern—an eschewing of artifice and manipulation, a determination to let multiple voices speak for themselves, and so on—but this claim cannot be pushed very far in the case of *The Storm.*

But it is an ill wind that blows no good, and one of the ironies of *The Storm* is to read about all the roofs of thatch, tile, and lead that got blown away, and to realize that Defoe's own brick and tile works in Essex, which must have been a goldmine in the aftermath of the hurricane, had in fact been seized from him just months before, a casualty of his period of hiding and imprisonment for writing *The Shortest Way with the Dissenters*. One of the strengths of *The Storm*, in fact, is Defoe's shrewd awareness that a hurricane can be bad for some yet good for others. This way of looking at disasters is certainly sardonic but not necessarily cynical: a similar pattern is to be found toward the end of *A Journal of the Plague Year*, where Defoe devotes twelve pages to the impact of the plague on business.

In 1665 most domestic as well as foreign trade was very depressed, and Defoe shows that even some apparent boons turned out to be misfortunes. Thus during the plague summer "there was a most excessive Plenty of all Sorts of Fruit, such as Apples, Pears, Plumbs, Cherries, Grapes; and they were the cheaper, because of the want of People; but this made the Poor eat them to excess, and this brought them into Fluxes, griping of the Guts, Surfeits, and the like, which often precipitated them into the Plague" (222). So cheap and abundant fruit furthered the plague rather than offsetting it. Defoe goes on to show that the stoppage of business in London caused a stagnation of trade throughout the country, so that "the Poor were pinch'd all over *England* by the Calamity of the City of *London* only" (223). But his conclusion is rather remarkable:

> It is true, that the next Year made them full amends by another terrible Calamity upon the City; so that the City by one Calamity impoverished and weaken'd the Country, and by another Calamity even terrible too of its Kind, enrich'd the Country and made them again amends: For an infinite Quantity of Household Stuff, wearing Apparel, and other Things, besides whole Ware-houses fill'd with Merchandize and Manufactures, such as come from all Parts of *England*, were consum'd in the Fire of *London*, the next Year after this terrible Visitation: It is incredible what a Trade this made all over the whole Kingdom, to make good the Want, and to supply that Loss:

So that, in short, all the manufacturing Hands in the Nation were set on Work, and were little enough, for several Years, to supply the Market and answer the Demands; all Foreign Markets, also were empty of our Goods, by the stop which had been occasioned by the Plague, and before an open Trade was allow'd again; and the prodigious Demand at Home falling in join'd to make a quick Vent for all Sorts of Goods; so that there never was known such a Trade all over *England* for the Time, as was in the first seven Years after the Plague, and the Fire of *London*. (223–24)

In this passage Defoe is not at all elegaic about the losses of life or property in the plague or the fire. Instead, he is intrigued by the complex connections between disasters and trade, and his habitual keenness for paradox is strikingly at work. For him the Mandevillian linkage between private vices and public benefits—the argument that prosperity and civilization require the production and consumption of morally suspect luxuries—is valid but too narrow. His own more sweeping paradox is that out-and-out disasters, however dismal or lethal for those on the spot, are wonderful economic stimulants, with long-term gains not only outweighing but also depending upon short-term losses.[4] Today, post-Kobe, the linkage may seem obvious, but I know of no earlier account of it than Defoe's.

Disasters can thus be turned to account in a commercial sense, which some would regard as a modern way of looking at them. But it is equally characteristic of Defoe to present them from a much more primitive perspective, as he does in the first half of *Due Preparations for the Plague*, through the story of the family that survives by shutting itself up in its London house. Just as the mechanism by which the plague was propagated was debated during Defoe's lifetime and long afterward, so too there was disagreement about the efficacy of various measures to prevent its spread that had been adopted in 1665 and were proposed again in 1721, such as exterminating household pets as well as rodents, burning bonfires at street corners, and so forth. As to Defoe's position on many of these questions, the evidence presented in *Due Preparations for the Plague* and *A Journal of the Plague Year* is abundant but ambiguous.

He seems to have believed, for example, that if flight is an option, it is the most effective antiplague measure; yet the people whose responses to the plague of 1665 interest him do not flee, but remain in or near London throughout their nearly year-long ordeal. One might explain this by arguing that even when he writes about peripatetic figures, his point of view, theirs, and the assumed reader's all tend to be that of a Londoner; or that the real subject of the plague is so much an urban crisis that he could not have dealt with it by following the fortunes of those who left town; or that (as various passages in *A Journal of the Plague Year* indicate) he looked somewhat askance at those who fled, particularly members of the court and the legal, medical, and clerical professions, whom he regarded as having abandoned their civic responsibilities; or that as a shrewd man of letters he realized that those who put themselves beyond the reach of the plague also put themselves beyond narration—just as Robinson Crusoe would have done if he had followed his father's sensible advice to content himself with "the middle station of life" in Yorkshire. Only by imprudently running away from home does Crusoe become worth writing or reading about; only by imprudently *not* running away from London do the dramatis personae of Defoe's plague books make their stories worth telling.

His desire to offer practical guidance in case the plague should recur no doubt entered into his decision to focus on those who stayed behind. Yet a more crucial factor may have been his deep and long-standing fascination with the possibility of secure refuges within a world perceived as alien, inscrutable, and threatening even at the best of times. Crusoe's construction of a totally self-sufficient, impregnable fortress may be the fullest and best-known realization of this fantasy in English literature, but the account in the first half of *Due Preparations for the Plague* of the man who shuts up his family in his amply stocked and barricaded London house is comparable in spirit and effectiveness. As in *Robinson Crusoe*, a preoccupation with the details of shutting out invasive enemies cannot be ascribed to mere paranoia, since the threat from without is genuine and terrifying. At the same time, there is a sense in which the plague (like Crusoe's cannibals) seems almost welcome, as an occasion for defensive contrivances that give great satisfaction to those who create them (or write or read about them). The head of the family in *Due Preparations* shares a siege mentality with Defoe's other protagonists, yet his mood tends to be one of steely equanimity: at his lowest point "the good man was almost discouraged" (XV: 62), but like Crusoe amidst his travails he is often cheerful and never despondent. To enjoy a respite from anxiety, to achieve a degree of security within fortifications of one's own erecting, is as close as most of these harried heroes ever come to happiness. (Colonel Jack, fearful of being recognized and betrayed by some Preston rebels transported to Virginia, is similarly relieved at being shut up safely in his own room, and virtually swaddled, by his resourceful and maternal final wife.)

If thinking about the plague in religious terms in the 1720s is evidence of a conservative outlook, and if thinking about it in scientific or commercial terms is a sign of a progressive, "enlightened" outlook—associations posited by at least one fellow contributor to this volume—then Defoe must be transitional, confused, or both. But what, then, are we to make of his conception of the plague as bringing about a gratification not attainable at other times: that is, the pleasure of retreating into a totally self-contained, private, sealed-off world where you are (to use a word favored by Defoe but deemed "low" by Johnson) completely "uncomeatable"? Surely this is symptomatic of a mentality not easily reducible to such categories as traditional or modern. Defoe plays upon primitive fears and longings that may be provoked by modern urban life. Over against that life, however, he does not set up some chronologically or geographically remote golden-age alternative, but its own quintessence: that is, he represents a state of absolute alienation and isolation as a kind of utopia. This pattern of guarding oneself by obsessively sequestering oneself is remarkable, and it is realized as dramatically in the first part of *Due Preparations for the Plague* as in *Robinson Crusoe*. Defoe concludes his story of the family that survives by immuring itself by declaring that

> next under the protection of God's providence, a complete retirement from the street, and from conversing on any account whatever

with the rest of the people, separating from them, and having, as we may say, nothing to do with them, neither to buy or sell, or speak or sit with or near them, has been approved to be capable of effectually preserving a man or a family in the time of an infection. (XV: 76)

This is a fair summary of the preceding narrative, insofar as its purpose is simply to demonstrate through a case history the efficacy and the practicability of one way of dealing with the plague. But my point about this case history is that in addition to having a sober rhetorical function, it must be seen as a venture into utopian fantasy of a peculiarly Defoean sort. The passage just quoted spells out the recommended means to survival, but does not capture the underlying paradox—that a policy of self-imposed confinement, which many readers might find almost as grim and dehumanizing as the disease it is designed to avoid, is undertaken and executed with the same zest and indefatigability that Crusoe and Defoe's other heroes and heroines bring to their exercises in self-preservation.

The passage just quoted, however, is retrospective and general; Defoe's relish for this brand of voluntary imprisonment emerges much more forcefully when he is dealing with its concrete features—either prospectively, in the pages that carefully itemize the plentiful provisions laid in so that the besieged family will be able to sustain itself, or in the subsequent chronicle of specific steps taken to minimize danger. A typical paragraph traces the precautions over receiving mail:

His letters were brought by the postman, or letter-carrier, to his porter [ensconced outside the street-door in a little booth], when he caused the porter to smoke them with brimstone and with gunpowder, then open them, and to sprinkle them with vinegar; then he had them drawn up by the pulley [to an upstairs window], then smoked again with strong perfumes, and, taking them with a pair of hair gloves, the hair outermost, he read them with a large reading-glass which read at a great distance, and, as soon as they were read, burned them in the fire; and at last, the distemper raging more and more, he forbid his friends writing to him at all. (XV: 61–62)

Individually these actions are trivial and prosaic, yet cumulatively they acquire considerable momentum, and Defoe's own fixation on circumstantial detail is the perfect stylistic complement to the finical obsessiveness of the conduct he is describing. Just as the man cannot feel secure wearing hair gloves unless the hair is on the outside, so too Defoe as narrator cannot be content to identify them merely as hair gloves but must specify "the hair outermost." As with Crusoe, a great deal in this man's predicament is out of his control and would dismay and incapacitate many people put in the same position; and this man is also like Crusoe in that an ability to fasten on small things that *are* within his control tends not only to offset the dreadfulness of his situation but also to transform it into something almost idyllic. Once again, if we believe with some historians that there is value in the taxonomic exercise of attaching labels such as "Enlightenment" to eighteenth-century behavior, we might regard this man (who happens to be a grocer) as embodying a resilience and resourcefulness that are "modern" rather than "traditional," because they are fostered by commercial and thus putatively forward-looking ways of thinking and acting.[5] Whatever the inherent usefulness of vague and sweeping period labels, I have tried to suggest that they are nugatory in the present context. Improvising one's way through disasters with pulleys, reading glasses, brimstone, and hair gloves reflects a mentality no less primitive than progressive. Insofar as this phoenix mentality is associated with commerce, Defoe traces it back to the Phoenicians;[6] to persuade readers of the importance and value of trade, he usually chose to emphasize its long and dignified pedigree rather than its modernity.

Intent on finding mechanisms for distinguishing the natural from the merely local, temporary, and contingent, some eighteenth-century writers tried to think how contemporary English and French mores would strike a visitor from China or Peru; others tried to imagine extreme situations, on the assumption that once the customary and conventional had fallen away, the essential would emerge in all its clarity. One way was to hypothesize a state of things prior to civilization; another way was to investigate cultures perceived as primitive in various newly discovered corners of the world; and still another way was to ponder what was left when the trappings of civilization were snatched away by the heavy hand of disaster. Seasons of disaster, like seasons of carnival, thus opened up the possibility of arriving at hidden truths through drastic subtraction. The real objects of analysis were not disasters themselves, but man and society. From disasters, then, what message did Defoe extract about "unaccommodated man," to use another phrase from *King Lear*?

A popular nineteenth-century disaster narrative, Bulwer-Lytton's *Last Days of Pompeii* (1834), raises in a penultimate chapter the question, "Who in that hour spared one thought to his neighbor? Perhaps in scenes of universal horror, nothing is more horrid than the unnatural selfishness they engender." With some of this Defoe would have agreed. He too thought that under stress, people tend to lose their generosity and look out for themselves; the law of self-preservation supersedes whatever benevolence or altruism the civilizing, moralizing process has been able to induce in better times. For Defoe, moral behavior is a luxury, splendid for those who can afford it, but not to be expected of those who cannot. Under pressure, then, selfishness is bound up with survival and thus—as Defoe sees it—so natural as to be beyond reproach. The plague drives people into themselves, not merely isolating them from one another, but inducing the kind of wary, edgy callousness that typifies most of Defoe's characters. Being foxy and self-centered helps them to endure and get on, but makes them less lovable than, say, a Tom Jones, who endears himself precisely by forgetting himself. In preferring survival over amiability, Defoe's characters seem to be at one with their shady creator.

A disaster like the plague imposes on everyone, at least for a time, the struggle for self-preservation that his heroes and heroines are always engaged in. If Defoe is not as horrified as Bulwer-Lytton by the spectacle of *sauve-qui-peut* during a disaster, one reason may be that he tended to see disasters as the norm, as if they were his own everyday struggle writ large. For him a disaster is not an interruption or reversal of quotidian existence but a more inclusive, more extreme version of it. For him a disaster is literally *extra*ordinary—not some antithesis to the ordinary that turns it topsy-turvy, or some gap in the ordinary that halts or suspends it, but an extension of the ordinary to the furthest point imaginable. This would imply that for Defoe there is no such thing as a "true" disaster, an utterly anomalous event, that differs qualitatively as well as quantitatively from prior experience. For him, to speak of chaos or disorder in nature does not mean that laws do not cover the phenomenon, or have stopped operating; it is merely a way of disguising one's ignorance about those laws. Among the figures of speech in the book of nature, disasters are to be read as hyperbolic specimens of *amplificatio* or *reductio*—a bit bombastic and stagy for neoclassic taste, but by no means nonsensical.

Over and over, *A Journal of the Plague Year* describes people looking out for themselves at the expense of others, suggesting that this was understandable and hardly blameable. Yet those who go beyond this, seeking not merely to survive but to profit from the helplessness of plague victims and the breakdown of law enforcement, do provoke the narrator's censoriousness. There are more chilling stories, too, about people who wantonly infect others, or nurses who murder their patients, but these always seem to have taken place in remote parts of town and are reported skeptically as mere hearsay, as if such gratuitous malice is scarcely credible. All the same, despite these distancing devices, such passages possess an emotional intensity beyond anything that the plague itself arouses in the narrator, H.F. And similar moments of highly charged beastliness occur in Defoe's other writings as well. Think of Robinson Crusoe, who is shipwrecked in a Caribbean hurricane and nearly buried in an earthquake: for him a single footprint in the sand is much more unnerving, and the sight of leftovers from a cannibal feast makes him vomit.

Crusoe stands in some awe of the power of nature, but scarcely dreads it. His fear and loathing, like Gulliver's, are directed mainly toward his fellow Yahoos. Being swallowed up or buried alive seems to be the worst fate Defoe can imagine: in his books, storms at sea and earthquakes pose this threat most frequently, but cannibalism does so most virulently. For Defoe, the heart of darkness is man's handiwork, not nature's; the worst disasters have humans not only as victims but also as perpetrators. It follows that within the plague narratives the chief drama lies in a conflict, not so much between contagionist and miasmatic theories of infection as between sunnier and more somber visions of man. On balance, H.F. sides with the contagionists and with those who see more grievances than benefits in shutting up infected houses. In all such controversies he gives both sides their due, and he is similarly ambivalent about human nature. H.F. himself is consistently humane and decent: not at all saintly or noble, yet reassuringly ordinary amidst extraordinary circumstances. Part of the *Journal*'s subtitle is *Observations . . . of the most Remarkable Occurrences* during the plague. But more remarkable than *what* H.F. observes or thinks is *that* he goes on observing and thinking amidst such scenes. He is not impervious to what goes on around him, but he can register all the chaos, take it in and feel threatened by it, and nevertheless retain his own normality. In short, he is heroically unheroic, and in this respect he and Robinson Crusoe are more closely akin to one another than to any of Defoe's other characters.

H.F. is pleased to be able to report that some people behaved well, but he presents much more evidence, although often at pains to qualify or discount it, of people behaving cravenly or harshly, and he has some downright horror stories. H.F.'s moderation, evenhandedness, and general probity give him greater authority than the professional experts whose theories he reports, and serve in a modest but effective way to counteract the very breakdown of order and authority he writes about. For Defoe, in any case, what is grimmest about this and other disasters is not what they do to people, but what they cause some people to do. It is always savages, fanatics, extravagantly *outré* characters who behave madly or fiendishly, never Defoe's narrators; and it is along these lines, at least as much as racial or class ones, that "otherness" is defined in his works.

Alongside confinement in Newgate or on a desert island, or treks across dark continents, disasters thus serve in Defoe's imaginative universe as ordeals that distinguish "them" from "us"—those who collapse or turn feral or otherwise become deranged from those who doggedly and resourcefully and more or less decently come through. If catastrophes are among the "Inscrutables of Nature," opaque in their causes and operations, they are nevertheless "expressive" of something more than God's existence and power. When passed through such a prism as *A Journal of the Plague Year*, they reveal a broad spectrum of human behavior, much of it nearer the diabolic than the saintly end of the scale. But squarely in the middle, impressive in his sheer representativeness, his unimpeachable typicality, stands Defoe's narrator—as alive and as principled as ever, as if-to suggest that uprightness and survival are naturally associated. Elsewhere, as in *Moll Flanders* or *Roxana*, Defoe often shows them at odds. Despite all the dire events it chronicles, *A Journal of the Plague Year* is ultimately less bleak than either of the novels about women, because Defoe makes human nature count for so much more than external nature, and because he makes his everyman, H.F. the saddler, at once so ordinary and so admirable.

NOTES

1   *The Compleat English Tradesman,* vol. 2 (London, 1727), 198–99, 201, 188, 184–85. Subsequent references in the text to *The Storm* are to the original 1704 edition; those to *Due Preparations for the Plague* (1722) and to the article on Saint Vincent in *Mist's Journal* (1718) are to *The Romances and Narratives of Daniel Defoe,* ed. George A. Aitken, 16 vols. (London and New York, 1898); those to *A Journal of the Plague Year* (1722) are to the Oxford English Novels edition, ed. Louis A. Landa (London, 1969). Landa's introduction provides an excellent historical account of medical thinking about plagues and particularly the competing miasmatic versus contagionist theories of its propagation (labeled "vertical" and "horizontal" theories elsewhere in this volume). For thoughtful suggestions I am indebted to Kay Flavell.

2   See chapters 4–6 of T. D. Kendrick's *The Lisbon Earthquake* (Philadelphia and New York: J.B. Lippincott, 1955).

3   The problem of the appropriate distance from a disaster can be posed in terms of reception as well as narration: as readers of disaster narratives, we are in the same emotionally and morally equivocal position that theorists of the sublime have identified through the image of watching a shipwreck at sea from a vantage point on dry land. The spectacle may arouse various strong feelings, including compassion for the victims, yet it is after all only a spectacle. To say this is not to trivialize the experience, however, but to aestheticize it, to suggest that it is possible (or at any rate pleasurable) only at a secure, contemplative distance. Defoe himself seems to have had some misgivings about gratifications of this sort: his idea of a perverse hedonist is "a Man that would Blow up a House, and the whole Family in it, for the meer Satisfaction of hearing the Bounce; and please himself with it afterward, upon the meer Pleasure of seeing the innocent Wife and Children fly up in the Air, and be dash'd in Pieces with the Fall" (*Conjugal Lewdness* [London, 1727], 335).

4   Defoe saw that a plague could serve as an economic stimulus not only where it occured at a later time, but elsewhere at the same time. Writing later in the 1720s about

"such Accidents as may raise or sink our Manufacture," his first example is the plague at Marseilles:

> Upon that sad Occasion, the Commerce being entirely stop'd between *France* and *Spain,* and indeed all other Parts of the World, the Manufactures of the City of *Marseilles* in particular, and the Country adjacent, being wholly interrupted, occasion'd a very great Addition to the Trade of *Great Britain;* particularly for such Manufactures as the *French* used to send to *Turkey,* to *Spain,* and to *Italy;* and the Merchants Commisions from Abroad were visibly enlarged hither for near two Years, upon that particular Occasion: It was plain they cou'd have no Goods from *France.* (*A Plan of the English Commerce. Being a Compleat Prospect of The Trade of this Nation, as well the Home Trade as the Foreign* [London, 1728], p. 259)

5   As my initial quotations from *The Compleat English Tradesman* suggest, Defoe regarded resilience and resourcefulness as ideals fostered by commerce. He was not so partial to his fellow tradesmen, however, as to suppose that they monopolized these traits: for example, he admired William III on grounds that "*Antaeus* like, from every Fall he rose, / Strengthen'd with double Vigour to oppose" (*The Mock Mourners,* in *A True Collection of the Writings of The Author of the True Born English-man* [London, 1703], 54).

6   See Defoe's assessment of the destruction of Tyre and its aftermath: "It is a Question in matters of Commerce, whether the destruction of *Tyre,* by *Nebuchadnezzar,* did good or hurt. If I may give my opinion, I think it was rather good than harm; for tho' it is true, that the Citizens had a very great loss in the demolishing their Houses, and ruining their public Edifices; yet as it scatter'd a diligent and useful People into divers parts of the World, where they settled immediately to business, some in one place, and some in another: They were as so many Instructors to the Nations wherever they came, to pursue the same Industry, and maintain themselves by Trade, which before, 'tis very likely, they knew little or nothing of" (*A General History of Discoveries and Improvements, In useful Arts, Particularly in the great Branches of Commerce, Navigation, and Plantation, in all Parts of the known World* [London, 1725], 72).

Defoe puts the same positive construction on two disasters suffered by industrious trading people nearer his own time: namely, the persecution of Protestants in the Spanish Netherlands in the reign of Queen Elizabeth, whose flight to England first enabled the woolen manufacture to "c[o]me up to its full Maturity" (*A General History,* 213–14); and the persecution of Protestants in France following the Revocation of the Edict of Nantes, whose emigration similarly enhanced English expertise in various arts. Along with the Tyrians, the Walloons and the Huguenots exhibit, in Defoe's view, the distinctive capacity of the tradesman to "rise out of his own Ashes," and also the paradoxical phenomenon of disasters turning out to do more "good than harm" from a commercial perspective.

3

Safety and Reconstruction of Noto after the Sicilian Earthquake of 1693— The Eighteenth-Century Context [1]

STEPHEN TOBRINER

On Sunday morning, 11 January 1693, one of the strongest European earthquakes in recorded history struck southeastern Sicily.[2] Its epicenter was in the island's limestone Hiblean mountains, overlooking the southeastern coast, where intense shaking ruined forty cities in an instant and killed 54,000 people. In the city of Noto, a historic, rich, inland fortress crowning a rocky outcrop, one citizen remembered: "Then came an earthquake so horrible and ghastly that the soil undulated like the waves of a stormy sea, the mountains danced as if drunk, and the city collapsed in one miserable moment killing more than a thousand people."[3] The shaking was felt from the island of Malta in the south, where it ruined the city of Mdina, to Calabria in the east, and across the entire island of Sicily to Palermo, where the walls of several palaces collapsed. Southeastern Sicily was devastated.

As survivors found their way out of the ruins in Noto, Catania, Avola, Ragusa, and scores of other Sicilian cities, they prayed and confessed, hoping for protection and deliverance. An officer of the Spanish viceroy in

Messina wrote to his king that "the processions and harsh penitences which have been made are without equal in the world."[4] Although the Spanish officer may have thought the processions he saw were extraordinary, each earthquake of the seventeenth and eighteenth centuries called forth such responses of extreme piety.[5] Catholics invoked local saints particularly powerful in stopping earthquakes like Alexis and Emidio, and of course the Virgin herself.[6] The specter of the Last Judgment or the destruction of Sodom and Gomorrah was always close at hand. Religious leaders and commentators saw earthquakes as God's will. Protestant preachers, like John Shower, saw the 1692 Jamaica earthquake and 1693 Sicilian earthquake as a sign of God's displeasure with wanton ways and exhorted the English to repent.[7] To explain the Lisbon earthquake of 1755 Chevalier Joseph Cuers de Cogelin wrote of God's anger at the people of Lisbon for being too proud.[8]

Whatever their theological attitudes toward the meaning of earthquakes, seventeenth- and eighteenth-century architects and builders did attempt practical measures to make buildings and cities seismically safe, just as people in cultures around the world had done long before the Enlightenment. Evidence suggests that the inhabitants of the island of Santorini employed architectural strategies for resisting earthquakes as early as 1650 B.C.[9] Knowledge of seismically resistant construction existed in China and probably in Japan in the twelfth century.[10] Theories inspired by Aristotle's *Meteorologica* about the origin of earthquakes influenced generations of scholars and architects; this influence is apparent in the only surviving architectural treatise from antiquity, written by Vitruvius.[11] Many Renaissance architects, among them Filarete, Palladio, and Leonardo da Vinci, wrote about seismically resistant design, but one of the most insightful pre-eighteenth-century treatises on the subject was written by the Mannerist architect Pirro Ligorio in sixteenth-century Ferrara. While embracing Aristotelian explanations for the cause of earthquakes, Ligorio, in his careful observation of postquake damage, also anticipated the scientific method of a later age.

The eighteenth century is traditionally viewed as the cradle of modern

European scientific inquiry; it is often portrayed as an age obsessed with finding explanations for curious and unpredictable natural events in the hope of understanding them and eventually controlling their effects.[12] This century also saw the birth of modern engineering with the founding of the French corps of Ponts et Chaussées in 1716.[13] For the first time, building upon experiments undertaken by Galileo, reliable tests of strengths of material had been devised and forces calculated.[14] Giovanni Poleni wrote a book dedicated to outlining the causes of cracks in the dome of St. Peter's and posited a way of understanding the strength and failure of domes.[15] Modern engineering feats begun in the seventeenth century with the creation of vast canals and ports made way for even more sweeping projects in the eighteenth century.

The specter of earthquakes loomed large in the Enlightenment consciousness, challenging this newfound technological confidence. Between 1693 and 1783 earthquakes in Europe killed more than 130,000 people and destroyed as many as one hundred cities, including one of the continent's richest capitals, Lisbon. This chapter asks how architects and engineers of the period responded to earthquake danger by following the history of the city of Noto in Sicily and comparing the response in Noto to that of other cities damaged in the eighteenth century.

Noto was moved to its present location after the earthquake of 1693 and rebuilt over the course of the eighteenth century; it stands today as one of the most beautiful Baroque cities in Italy and remains largely unchanged since the eighteenth century, thereby offering a rare opportunity to study construction and seismic safety techniques of that period. Here, we will examine Noto's reconstruction, which took place in several phases, with individual buildings continuously rebuilt, enlarged, and repaired up through the 1780s, and we will compare this effort to that of Noto's sister cities in southeastern Sicily. The chapter's focus then shifts to recovery policies in Lisbon and Calabria after earthquakes struck these places. We ask: How does the reconstruction of Noto, begun as one of many colonial cities under the Spanish Hapsburgs, compare with strategies undertaken by the Marquês de Pombal in Lisbon or the Neapolitan Bourbons in Calabria? How do these strategies relate to the perception of earthquake danger and the scientific understanding of buildings' responses to earthquakes in the Age of Reason?

What Architects, Engineers, and Builders Could Have Known about Seismically Resistant Design and Safe Urban Planning at the End of the Seventeenth Century

Practical antiseismic urban and architectural strategies characterize responses to the three most destructive European earthquakes in the eighteenth century: the Sicilian earthquake of 1693; the Lisbon earthquake of 1755; and the Calabrian earthquake of 1783. Because engineers and architects involved in reconstruction cite neither architectural treatises nor precedents and rarely explain their reasoning, it is difficult to reconstruct their decision-making process. They seem to have observed damage and attempted to confront it pragmatically. Even though they may not have correctly deduced the cause of earthquakes, they could see their results. Such analysis of direct observation, which occurred even before the Enlightenment, should be seen as an ongoing, if sporadic, attempt to understand a dangerous situation and to design a response to it. What did these engineers and architects deduce from the evidence at hand? The Mannerist architect Pirro Ligorio (1510–1583) provides an example.

Ligorio died more than one hundred years before the earthquake of 1693, but his manuscript treatise illustrates what a trained and curious architect could observe about earthquake damage.[16] Ligorio, a learned antiquarian who is probably most famous as the architect who designed the Este villa gardens at Tivoli, worked on St. Peter's. He was in the employ of Duke Alfonso II d'Este when an earthquake badly damaged the city of Ferrara, the Este family's ancestral seat, in 1570. Although Alberti, Filarete, Leonardo da Vinci, and Palladio had suggested ways of building safer, seismically resistant structures before Ligorio, their comments were cursory compared to his treatment of the subject.[17]

Ligorio, like other Renaissance architects and scholars, believed that Aristotle had correctly identified the cause of earthquakes in his *Meteorologica*. According to Aristotle the subterranean release of *pneuma*, or spirit, a kind of wind that collected in underground caves and fissures, caused earthquakes.[18] Aristotle's complex theory became simplified over the years. Pneuma was directly equated with underground winds that sought release. If arrested or compressed, they caused earthquakes. Roman authors like Varro, Pliny, and Vitruvius posited an antiseismic remedy: earthquake shaking could be mitigated by providing an artificial release for these winds in underground cavities like wells or sewers. To prove this theory Ligorio recounts that an earthquake that struck Naples in December 1456 did the least damage to areas constructed over subterranean voids.[19] This theory of the efficacy of subterranean voids, endorsed by philosophers like Descartes, was popular throughout the seventeenth and eighteenth centuries.[20]

Although Ligorio embraced Aristotle's theories, which now appear fanciful, his keen observation of damage and his pragmatic approach to designing an antiseismic structure illustrate how an observant professional anticipated modern concepts of building safety in earthquakes. He described damage in the most vulnerable part of Ferrara, the old medieval quarter built on alluvial river soils. The more modern quarter of the city, the Terranova, added by Ercole III d'Este in 1494 and planned by Biagio Rossetti (1447–1516), is excluded from his narrative: first, because the area was less damaged; second, perhaps because damage in the older section of the city—away from the aristocratic palaces—was politically safer to describe. Ligorio criticized buildings that were simply too old, built with thin walls, lacking in reinforcement, and bonded with inferior mortar. He blamed the craftsman guilds working without the guidance of a trained architect (like himself, of course) for the poor design and execution of the buildings that failed. As a result, he stressed building well with the best of materials and using iron ties where necessary to bond walls together. When Ligorio saw evidence of heavy exterior walls oscillating at different frequencies and striking one another, he suggested heavier than usual internal partitions to stabilize these walls and proposed uniform wall thickness as a way of ensuring that buildings moved together in earthquakes. Regular ground plans, he hypothesized, were far more resistant to shaking than irregular ones. Ligorio's reasoning thus significantly foreshadows modern ideas for making buildings earthquake resistant.

Other published treatises as complex as Ligorio's that considered both earthquakes and architecture did not appear until the mid-eighteenth century. Giovanni Gentili described an earthquake at Livorno in a paper published in 1742; he proposed that antiseismic structures be as solid and symmetrical as possible.[21] Eusebio Sguario's *Specimen physico-geometricum de terraemotu ad architecturae* (1756) for the first time rightly described the dynamic movement of a building in earthquake shaking.[22] Walls equal and parallel to one another move together like inverse pendulums while unequal walls oscillate at different rates, pounding one against the other. Sguario's dynamic theory therefore dictated symmetrical construction, again according with modern engineering ideas about the best building configuration in earthquakes. This period also saw an increased interest in antiseismic buildings constructed of wood. Christian Wolff described a rigid wooden framework for roofs and foundations,[23] and the most famous Italian architectural treatise of the late eighteenth century, Francesco Milizia's *Principii di Architettura Civile* (1781), described an antiseismic house in which each piece of wood is tied to the next so that the entire structure works as a unit.[24] Milizia further stated that a building should be wider than it is tall, thereby ensuring a low center of gravity. For good measure he added that the site should have caves, cisterns, and wells around it to allow dispersal of the underground winds.

THE SICILIAN EARTHQUAKE OF 1693

Neither Ligorio's manuscript nor the later work of Sguario would have been available to the architects, engineers, and administrators working in Sicily in 1693, yet these planners' decisions addressed earthquake mitigation with a similar acuity. The Spanish viceregal government faced the January disaster with surprising efficiency, dispatching several officials to assess the damage and oversee reconstruction and establishing a governing body to conduct recovery operations.[25] No stated seismic policy or procedure for the vast reconstruction that would follow has been uncovered, but the outcomes of numerous town councils and their ad hoc decisions were surprisingly similar in response to earthquake danger. In certain cases there is no doubt that administrators considered whether a city's site or street plan could or should be changed or regulated to prevent future catastrophe. Three prominent cities illustrate this strategy: Catania, Avola, and Noto.

Citizens and officials endorsed an antiseismic strategy for redesigning the city plans of Catania and Avola to increase safety by widening streets and enlarging piazzas. Catania was so badly damaged in 1693 that one observer said that it was "as flat as the palm of your hand." [26] The sloping site with a beautiful harbor was commercially profitable, but geographically dangerous. It had been ruined before—partially inundated in 1669 by a lava flow from Etna's flank—but the citizens wanted to remain on the site even after the earthquake had leveled the city. Instead of moving the city, the council focused on the narrow, curvilinear medieval streets of the old town as its most hazardous and correctable feature. The council is recorded as condemning the narrow, twisting streets so easily closed by falling rubble and endorsing the straight and wide streets that were eventually built in the reconstructed city. These streets were to be wide enough to enable people to leave their houses after debris had fallen. The council also planned extremely large piazzas as places of refuge after earthquakes; they would serve as camping areas so people could remain close to their possessions to prevent looting and yet be protected from the danger of falling walls.

Unlike Catania, Avola was rebuilt in a new location on the flat plain southwest of its former mountainous site. According to a contemporary report, medieval Avola's site (Avola Vecchia) was dangerously narrow. [27] The steepness of the site had led to houses being built close together, terraced down the slopes, perhaps looking similar to present-day Ragusa Ibla. When one house fell, the report continues, it pulled down its neighbors. The report also questioned the seismic vulnerability of the rocky site, noting that part of the promontory actually broke apart during the earthquake. [28] The medieval city of Avola, like Catania, was rebuilt with straight streets and extremely large piazzas (Figure 1). The hexagonal plan incorporated many open spaces that would provide safe refuge during a seismic event.[29]

In areas affected by the earthquake of 1693, tortuous, constricted medieval streets were largely condemned and wide, straight streets uniformly adopted. The change in structuring cities was not just the result of aesthetic preference but also of the documented observation that narrow, curving streets were hazardous in earthquakes. Eighteenth-century architects and engineers realized that after a temblor, open spaces were necessary in order to provide escape routes and to facilitate the delivery of emergency services. In Catania and Avola, as well as in Lisbon and Calabria, open spaces were thus knowingly incorporated into reconstruction plans in hopes of improving seismic safety. Rather than abandoning a city after an earthquake, citizens could remain near their damaged houses

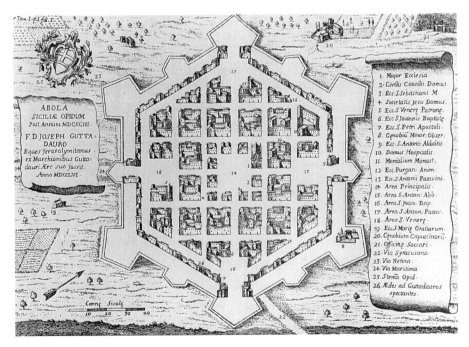

FIGURE 1. Plan of Avola (V. Amico, *Lexicon Topographicum Siculum*, vol. II, Palermo and Catania: P. Bentivenga, 1757–60)

and workplaces if open sites were available for temporary housing; supplies could be stockpiled and food dispensed. Obviously, to provide safety, these spaces needed to be big enough to provide proper clearance from surrounding structures—during the Lisbon earthquake of 1755 many people ran into the plazas only to be killed by falling facades.

Abandonment of a site was also used as an antiseismic strategy. The old site of Noto, now called Noto Antica, like Avola Vecchia, was said to have broken apart in the 1693 earthquake. It was abandoned partly for political and economic reasons—to move closer to the rich coastal plains and to provide easier access to transportation by road and by sea—but most notably because of the inherent difficulties of its terrain, which was judged to be unstable and therefore dangerous after the January temblor.[30] People began to assess keenly the safety of given sites by looking for what damage could be seen on the ground or in the soil itself, and their observations at Noto and Avola, well founded or not, led to the abandonment of the old sites. Architectural treatise writers beginning with Vitruvius extolled the virtues of healthy and safe locations for founding cities, but often practical market considerations prevailed; economically successful sites were rarely abandoned even if they were found to be unhealthy or seismically vulnerable. Yet, surprisingly, in the seventeenth and eighteenth centuries, abandonment was often the first option considered when disaster struck. While many cities were transferred to new sites after the Calabrian earthquake of 1783, the option was discussed and dismissed in Catania in 1693 and vetoed in Lisbon in 1755 as too costly. In the Americas, the Spanish moved the capital of Guatemala three times before they settled on the site of what is now Guatemala City.[31] The first site was attacked by Indians, the second was destroyed by a mud slide, and the third struck by three earthquakes in 1717, 1751, and 1773. After the last quake the viceroy decided to move the city to what his engineers thought would be a better site, present-day Guatemala City, but many citizens defied his orders and stayed in the old city, now called Antigua Guatemala. In Noto a similar difference of opinion led to the temporary settlement of three separate sites, all intended to become the new city.

THE CITY PLAN OF NOTO

While Catania and Avola represent relatively unified preventative strategies, Noto's story is more complex, and is preserved in the plan of the city as it appears today (Figure 2).[32] Seismic safety does not seem to have played as large a role in Noto's urban plan. The Notinese, like the Avolese, transferred their city to a new location, but not all the citizens wanted to move. For ten years a dispute raged between those who supported the new town and those who wanted to return to the old. Simultaneously, another dispute erupted between the Spanish planners, who had intended the summit of the area, called the Pianazzo, to be the center of the town, and most of the people who settled on the lower slope of that general area, called the Meti. The summit was flatter and therefore safer during earthquakes, but it was also a steep

FIGURE 2. Air View of Noto, 1972 (Author)

climb from the plains and too small to accommodate the whole city. Two distinct grid plans developed, the first on the Pianazzo, the second on the slope. The architect Fra Angelo Italia, planner of Avola, was called to Noto; it was he who linked these two grids together in the unified plan we see today in which the four major squares in Noto balance one another, one on the summit and three on the slope below. Notwithstanding Italia's attempt to unify the city, the slope and the Pianazzo retain very different characters.

Around the time of Italia's visit, in the last years of the seventeenth century, the Spanish government, anxious to end the dispute over the location of the city once and for all, arranged a plebiscite.[33] All the remaining citizens of Noto, now ensconced on the new site, were polled. They had suffered plague, lack of water, and squalid living conditions on the Meti. Therefore it is no surprise a majority wanted to leave. But this majority was overruled by members of the aristocracy and the church. Michele Luminati has rightly pointed out that the vote itself was a victory for a peaceful legalistic solution to what could have become an internecine battle between the few dissenting aristocrats and the majority of aristocrats, and between the aristocrats and the commoners.[34] The transition and final confirmation of the new site, by declaration of the Spanish government, ended all debate in 1702.

The triumph of the upper classes is recorded in the city itself. It is a perfect artifact of the ancien régime, where class dichotomy is stamped onto the streets of Noto: The upper classes built palaces and baroque churches on the grid plan, while the lower classes built their humble dwellings within the blocks formed by the wide, straight streets. In order to gain access to the centers of the blocks, random, curving medieval alleys were built. Paolo Labisi, one of the official city architects of Noto charged with assessing buildings and regulating construction on vacant lots, mentions the importance of having piazzas as refuges during earthquakes, but the hazardous slope of the Meti and the existence of these narrow, curvilinear alleys in the plan show a lack of cohesive, systematic seismic planning.[35] In the case of Noto the most significant antiseismic strategy was not the design of the new town but the abandonment of Noto Antica.

REBUILDING NOTO

As it was being rebuilt Noto was rocked by earthquakes in 1727, 1738, 1766, 1767, and 1780.[36] Major earthquakes struck in other European cities during this time as well: in central Italy in 1703, Palermo in 1726, Lisbon in 1755, and, after Noto was complete, in Calabria in 1783. What effect did these earthquakes have on the reconstruction of Noto? Were additional mitigation efforts made in building practices?

Noto was first reconstructed as a temporary city largely built of wood. Then, around 1702, after the first decade on the new site, a second reconstruction in modest stone structures began. But many of these buildings were demolished and enlarged again from about 1730. During its first period of reconstruction Noto's citizens were concerned enough about future earthquakes to build cautiously. Chroniclers tell us that the first buildings of the city were small and low because of the fear of future shocks.[37]

Excavations of these first structures have uncovered a peculiarity that might be related to attempts to make the site of Noto and individual structures seismically resistant. There are scores of artificial caves carved under major structures. Some can be explained as cisterns for collecting rainwater, but some were never used as cisterns and never closed. Buildings were purposely constructed over them, often with major walls positioned over the voids. Could these voids be the antiseismic caves recommended by every author discussing seismic safety in the Renaissance? Although no direct supporting evidence has emerged in the documents, this is not an unlikely hypothesis.

It is still unclear whether the architects of Noto learned anything from the experience of the 1726 earthquake in Palermo, where damage assessment and reconstruction methodology were surprisingly ahead of their time. After that quake, antiseismic solutions for cupolas made of stucco and wood instead of stone were discussed and implemented. Strengthening of damaged structures through the copious use of iron was introduced.[38] Even a law prohibiting the use of heavy balconies was promulgated.[39] And the connection between poor alluvial soil and building damage was considered, as Domenico Campolo's map of Palermo demonstrates.[40]

A year later, in 1727, an earthquake damaged several newly recon-structed buildings in Noto: the facade of the church of S. Francesco broke apart; the vault of S. Agata fell; the cross of the church of SS. Trinità tumbled off; S. Maria di Gesù was damaged; a portion of the facade of the Jesuit seminary facing the present Piazza XVI Maggio collapsed; and the newly erected Chiesa Madre facade doorway fell in.[41] What effect did the lessons of the Palermo earthquake have on reconstruction in Noto? Rosario Gagliardi, the most famous architect working in eighteenth-century Noto, left us little written information about his views on architecture, much less earthquakes. Nevertheless, his work in Noto reflects his knowledge and concern about seismic safety. Gagliardi had been employed to strengthen the damaged church of S. Maria la Rotonda in Noto, where he reinforced walls by inserting iron bars and keys, just as architects in Palermo had done. Whether a reflection of post-earthquake observations in Palermo or in Noto itself, in Gagliardi's work and throughout Noto there is a lack of large cupolas, tower facades, and high towers. Furthermore, most domes in Noto, like the one atop the Jesuit church of S. Carlo, are Lombard domes with framed timber roofs and interiors of wood, bamboo, and stucco. Evidence of the architect's acknowledgment of seismic problems might also be revealed in his church of S. Domenico, which was unusually squat, and in his method of miniaturization in his tower-facade churches elsewhere in Sicily, which reduced how far the last story projected above the roof. We do know that Gagliardi took the threat of temblors into account because of a document of 1750 in which he discussed wood and stucco vaults as opposed to stone vaults for the church of S. Michele in the town of Scicli in relation to earthquakes;[42] he advised that wood and plaster vaults would resist earthquake shocks more effectively than stone vaults. Perhaps his wooden and plaster vault of the convent of S. Chiara in Noto was just such a response to the earthquake of 1727.

The other main architect involved most prominently in Noto's recon-struction, Paolo Labisi, certainly read about antiseismic architecture. In a treatise of Christian Wolff's, *Elementa Matheseos Universae* (1715–1717), translated for Labisi in 1746 as *Elementi dell'Architettura Civile*, there is a discussion of lateral bracing in roof systems and a depiction of the *cratico-la*, or wooden grate, used in foundations, which served "*ad impedire ne' tremuoti lo scompaginamento delle parti*" (to prevent the breaking up of parts in the event of an earthquake), but in Labisi's own work we see no use of wood armatures or iron tie bars.[43] Likewise in his 1750 plans for the House of the Crociferi Fathers, the last great religious house to be built in eighteenth-century Noto, we see no evidence of antiseismic construction.[44] How can this be explained? We can only guess, but the reasons might be many. Judging from contemporary and historical experience, people tend to ignore or forget earthquake danger after a few years. Aesthetic values and short-term economic exigencies usually outweigh seismic precautions. Information about actual earthquakes and antiseismic methods may not have seemed germane to Noto. Labisi knew of no prestigious models for designing differently, so he built well, perhaps believing in solid building technique as an antiseismic strategy—a belief shared by some architects and engineers from the Renaissance up to our own time.

Lisbon Earthquake of 1755

The most famous earthquake of the eighteenth century, the great Lisbon earthquake, struck Lisbon at 9:40 A.M. on All Saints' Day, 1 November 1755.[45] Houses and shops in the lower city (present-day Baixa), built on alluvial soil, were razed. Thirty-five of Lisbon's forty parish churches were destroyed. Thousands of people, many in church at the time, perished on a sacred religious day in one of the most resolutely Catholic cities in Europe. Even strategies that should have saved lives failed: crowds trying to escape the earthquake ran to the safety of the vast expanse of the Terreiro do Paço, but this was not a safe refuge. Lisbon lies inland from the Atlantic coast along the northwestern bank of the Tagus River estuary. The waters of the Atlantic, at the mouth of the estuary, receded during the shaking of the earthquake only to return as a seismically generated wave, a tsunami. The 40-foot tsunami rolled down the estuary at incredible speed and broke over the crowds seeking safety at the Terreiro do Paço. By afternoon, fires that began shortly after the earthquake incinerated surviving and ruined buildings alike. As many as 30,000 people died in Lisbon. The earthquake was felt as far away as Algiers, Madrid, and Strasbourg.

The psychological effect of the disaster corresponded to the magnitude of the damage it caused. Religious and philosophical tracts appeared by the dozens, trying to make sense of the enormous disaster that occurred. Philosophers of the Optimist School, who held that the laws of nature constituted the revelation of a divinely ordered and harmonious world, "the best of all possible worlds," were baffled. Voltaire attacked them with sarcasm in his novel *Candide*: "If this is the best of all possible worlds, whatever must the others be like?"

Not as well known as Voltaire's literary response to the Lisbon earthquake is the sophisticated antiseismic response authored by the tyrannical and brilliant Secretary of State for Foreign Affairs and Welfare Sebastião José de Carvalho e Melo, who later became the Marquês de Pombal. Systematic earthquake mitigation methods are thought to date from the Marquês de Pombal's Enlightenment initiatives for the reconstruction of Lisbon. However, many of the decisions and strategies in the urban redesign of Lisbon had already been put into practice in Sicily. Pombal's military architects, headed by Manuel da Maia, presented him with several reconstruction schemes for Lisbon, each a direct outcome of the destruction they had seen. First, they suggested that the city be moved to a safer location, an idea that was vetoed because of the city's size. Second, they suggested that the whole city be redesigned with wide, straight streets, as Catania had been. But this idea was vetoed by the landowners and considered impractical. The third proposal was to leave the street pattern unaltered and rebuild the buildings in their former locations. The fourth proposal was to rebuild the most damaged section on a new plan and to rebuild the rest of the city on the pre-earthquake plan. And it was this proposal—in effect a compromise solution—that Pombal endorsed. The central low-lying area of the city, the Baixa, was redesigned with straight streets linking the Terreiro do Paço and the Rossio squares, the blocks between them repeated rectangles. Da Maia wanted building height limited to two stories for earthquake safety and no building to be taller than the streets were wide, in order to keep streets passable after earthquakes. Both of these regulations failed to be enacted.

The major technical breakthrough in the rebuilding of Lisbon was the invention of the *gaiola*, a flexible, diagonally braced wooden skeleton around which masonry walls were built (Figure 3).[46] The flexible wooden skeleton was designed to hold the brittle masonry in place when the structure was shaken while the encasing masonry was supposed to protect the wood from fire. This is the first antiseismic building system to have

FIGURE 3. Modern Model of *Gaiola* Construction (J.-A. França, *A Reconstrução de Lisboa e a aquitectura pombalina*, 2nd ed., Biblioteca Breve, vol. 12, Lisbon: Instituto de Cultura e Língua, Portuguesa Ministério da Educação e Ciência, 1981)

been tested (soldiers stamped randomly on the floors) and to have been stipulated by law. Lisbon's new city plan successfully employed older strategies such as the straightening of streets and the creation of open spaces in the central part of the city, but the plan's greatest innovation was its focus on building technology and codes. The inventors of the *gaiola* had faced the question of antiseismic construction, which Noto's architects had largely ignored.

CALABRIAN EARTHQUAKES OF 1783

Six strong earthquakes struck Calabria between 5 February and 28 March, destroying scores of towns and killing 35,000 people.[47] Since the earthquakes recurred over months, scientists flocked to the ruined province to observe their effects. For the first time in modern history many people's observations of earth movements were integrated into a graduated scale so that damage could be assessed. Also for the first time, a scholarly commission was appointed by the government of Naples to study the earthquakes and to recommend reconstruction policy. The studies were initiated by the Reale Accademia delle Scienze e delle Belle Lettere of Naples under the aegis of the Bourbon government, which ruled southern Italy and Sicily in the late eighteenth century. The royal physician, Giovanni Vivenzio, correlated much of the commission's material and published an exhaustive analysis of the earthquake entitled *Istoria de' Tremuoti*, with plans for the reconstruction of towns and buildings.

Vivenzio's work contains the only known diagram of a specially designed antiseismic building system called *la casa baraccata* (Figure 4), a system peculiar to Calabria that does not follow the form of the earlier Portuguese *gaiola*. Drawn by Vincenzo Ferraresi and published with a commentary in *Istoria de' Tremuoti*, the system works upon the basic principle that the masonry structure is tied together by an internal wooden framework. But whereas the lateral resistance of the *gaiola* is in the internal walls, the lateral resistance of the *casa baraccata* is in the external walls, in the form of X braces. The system was an attempt to remedy observed

FIGURE 4. The *Casa Baraccata* (G. Vivenzio, *Istoria de' Tremuoti avvenuti nella provincia di Calabria Ulteriore e nella città di Messina nell'anno 1783, e di quanto nelle Calabrie fu fatto per lo suo risorgimento fino al 1787. Preceduta da una teoria, ed istoria generale de' tremuoti*, Naples: Stamperia Regale, 1788)

failures in pure masonry construction by proposing height limitations, symmetrical configuration, and the use of linked, X-braced wooden members.[48]

Ferraresi's design, published by Vivenzio, also illustrates a hidden anti-seismic feature that takes us back to the theory of earthquakes discussed by Aristotle. A majority of scholars still believed that some form of underground heat, explosion, or winds caused earthquakes. But another school of thought that arose in the late eighteenth century seized on the notion that electricity might be the culprit. A great debate ensued regarding the cause of the Calabrian earthquakes. Hence the lightning rods that adorn the eaves of the *casa baraccata* indicate that Ferrari or Vivenzio did not discount this theory. The engineer Francesco La Vega is credited with writing the guidelines that were adopted as law by the Bourbon government in 1785 and which prescribed the *casa baraccata*. The actual buildings erected in Calabria had far less elaborate internal wooden frameworks than the one illustrated by Vivenzio, and the real antiseismic value of their designs is debatable.[49] Nevertheless, the *baraccata* system was the first known antiseismic system prescribed by code for an entire region.

The Bourbons, who were intent on bettering the backward province of Calabria, used the 1783 earthquake as a pretext to seize church property while creating a safer, more hygienic urban environment. A good example of seismic reforms is the town of Filadelfia (Figure 5), founded after the earthquakes. The Bourbons moved the population of the medieval town of Castelmonardo, on a hill some miles away, to a new, symmetrically planned town. Safer in its street plan and piazza configuration, more centrally located, with easier access, Filadelfia was the Bourbons' attempt at creating an ideal community. Construction costs were partly financed through governmental recovery funds, which derived from revenues secured from the Catholic Church. The fund, called the Cassa Sacra, was the product of the Bourbon government's attempt to use the earthquake as a means of social reform by limiting ecclesiastical power and raising the standard of living. As a result, Filadelfia, like the other cities of Calabria, has fewer churches than its predecessor, Castelmonardo, did before the earthquake. Special laws limited the number of churches by stipulating a population ratio to each built. A contemporary view of the town shows neat, nearly uniform dwellings evenly distributed around five piazzas in a quincunx plan. The five spireless churches are designed as classical temples.

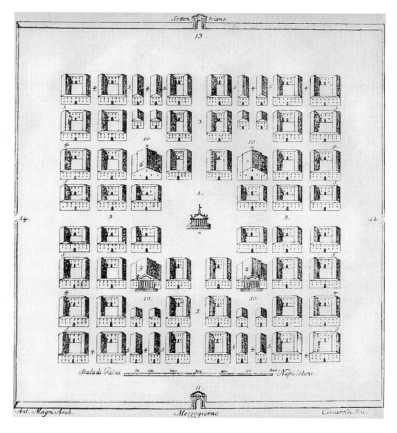

FIGURE 5. Project for the City of Filadelfia (E. Serrao, *De' tremuoti e della nuova Filadelfia in Calabria*, Naples: Raimondi, 1785)

Filadelfia provides an antithetical example to that of Noto; in Filadelfia's design, an Enlightenment humanism prevailed over the interests of the church, and central government and bureaucracy overrode the power of local aristocrats. Nothing could be starker than the contrast between Paolo Labisi's *veduta*, or view, of Noto, drawn in the 1760s and redated 1783 (Figure 6), and the project for Filadelfia, dated 1785. Labisi illustrated scores of churches, monasteries, and palaces amid the backdrop of haphazard lower-class dwellings. Although they are of the same decade, the rational design for Filadelfia and Labisi's Noto seem to belong to very different

FIGURE 6. The Veduta of Noto Drawn by Paolo Labisi in the 1760s and Redated 1783 (Formerly in the Biblioteca Comunale di Noto, Now Lost [Author])

eras. With regard to seismic safety, every building in Filadelfia was constructed employing the *casa baraccata* according to government code, while Noto's builders remained faithful to their traditional masonry construction.

NOTO AND THE EARTHQUAKES OF 1755 AND 1783

A little more than ten years after the 1755 Lisbon earthquake, two more earthquakes struck Noto in 1766 and 1767. The House of the Crociferi, still under construction, was severely damaged. The commission to construct the building had been taken away from the architect Paolo Labisi, an aspiring aristocrat, and reassigned to Vincenzo Sinatra, a crafts-man who made his way up through the ranks, perhaps aided by his father-in-law, Rosario Gagliardi. Although the ensuing legal battle between Labisi and Sinatra spurred Labisi to write his own treatise on architectural law (completed c. 1773), he made no mention of antiseis-mic construction.[50] Perhaps a system like the *gaiola* or a far less ambitious plan of open interiors could have saved the building. Or perhaps the con-struction was flawed, as Labisi claimed, by Sinatra's incompetence. The damage to the structure made it impossible to finish this building as planned and probably played a part in later partial collapses.

Again in 1780 Noto was struck by an earthquake, this time causing the new dome of S. Nicolò, Chiesa Madre, to collapse.[51] This dome was the first of a series of three domes that would collapse; the second fell in an earthquake in 1848, the third in a rainstorm in 1996. The collapse of 1780 is particularly puzzling because it occurred in the third Chiesa Madre built on the site, a structure that was supposed to have been an improvement over the earlier second church. The first church was a temporary wooden and stone structure; the second church was a smaller stone building, which was damaged in the earthquake of 1727. By 1753 Gagliardi judged the sec-ond church to be constructed improperly of soft stone, completely against the rules of architecture. This church was demolished around the time of Gagliardi's death. The new, grander third church, which rose on the site of the second and was perhaps based on Gagliardi's designs, proved technical-ly flawed. Construction of the pillars supporting the arcade was substan-dard, due partly to the use of smooth round river stones to which mortar would never adhere and partly to the soft, damp limestone and poor mor-tar itself. It is ironic that the second church, denounced by Gagliardi, should be followed by one that repeated the very mistakes he had pointed out years before. The Chiesa Madre not only lacked an antiseismic design but also basic solid construction as well. The most important and last of the great structures in Noto, the Chiesa Madre was unfortunately built more poorly than the churches and monasteries that preceded it.

A contemporary aerial view of Noto (Figure 2) illustrates that it still closely resembles the image Labisi recorded in his *veduta* (Figure 6). As we look back on this eighteenth-century city in southeastern Sicily it is worth asking how we can place it in relation to earthquake mitigation strategies. Let us first consider earthquake mitigation decisions based on site assessment. Did the moves of Noto and Avola increase the safety of these cities? How dangerous was a site like Noto Antica? Contemporary observers saw rock slides and fissures after the earthquake of 1693. Further, the danger of the site would have been confirmed because it was the epicenter of a score of earthquakes in the eighteenth century.[52] Nevertheless, the rock outcropping of Noto Antica, like the site of Avola Vecchia, possibly could be preferable to alluvial soil, with its increased risk of shaking and liquefaction. In Noto the gradual filling and leveling of the site—as the first temporary city was replaced by permanent constructions built on filled foundations—added to potential wave amplification and possible earthquake danger. By comparison, the introduction of wide, straight streets in Catania, Avola, and Noto improved escape and access routes. Whereas, in the Baixa district of Lisbon and in Catania such sweeping urban revisions were accomplished on the original sites, in Avola Vecchia and Noto Antica, constructed on narrow sites covered in ruins, rebuilding with wide straight streets was impossible. Moving these two cities proved crucial in this regard.

The initial phase of urban design immediately following the earthquake of 1693 incorporated sound concepts for seismic safety: wide, relatively level, and straight streets were safer during and after earthquakes. The immense piazzas like those of Avola provided places of refuge during the shaking and safe camping sites after the shock. These basic practices were repeated in Lisbon and Calabria. Unfortunately the safety of urban spaces can only be maintained through code enforcement; for example, the institution and maintenance of limited building heights. As noted earlier, immediately after the 1693 earthquake apprehensive citizens only built low masonry buildings in Noto. If the facades of these low structures fell in an earthquake, they would not have blocked the new wide, straight streets. But with the passage of time in Noto and Catania, facades were built higher and higher, and the danger of blocking the streets increased. Similarly, the open spaces, which the Catanese felt would guarantee safe havens after earthquakes, became endangered by the high buildings surrounding them.

What can we say about building practice in Noto in relation to earthquakes? Noto was rebuilt largely as it had been built prior to 1693, with no consistent improvements in its building technology. Apparently Gagliardi made attempts to lighten some of his masonry structures by using wood and plaster vaults, but he rarely introduced either iron or wood to help hold the buildings together. Neither Paolo Labisi nor Vincenzo Sinatra seems to have been interested in the problem. There was no new technology and no new law to direct how buildings might be constructed more safely, illustrating that Noto was far behind Pombal in Lisbon or the Bourbons in Calabria, both inspired by the model of the French corps of engineers. These governments assigned groups of engineers and architects to solve seismic problems. After adequate solutions were found, each government then invested its full authority in regulating new construction. True, neither the *gaiola* nor the *casa baraccata* proved the perfect solution, but both illustrate attempts to remedy problems inherent to masonry buildings. Both might be classified as Enlightenment solutions because of their rational approach to earthquake safety based on observation—but let us not forget Pirro Ligorio, who wrote more than a century earlier. What distinguishes the *gaiola* and the *casa baraccata* from earlier antiseismic systems is that both were implemented and required by law. While the *gaiola* was confined to the Lisbon area, the *casa baraccata* was an antiseismic building technology adopted across an entire region. No similar strategy evolved in Sicily, in part because the island was ruled by foreign governments (including the Bourbons of Naples) throughout the eighteenth century. These governments, far more concerned with economic exploitation and maintaining order, did not have the power or the will to influence local practices except in setting standard fees and taxes. The result is that to the present day, Noto's masonry buildings are extremely vulnerable to earthquake damage, as are those of all the cities of southeastern Sicily. Noto is a magnificent city faced throughout in a golden limestone whose apparent permanence is belied by its own history. Paolo Labisi's *veduta,* redated 1783, was probably meant to be a testament of Noto's survival, proving that it was not damaged by the Calabrian earthquakes of 1783. The city lives in the *veduta* as it did in the eighteenth century—a fragile artifact of Sicilian culture touched by Enlightenment ideas but still firmly planted in an earlier tradition.

NOTES

1   This article appeared in an earlier form in *Storia dell'urbanistica/Sicilia II, Le città ricostruite dopo il terremoto siciliano del 1693*, eds. A. Casamento and E. Guidoni (Rome: Edizioni, Kappa 1997), 26–41. It has been entirely rewritten and updated for this publication.

2   This was the second earthquake in a series. The first occurred on 9 January 1693. The best scientific account of the 1693 earthquake can be found in *Catalogo dei forti terremoti in Italia*, eds. Enzo Boschi et al. (Bologna: Istituto Nazionale de Geofisica, SGA Storia geofisica ambiente, 1995), 291–297.

3   S. Tobriner, *The Genesis of Noto, an 18th-Century Sicilian City* (London: A. Zwemmer Ltd and Berkeley: University of California Press, 1982), 25.

4   Tobriner, *Genesis,* 25.

5   For example, see T. D. Kendrick, *The Lisbon Earthquake* (Philadelphia and New York: J.B. Lippincott Co., 1955), 113–69; A. Placanica, *Il filosofo e la catastrofe; un terremoto del Settecento* (Turin: Casa del Libro Editrice, 1985), 143–61.

6   For the saints of earthquakes see above and C. Margottini and J. Kozak, *Terremoti in Italia, dal 62 A.D. al 1908* (Rome: Ente per le Nuove Tecnologie, l'Energia e l'Ambiente 1992), 11.

7   J. Shower, *Practical Reflections on the Late Earthquakes in Jamaica, England, Sicily, Malta & c. Anno 1692* (London: J. Salusbury,1693).

8   Kendrick, *Lisbon,* 142.

9   Dr. Pano Touliatos described seismically resistant Minoan architecture at Akrotiri on Santorini and on Crete itself at the international convention entitled *Piano e progetto nelle aree a rischio sismico,* Catania, 1994. For a good summary of the literature and the debate concerning antiseismic architecture in antiquity see S. C. Stiros, "Archaeological

Evidence of Antiseismic Constructions in Antiquity," *Annali di geofisica*, 38, no. 5-6, (Nov.–Dec. 1995): 723-36.

10   S. Tobriner, "Response of Traditional Wooden Japanese Construction," *Seismological and Engineering Aspects of the 1995 Hyogoken-Nanbu (Kobe) Earthquake*, Earthquake Engineering Research Center, Report no. UCB/EERC-95/10 (Berkeley, November 1995), 61–80. H. Shiping, "The Earthquake-resistant Properties of Chinese Traditional Architecture," *Earthquake Spectra* 7 (1991): 355–89.

11   S. Di Pasquale, *Architettura e terremoti; Il caso di Parma: 9 november 1983* (Parma: Istituto per i beni artistici, culturali e naturali della regione Emilia-Romagna, Dipartimento di costruzioni dell'università degli studi di Firenze, 1986), 18.

12   This drive to understand and control natural phenomena can be seen in the debates surrounding the cause of earthquakes described in Placanica, *Il filosofo*.

13   A. Picon, *French Architects and Engineers in the Age of Enlightenment*, (trans. Martin Thom (Cambridge: Cambridge University Press, 1992), in particular 100–206, 300–39.

14   S. P. Timoshenko, *History of Strength of Materials* (New York, Dover Publications, Inc., 1983), 7–66.

15   G. Poleni, *Memorie istoriche della gran cupola del tempio vaticano e de' danni di essa, e de' ristoramenti loro, divise in libri cinque* (Parma: Stamperia del Seminario, 1748).

16   E. Guidoboni, "An Early Project for an Antiseismic House in Italy: Pirro Ligorio's Manuscript Treatise of 1570–74," *European Earthquake Engineering, Journal of European Association for Earthquake Engineering* 2 (1997): 13–20.

17   Di Pasquale, *Architettura*, 19; F. Di Teodoro and L. Barbi, "Leonardo da Vinci: del riparo a'terremoti," *Physis, Rivista internazionale di storia della scienza* 25, no. 1 (1983): 5–39, for other architects see p. 12; U. Barbisan and F. Laner, "Wooden Floors: Part of Historical Antiseismic Building Systems," *Annali di geofisica* 37, no. 5–6 (Nov.–Dec. 1995): 775–84, and E. Guidoboni, "Pozzi e gallerie come rimedi antisismici: la fortuna di un pregiudizio sulla città antiche," in *I terremoti prima del Mille in Italia e nell'area mediterranea*, ed. Guidoboni (Bologna: Istituto Nazionale de Geofisica, SGA Storia geofisica ambiente, 1989), 127–35.

18   Guidoboni, "Pozzi," 127–35.

19   Guidoboni, "An Early Project," 17.

20   For Descartes see Di Pasquale, *Architettura*, 19; Giudoboni, "Pozzi," 132, quotes G. A. Casagrande (*Saggio sopra la diversità della natura, cagione ed effetti dei terremoti*, Jesi, 1782) advising the excavation of wells as an antiseismic measure.

21   Di Pasquale, *Architettura*, 26.

22   Di Pasquale, *Architettura*, 27–28; Barbisan and Laner, "Wooden Floors," 776–77.

23   C. Barucci, "Aspetti delle tecniche costruttive nelle ricostruzioni siciliane e calabrese tra XVII e XVIII secolo," in *Storia dell'urbanistica/Sicilia II, Le città ricostruite dopo il terremoto siciliano del 1693*, eds. A. Casamento and E. Guidoni (Rome: Edizioni Kappa, 1997), 42–49.

24   Di Pasquale, *Architettura*, 23.

25   Tobriner, *Genesis*, 27.

26   Ibid., 25–26, 103–104.

27   S. Tobriner, "Angelo Italia and the Post-Earthquake Reconstruction of Avola in 1693," *Le Arti in Sicilia del settecento: Studi in memoria di Maria Accascina* (Palermo: Regione Siciliana, 1985), 75–86; and L. Dufour and H. Raymond, "La Riedificazione di Avola, Noto e Lentini: Fra Angelo Italia, maestro architetto," *Il Barocco in Sicilia*, eds. M. Fagiolo and L. Trigilia (Siracusa: Ediprint, 1987), 11–31; see also their *Dalla città ideale alla città reale. La ricostruzione di Avola 1693–1695* (Caltanissetta: Ediprint, 1993). Also see F. Gringeri Pantano, *La città esagonale* (Palermo: Sellerio, 1996), 95–133.

28   Tobriner, "Angelo Italia," 75.

29   Ibid., 78.

30   Tobriner, *Genesis*, 32.

31   V. L. Annis, *The Architecture of Antigua Guatemala* (Guatemala: University of San Carlos of Guatemala, 1968); D. H. Popenoe, *The Story of Antigua Guatemala* (Dalton, Mass.: Studely Press, 1975) are the sources for the material on Antigua Guatemala. Where disagreements arose between the authors, as in opinion about the cause of the mudslide at Almolonga, I have followed Annis.

32   Tobriner, *Genesis*, 41–65.

33   Ibid., 47.

34   M. Luminati, *Erdbeben in Noto; Krisen- und Katastrophenbewältigung im Barockzeitalter*, Zürcher Studien zur Rechtsgeschichte 27 (Zürich: Schulthess Polygraphischer Verlag, 1995).

35   Tobriner, *Genesis*, 97.

36   For earthquakes see E. Boschi, E. Guidoboni, and D. Mariotti, "I terremoti dell'area siracusana e i loro effetti in Ortigia," *Sicurezza e conservazione dei centri storici, Il caso*

Ortigia, ed. A. Giuffrè (Rome: Laterza, 1993), 15–36, in particular 18 and 19; E. Guidoboni, V. Petrini, P. Riva, G. Lombardini, A. Madini Moretti, and M. Forte, "Quantitative Measurements and Structural Analysis in Seismic Archaeology: The Walls of Noto and the 1693 Earthquake," paper delivered at Terremoti e civiltà abitative: dieci anni di ricerche Istituto Nazionale di Geofisica, Accademia Nazionale dei Lincei, Rome, October 1993; Cleofo Canale, *Noto—La struttura continua della città tardo barocca* (Palermo: S.F. Flaccivio, 1976), 58, 363, 288–89.

37   Tobriner, *Genesis,* 6.

38   I am preparing an article on the antiseismic measures used by architects after the 1726 earthquake. The use of iron rods to strengthen damaged buildings was widespread. One prominent example is the church of SS. Salvatore.

39   R. La Duca, "Terremoti, norme antisismiche ed architettura a Palermo tra Settecento e Ottocento," *Laurea Honoris Causa* (Palermo: Facoltà di Architettura, Università degli Studi di Palermo, March 1995), n.p.

40   Ibid. The map illustrates the correspondence between filled-in river beds and damaged structures. The conclusion is obvious: the heaviest concentration of damaged buildings is on alluvial soil. The danger of intense shaking on alluvial soil was demonstrated dramatically in the failure of the Cypress Freeway in Oakland during the 1989 Loma Prieta earthquake in California. This is the first known map to demonstrate the relationship between damage and soil type.

41   C. Gallo, "Noto agli albori della sua rinascità dopo il terremoto del 1693," *Archivio Storico Siciliano,* 1964, 116–21; and Canale, *Noto,* 58, 263.

42   P. Nifosì, *Scicli: Una vita tardobarocca* (Scicli: Comune di Scicli, 1988), 32, 37.

43   For Labisi's work on the House of Crociferi and his use of Wolff see Tobriner, *Genesis,* 184–96.

44   The iron tie-bars in the southwest part of the building are of a much later date, the drawings illustrate no seismic features, and the recently excavated foundations in the courtyard indicate faulty construction.

45   The description of Lisbon is based on J.-A. França's *Lisboa Pombalina e o iluminismo* (Lisbon: Livaria Bertrand, 1965); F. L. Periera de Sousa, *O Terrement de 1 de Novembro de 1775 em portugal e um Estudo Demográfico,* 4 vols. (Lisbon: Serviços Geologicas, 1919–32); J. R. Mullin, "The Reconstruction of Lisbon Following the Earthquake of 1755: A Study in Despotic Planning," *Planning Perspectives* 7 (1992): 157–79; Kendrick, *The Lisbon Earthquake,* 45–70; and M. Levy and M. Salvadori, *Why the Earth Quakes: The Story of Earthquakes and Volcanoes* (New York and London: W. W. Norton, 1995), 61–65.

46   Tobriner, "History of Reinforced Masonry," 126–27.

47   *Catalogo dei forti terremoti,* 334–46, for the earthquake itself. For the reconstruction the basic work is I. Principe, *Città nuove in Calabria nel tardo Settecento* (Chiara valle Centrale: Edizioni EFFE EMME, 1976).

48   S. Tobriner, "La Casa Baraccata: Earthquake-Resistant Construction in Eighteenth-Century Calabria," *Journal of the Society of Architectural Historians* XLII, no. 2 (May 1983), 131–38. C. Barucci, "Aspetti," 42–49; and C. Barucci, *La casa antisismica. Prototipi e brevetti. Materiali per una storia delle tecniche e del cantiere* (Rome, Reggio Calabria: Gangemi, 1990), 30 ff.

49   Tobriner, "La Casa Baraccata," 136–38.

50   Tobriner, *Genesis,* 196.

51   At the writing of this article I am directing a project for compiling the history of the construction and multiple failures of S. Nicolò, the present cathedral of Noto, for the engineers who are working on a project to reconstruct it after the failure of its nave and dome.

52   E. Boschi et al., *I terremoti dell'area, 15–36.*

PART II

Colonial Perspectives
and
New World Calamities

4

Hunger in the Garden of Plenty

The Bengal Famine of 1770

David Arnold

*I*n Europe's Age of Enlightenment India remained an enigma. Judged by the apparent fertility of its soil, the wealth of its natural products, and the skill of its artisans, it ranked among the most favored and productive locations on earth. Considered, too, in the light of what Western Orientalist scholarship was beginning to uncover of the antiquity and sophistication of its literature, philosophy, and sciences, India—more especially Hindu India—seemed fit to rival the cherished achievements of ancient Greece and Rome. The founding of the Asiatic Society of Bengal in 1784 was one of the clearest expressions of the belief that India had a noble, if long neglected, place among the family of civilized nations.[1] And yet, from the 1750s, as the English East India Company began, by conquest and by stealth, to establish its dominion over South Asia, an alternative understanding of India was emerging, one that emphasized the moral and material poverty of India, the alien, even unfathomable, nature of its peoples and cultures, and so called into question its place among the "civilized" and "enlightened" nations of the globe.[2] The devastating Bengal famine of 1770 was not alone in generating this alternative vision, but the magnitude of the crisis, in which as many as ten million people may have perished, helped propagate an image of India as a land still subject to the capricious sway of nature (at a time when Europe grew yearly more confident of its mastery) and as a society too feeble and fatalistic to fend for itself. While the famine stimulated intense criticism of company exploitation and mismanagement, it also, paradoxically, strengthened belief in the intrinsic superiority of the West and in its imperial mission.

"So Great a Calamity"

In an age when India was passing rapidly under Europe's control and fell increasingly subject to its curiosity and scrutinizing gaze, there were many Europeans who either witnessed the famine that devastated eastern India in 1770, or who reflected on its significance from afar. John Shore, recently arrived in Bengal as a servant of the East India Company, was one eyewitness, and so deep was the impression that the famine made on him that nearly forty years later, after a long career in Indian affairs, he was moved to write:

> Still fresh in memory's eye, the scene I view,
> The shrivell'd limbs, sunk eyes, and lifeless hue;
> Still hear the mother's shrieks and infant's moans;
> Cries of despair, and agonizing groans.
> In wild confusion, dead and dying lie—
> Hark to the jackal's yell, and vulture's cry,
> The dog's fell howl, as midst the glare of day,
> They riot, unmolested, on their prey!
> Dire scenes of horror! which no pen can trace,
> Nor rolling years from memory's page efface.[3]

Another graphic account of the famine was given by an anonymous company official and published in London in 1771. Having explained how the famine began with "the dryness of the season" and the "approaching dearness of rice," the writer went on to describe how by April 1770, "many thousands" of hungry people had migrated to Calcutta, the principal seat of British power in India, "in hopes of finding relief amongst us." Within a fortnight, as conditions deteriorated still further, "many thousands [were] falling daily in the streets and fields," their corpses "mangled by dogs, jackals, and vultures." A hundred men were employed by the company and equipped with "doolys, sledges, and bearers"

> to carry the dead, and throw them into the river Ganges. I have counted from my bedchamber window in the morning when I got up, forty bodies lying within twenty yards of the wall, besides many hundreds lying in the agonies of death for want, bending double with their stomachs quite close contracted to their back bones.[4]

By June, as the price of rice rose still higher and hunger and scarcity became ever more widespread:

> One could not pass along the streets without seeing multitudes in their last agonies, crying out as you passed, "My God! My God! have mercy on me, I am starving": whilst on other sides, numbers of dead were seen with dogs, jackals, hogs, vultures, and other beasts and birds of prey feeding on their carcasses.[5]

Although the famine did not fully reach Calcutta until April 1770, the signs of impending disaster had been evident several months earlier, three hundred miles to the northwest, in the province of Bihar. Like many other famines in eighteenth- and nineteenth-century India, natural causes appeared to lie behind the famine of 1770. British officials blamed the exceptional drought and the consequent loss of the *aman*, or autumn rice crop, which normally provided 70 percent of the year's harvest. In Bihar in August 1768 the rainfall had been so heavy as to cause flooding, but thereafter the rains needed to water growing crops had been inadequate or had failed altogether, and by early 1769 there were reports of increasing drought, rising grain prices, and acute shortages. With only a few light showers falling in July, the prospects for the main harvest in December were bleak, and by the end of that year famine already stalked many districts of Bihar. By early 1770 drought and failed harvests had spread eastward into neighboring parts of Bengal, and the famine began in earnest. Several districts were said to be in a "terrible condition." For want of food and water villagers abandoned their homes in search of relief, flocking to Patna, Murshidabad, and Calcutta. In January 1770 there were an estimated 8,000 beggars on the streets of Patna, the capital of Bihar, and 50 people were dying every day. By March the daily toll had risen to 150. In October 1769 "great dearth and scarcity" had already begun to affect Murshidabad, where the Nawab of Bengal, now a virtual puppet of the company, resided with his court. The price of rice rose by May 1770 to four times the normal level and eventually to ten: but in many places it simply was not available at all. By July 1770, as the famine reached its height, 500 people were thought to be dying of starvation every day in Murshidabad.[6]

Suffering was even more widespread, if less visible to officials, in the surrounding countryside. In a pattern familiar from the more extensively documented famines of the nineteenth century, peasants tried to sell their possessions, even the plows and bullocks they would need in the future to till their fields. In desperation they ate their seed corn, then turned to eating grass, leaves, and bark. Children were sold to anyone who would buy them: some survived the famine only as slaves in European and Indian households. There were reports, as so often when the intensity of India's famine passed beyond normal comprehension, of hungry people driven to the extremes even of cannibalism: "There were persons who fed on forbidden and abhorred animals, nay, the child on its dead parent, the mother on her child."[7] Large numbers died of starvation or disease before they could find relief or because they were too worn out and malnourished to absorb the food they received. Mortality was greatest among agricultural laborers, poor peasants, and artisans (cotton and silk weavers, lime workers, and the like), with Bihar and western Bengal suffering most. Only toward the end of 1770 did the drought and famine abate. Rain came to Murshidabad in July and brought the further affliction of floods to some eastern districts. Before the end of September an "abundant" *aus* crop was reaped, followed by a plentiful *aman* harvest in December. On

Christmas Eve 1770, the governing council in Fort William, Calcutta, informed the company's court of directors in London that the famine had "entirely ceased." "Abundance," wrote W. W. Hunter of the Indian Civil Service ninety years later, "returned to Bengal as suddenly as famine had swooped down upon it."[8] But by then as many as a third of the population of Bengal and Bihar was already dead.

Precise figures for the number who died are impossible to ascertain. The East India Company had only taken de facto control of Bengal from the Nawabs since the battle of Plassey in 1757 and through assuming the powers of *diwani*, or revenue collection, in 1765. A system of "dual government" existed in which the company was formally responsible only for revenue collection. It had, as yet, gleaned little statistical information about its newly won territories. There was no census, no even halfway accurate tally of the numbers who lived and died. The extent of migration and the "desertion" of innumerable villages made it hard to establish who had perished or who had simply fled elsewhere. But there was no doubting the magnitude of the disaster. Richard Becher, the company's long-serving resident at Murshidabad, concluded as the famine drew to a close that "during the last year [1770] the provinces laboured under the most severe calamity that any country was ever afflicted with—a continued drought which produced such a famine and mortality among the inhabitants as I believe history does not furnish us with an instance of."[9] Becher did not attempt to number the dead, but John Shore, also at Murshidabad during the famine, reckoned that across Bengal as a whole at least one-fifth of the population had been lost.[10] As early as May 1770 it was believed that a third of the population in the "once plentiful province of Purnea" and in adjacent parts of eastern Bihar had died.[11] Two and a half years later, in November 1772, Warren Hastings, the new governor, wrote a lengthy report on the current state of Bengal, in which he described the impact of what had proved to be "so great a calamity." He reckoned, on the basis of his own observations and inquiries, that the province had lost "at least one-third of the inhabitants," and this figure has often been cited by subsequent historians.[12] In reviewing the evidence ninety years later, in a statistically more exacting age, Hunter calculated that the population at the time of the famine must have been about thirty million, and thus that "the failure of a single crop, following a year of scarcity, had within nine months swept away ten millions of human beings." This, he remarked, echoing Becher, represented "an aggregate of individual suffering which no European nation has been called upon to contemplate within historic times." [13]

Some recent assessments place the scale of mortality even higher. In 1970 the Bengali historian Nani Gopal Chaudhuri calculated that in the district of Rajshahi, which suffered only "moderately" during the famine by comparison with some localities, desertion and death together caused the disappearance of 66 percent of families: 47 percent of this loss was due to mortality alone. From figures for one part of Bihar, Chaudhuri estimated that in areas affected by drought and famine as many as half the total number of families were lost through death and desertion. He concluded: "It will not be far from [the] truth if we say that the famine of 1771 [*sic*] swept away near about half the population of the affected area." [14]

In terms of the enormous loss of life and the intensity and extent of human suffering involved, the Bengal famine of 1770 must count as one of the greatest catastrophes of the eighteenth century and, indeed, of modern times. It was, moreover, a crisis—not unlike the Lisbon earthquake of 1755—that had ramifications far beyond its immediate locality. [15] For reasons that will be examined shortly, the famine entered into a number of European accounts by French, Dutch, as well as English commentators; it even attracted the critical attention of the Scottish economist Adam Smith in *The Wealth of Nations*. [16] The famine fueled a vociferous debate about the operations of the East India Company, rapidly and rapaciously evolving from a trading organization into ruler of a vast empire in India, and prompted a greater degree of parliamentary scrutiny over the company's administration through the Regulating Act of 1773. The famine stimulated a radical reappraisal of what India, its people, and its environment represented, and provoked a searching critique of Britain's emerging role as an imperial power in Asia.

And yet, despite the enormous mortality and its impact on contemporary European attitudes, the Bengal famine had to a remarkable degree lapsed from official memory by the mid-nineteenth century. W. W. Hunter, whose research almost a century after the event uncovered a wealth of archival evidence, was partly motivated by the recent experience of the famine in neighboring Orissa in 1866. He discovered that "the disaster which from this distance floats as a faint speck on the horizon of our rule," stood out in contemporary records in "appalling proportions," and, indeed, provided "the key to the history of Bengal during the succeeding forty years." [17] Bureaucratic amnesia was matched by a paucity of Indian accounts, Ghulam Hussain Khan's Persian chronicle of these years, *Siyar-ul-Mutakharin* (1788), being a partial exemption. It is hard to believe that such a horrendous and widespread calamity did not live on in popular consciousness, as so many previous Indian famines had done. But it is suggestive of a lack of continuity, at least in middle-class awareness, that when Bankim Chandra Chattopadhyay used the famine as the backdrop to his celebrated novel *Anandamath* (1884), he drew not upon folk memories but on official descriptions extracted by Hunter and combined these with a vision of Bengal as a land suffering under the sway of the goddess Kali, destroying her own children through famine and pestilence. [18] Thereafter, the repeated famines of the late nineteenth century and mounting criticism of British rule revived interest in 1770 and strengthened the view that the famine was not a "natural" but a "manmade" disaster, and as such one of the most damning episodes in India's experience of colonial rule. [19] This interpretation gained further impetus from the Bengal famine of 1943, directly attributed to British bungling and in which three million lives were lost and which, with awful symmetry, scarred the final phase of British rule as that of 1770 had mutilated its very beginnings. Comparisons were inevitable between 1770 and 1943. That so many people died so rapidly in 1770, and in a province formerly renowned for its productivity, was, in the view of one Bengali writer, "due to the merciless exploitation of the English which had reduced a prosperous people to penury." [20]

During the past two hundred years, debate over causation and agency in the famine of 1770 has shifted back and forth between the twin poles of nature and culture.[21] If the consensus of recent opinion points the finger at human culpability, the famine nonetheless casts an illuminating beam of light on contemporary, or near-contemporary, interpretations of the place of nature in a catastrophe of such vast and tragic proportions.

"THE MOST FRUITFUL COUNTRY"

To some Europeans at the time, as later to many Indian nationalists, the Bengal famine of 1770 was so aberrant an event that it constituted a veritable crime against nature. It occurred at a time when Europe was beginning to develop a greater curiosity and a more informed understanding of the non-European world–of Asia, as of Africa, the Americas, and the Pacific. The second age of European exploration and political rivalry overseas stimulated a more scientific approach to the study of unfamiliar peoples and places. Expansion informed Enlightenment interest in trying to understand Europe's history and its political and social institutions, not only by reference back to the revered past of classical antiquity but also comparatively, through ethnographical observation of, and philosophical speculation about, other living societies around the globe. India was not entirely unfamiliar territory. Europeans had visited and traded there since the arrival of the Portuguese in the 1490s, and the accounts given by merchants, missionaries, doctors, and diplomats had already half fashioned occidental expectations of an exotic land. But from the mid-eighteenth century the great expansion of European trade and the meteoric rise of the English East India Company facilitated European access and provided fresh incentives for closer observation of India and the manners and customs of its inhabitants. New efforts were made to locate India within an expanding European conception of time and space. In the wake of Montesquieu's *De l'esprit des lois* in 1748, writers sought to identify and evaluate India's essential characteristics. Though individual assessments varied, there was a wide measure of agreement about what lay behind the exotic otherness of India—its timeless and unchanging nature, its long history of invading armies and despotic rulers, the rigidity of its religious and social divisions, the passivity of its Hindu population.[22] At a time when ideas of environmental, especially climatic, determinism were widely prevalent, European writers stressed the part played by the heat and humidity of India in molding its social institutions and religious beliefs; others located India within a dreamlike world of tropical abundance and luxuriance that might seem to us more appropriate to Tahiti or Ceylon than to India. One example of the latter representation was a French cleric, the Abbé Raynal, whose *Histoire philosophique des deux Indes* first appeared in 1772.

Like many of his contemporaries, the Abbé speculated that humans must have first established themselves in those regions of the world where, by dint of nature's abundance, they could live without "labour or anxiety." Only later did they migrate to cooler, more challenging, environments. It seemed reasonable to Raynal to suppose that "a part of the globe, best adapted to the human species, would be peopled the earliest, and that the first men would fix their abode in a delicious climate, pure air, and a soil too fertile to require much cultivation." He imagined "the plains of Indostan" to represent just such a location.

> The air is perfumed with the most delicious fruits, which afford a wholesome and refreshing nourishment; the trees form a shade impenetrable to the rays of the sun. While the living animals that are dispersed over the globe, cannot subsist in other parts without devouring each other, they share in India, in common with their master, the sweets of plenty and security. Even at this day, when the earth may be supposed to have been exhausted by the productions of so many ages, and their consumption in foreign countries, Indostan, if we except a few sandy and barren districts, is still the most fruitful country in the world.[23]

Like many Europeans of his day, Raynal believed that Bengal was the richest region of India and even of the whole of Asia. This was a view derived from the accounts of earlier European travelers, like the

Frenchman François Bernier in the seventeenth century, and from reports of the volume, variety, and value of the trade goods—from rice, sugar, and indigo to finely woven silks and painted cotton textiles—that originated in the province or flowed through its ports.[24] The catastrophe of 1769–1770 caused Raynal to wonder at the occurrence of "a drought of which there never had been an instance in those climates" and the reasons behind "a most dreadful famine in a country of all the most fertile." Quite apart from any influence ongoing Anglo-French rivalries over India might have had on his thinking, it was not surprising that, instead of blaming the "disturbance of the seasons" alone for the famine, Raynal accused the English East India Company, and the "most odious and most criminal of all monopolies" exercised by its merchants, for causing the shortage of grain and the resulting mortality.[25]

Among those critical of the company, nature was less the cause of the catastrophe than an index of its magnitude and abhorrence. The frequent references in contemporary accounts to dogs, pigs, jackals, and vultures devouring the dead, and even half dead, are a chilling reflection of the way in which the natural order had been inverted. Humans, instead of occupying their rightful place as the masters of nature, had, in a moment of extreme vulnerability and humiliation, become its sorry victims. The only consoling reflection, to the anonymous writer in the *Annual Register*, was that the great number of vultures, dogs, and jackals that descended on Calcutta on the "melancholy occasion" of the famine were "of great service" in leaving few human remains for company menials to dispose of.[26] But that wild animals and scavenging beasts should perform this task, in a society where pigs and dogs were particularly reviled, was a grisly parody of the funeral rites the living could no longer provide for the dead.

Superficially at least the return of the rains and the "abundant" harvests that followed helped restore Bengal to the semblance of its former prosperity. According to Hunter, the famine of 1770 was followed by three years of "extraordinary abundance, and nature exerted herself to repair the damage she had done." Because of the apparent speed of the recovery many Western observers in India and in Britain continued to regard

Bengal "in the light of a vast warehouse, in which a number of adventur-
ous Englishmen carried on business with great profit and on an enormous
scale."[27] But others, including many officials in Bengal, were fully aware
of how slow and faltering the process of recovery actually was.[28] In the eyes
of Europe, and in the perceptions of its own people, Bengal acquired an
image far more ambivalent than its old reputation for prosperity and
abundance. The travel narratives and landscape paintings of itinerant
British artists, like William Hodges in the 1780s, continued to present for
admiration the "luxuriant" vegetation and "picturesque" qualities of
Bengal and its western borderlands, "a country," Hodges remarked, "so
fertile in the beauties of nature."[29] T. B. Macaulay, law member of the
Calcutta government in the 1830s and an influential architect of British
opinion about India, lyrically described what had once been the richest
province of the Mughal empire:

> No part of India possessed such natural advantages, both for agricul-
> ture and for commerce. The Ganges, rushing through a hundred
> channels to the sea, has formed a vast plain of rich mould which,
> even under the tropical sky, rivals the verdure of an English April.
> The rice-fields yield an increase such as is elsewhere unknown.
> Spices, sugar, vegetable oils, are produced with marvellous exuber-
> ance. The rivers afford an inexhaustible supply of fish . . . . The great
> stream which fertilizes the soil is, at the same time, the chief highway
> of Eastern commerce. On its banks, and on those of its tributary
> waters, are the wealthiest marts, the most splendid capitals, and the
> most sacred shrines of India. The tyranny of man had for ages strug-
> gled in vain against the overflowing bounty of nature. In spite of the
> Mussulman despot and of the Mahratta freebooter, Bengal was
> known through the East as the garden of Eden. [30]

But the idea that Bengal could still, after the famine of 1770, represent
"the overflowing bounty of nature" was increasingly qualified or contest-
ed. British writers saw mounting evidence of the savage side of nature in
the recurrent famines and epidemics that swept the province. Even in

recent memory there had been droughts, floods, and famines (the latter, contra Raynal, as late as 1752), though they had not, apparently, tarnished the image of "golden Bengal." But several more calamities struck in the following thirty years, though not, mercifully, with as devastating a scale of mortality as in 1770. When epidemic cholera erupted in Jessore district of central Bengal in 1817 and began its century-long career of destruction in India and beyond, to be followed in the 1860s by "Burdwan fever" (malaria), the identification of Bengal with all manner of human misery was well established. To this, moreover, was added Bengal's economic decline in the face of British industrial competition, as silk- and cotton-textile manufacturing slumped, never to recover their former fame and prosperity.[31]

It was indicative of the perceptual shift away from the idea of Bengal as an abundant garden to a land of hardship and poverty that attempts, small enough in themselves, were made by the British to compensate for the apparent deficiencies of nature. In 1786 one of the most striking and hauntingly symbolic structures of early colonial India was completed at Bankipur near Patna. This was a giant domed *gola*, or public granary, built by the government to store grain in the event of any future famine.[32] A further indication of changing attitudes toward Bengal's natural capabilities was the proposal by Lieutenant Colonel Robert Kyd, also in 1786, for the establishment of a botanic garden across the River Hughli from Calcutta. One of the aims of the garden was to introduce into India food plants that might help to avert the kind of scarcity and loss of life caused in 1770 and again in 1784 by "the greatest of all calamities, that of desolation by famine, and subsequent pestilence."[33] Kyd's idea, which subsequently won approval from the court of directors, appealed to the eminent naturalist Sir Joseph Banks in London: he felt sure that future generations of Indians would "revere the names of their British conquerors to whom they will be indebted for the abolition of famine, the most severe scourge with which nature had afflicted the country."[34] The artificial contrivance of a botanic garden was thus to supplement the garden nature had made of Bengal, but which famine had found wanting. The garden, like the *gola,* illustrated the way in which, in an increasingly imperial-minded age, British claims to a mastery over nature were contrasted with Indians' abject subordination to it and so provided a legitimacy for empire itself.

By the time Hunter turned his attention to the famine in the 1860s, the idea was well established that control over nature epitomized the essential difference between India's hapless past and its present security under colonial rule. From his midcentury perspective the 1770 famine showed how little the economy of Bengal, at that time still in the murky twilight between "native government" and company Raj, was able to withstand the calamity of drought and consequent "natural scarcity." He contrasted this with the great improvements in transport and the sound adherence to the rational principles of political economy in the British India of his own day. Nature, barely checked by human agency, had ruled in 1770; by the time of the Orissa famine of 1866 (despite the fact that it, too, was marked by heavy mortality) nature had been tamed and made subservient to "modern civilization." [35] Equally, in Hunter's view, the depopulation and desolation caused by the 1770 famine had opened the way for the nihilism of unrestrained nature. Tigers (symbolizing nature at its most predatory and opportunistic) prowled and elephants plundered where once villages had thrived; impassable jungle (another expression of environmental negativity) sprang up where formerly fields and roads had been. The company, not renowned for its generosity, even had to pay villagers "tiger-money" to try to keep the rampant forces of nature at bay. So serious was the decline that in 1789 the governor general, Lord Cornwallis, declared one-third of the company's territories in Bengal to be "a jungle inhabited only by wild beasts." Nature had rushed in to fill the void created by human mortality and mismanagement. Its eventual containment and control was, conversely, for Hunter a measure of Britain's success in establishing "enlightened government" and freeing the people of India, unable or unwilling to help themselves, from the terrible scourge of hunger. [36]

"Resigned to Despair"

Surviving sources provide no evidence that the drought and famine of 1769-1770 were seen as a form of divine retribution. A sense of human culpability was, however, not uncommon. In the account of the famine published in the *Annual Register*, the writer found himself confronted by "poor creatures" who cried out "Baba! Baba! My Father! My Father! This affliction comes from the hands of your countrymen, and I am come here to die, if it pleases God, in your presence."[37] This would seem to suggest a clear identification of the famine as a "man-made calamity," and given the part played by company agents and merchants in extracting taxes and seizing or buying up grain, such a view may well have been widespread in Bengal in 1770.

The tone of official correspondence, too, was predominantly secular. Nature, not God, accounted for the abnormal "dryness of the season." But, once the drought had set in, there was an apparent acceptance among British and Indian officials alike that this had become a crisis beyond human rectification: only divine intervention could now save the starving inhabitants of Bihar and Bengal. Becher, the resident at Murshidabad, reported in August 1769 that, for want of rain, crops in the district north of Nadia were likely to be "very short indeed." He continued:

> Since the season for rain began they have hardly had any, and if God does not soon bless this country with plentiful showers the most fatal consequences will ensue—not only in a reduction in the revenues, but a scene of misery and distress that is a constant attendant on famine. God, of his infinite goodness, avert the dreadful calamity.[38]

Warning of an impending famine in its dispatch to the court of directors in November 1769, the council in Calcutta promised to "pursue every means in our power to relieve the miserable situation," but it added, perhaps in order to free itself of responsibility, that it doubted that "human means" alone would suffice.[39] References to ultimate dependence upon divine will also punctuated the reports of Indian officials. The Amil of Bishnupur, in southwest Bengal, gave an account of his efforts to collect the revenue despite the peasants' increasing hardship, adding that although he was "not negligent of the business committed to my care by the Government," it was "impossible to provide against the calamities inflicted by Heaven."[40] In May 1770, Muhammad Reza Khan, the company's Naib-Diwan, or principal revenue officer, in Bengal, observed:

> If the scarcity of grain and want of rain had been confined to one spot of the province, management and attention might find a remedy; but when evil is total, there can be no remedy but in the mercy of God. I know not what the divine will has ordained shall befall this country. The calamity is past the ingenuity of man. The Almighty alone can deliver us from such distress.[41]

The invocation of "God" and "Heaven" might indicate a deeply held conviction that human fate was determined by divine will; it might suggest, more pragmatically, an attempt to shrug off any personal responsibility for deficient revenues and an escalating crisis. There was, nonetheless, a belief, more marked among distant commentators than local observers, that the famine demonstrated the intense fatalism of the Indian people and so confirmed growing opinion in the West about the dependence of Indians on European energy and resolve to rescue them from the material and moral consequences of their own passivity. One statement of this view can be found in Raynal's account of the famine. After describing the effects of the famine and its resulting misery, the Abbé went on to observe that what he found "still more remarkable" than all the suffering and mortality was the lack of active response on the part of the Indian population. What seemed to him "to characterize the gentleness, or rather the indolence, as well mental as natural, of the natives" was that

> amidst this terrible distress, such a multitude of human creatures, pressed by the most urgent of all necessities, remained in an absolute inactivity, and made no attempt whatever for their self-preservation. All the Europeans, especially the English, were possessed of magazines [i.e., grain stores], and even these were not touched; private houses were so too; no revolt, no massacre, nor the least violence

prevailed. The unhappy Indians, resigned to despair, confined themselves to the request of succour they did not obtain, and peacefully waited the relief of death.[42]

We will see shortly how accurate this characterization of Indian responses actually was, but for the moment it should be noted how Raynal used this apparent display of Indian inertia to inform a wider understanding of Indian otherness by contrasting it with what he believed would happen in similar circumstances in Europe.

> Let us now represent to ourselves any part of Europe afflicted by a similar calamity. What disorder! What fury! What atrocious acts! What crimes would ensue! How should we have seen among us Europeans, some contending for their food with their dagger in hand, some pursuing, some flying, and, without remorse, massacring one another! How should we have seen men at last turn their rage on themselves, tearing and devouring their own limbs, and, in the blindness of despair, trampling under foot all authority, as well as every sentiment of nature and reason![43]

This led him to conclude that Indians were partly to blame for their own misery, for not responding with the kind of anger and active protest that would have characterized Europe's poor and hungry in similar circumstances. "Had it been the fate of the English to have had the like events to dread on the part of the people of Bengal," he suggested, "perhaps, the famine would have been less general and less destructive."[44]

A perception of Indian passivity also found some place in official discourse in the wake of the famine. In March 1770 James Alexander, the company's resident at Patna, reported "such is the disposition of the people that they seem rather inclined to submit to death than extricate themselves from the misery of hunger by industry and labour."[45] In his minute of 1789 John Shore observed that "in the pacific disposition and habitual subjection of the natives, we enjoy a security without example in the records of history. At this moment, no government can have a stronger appearance of permanency than our dominion in Bengal." But he did not believe that the British could count on this "pacific disposition" indefinitely unless the government gave its subjects in return security of property, freedom from oppression, and "a reasonable indulgence to their prejudices." The passivity of the people of Bengal was not, therefore, in his view absolute and unconditional.[46] Hunter, too, observed that during the famine "the people endured silently to the end," but, he acknowledged, "with a fortitude that casual observers of a different temperament and widely dissimilar race may easily mistake for apathy."[47]

Nevertheless, after 1770 European interpretations of Indian responses to the famine and to other calamities lent support to wider notions of Bengalis' passivity and their alleged physical and moral deficiencies. In an essay that included a lengthy description of the famine, Macaulay declared: "Whatever the Bengalee does, he does languidly. His favourite pursuits are sedentary. He shrinks from bodily exertion; and, though voluble in dispute, and singularly pertinacious in the war of chicane, he seldom engages in personal conflict."[48] In a subsequent essay, which also alluded to the famine as an exemplary moment of crisis, Macaulay claimed that Bengalis were feeble "even to effeminacy," and added that "the Bengalee . . . would see his country overrun, his house laid in ashes, his children murdered or dishonoured, without having the spirit to strike one blow."[49]

Racial and regional stereotypes apart, the attitude toward Indians in general developed in European accounts of the famine of 1770 suggested a deep, even unbridgeable, gulf between East and West. India, increasingly, was a land Europeans found hard to fathom. Indians were too strange, too perverse in their ways, beliefs, and customs, for Europeans, even in the Age of Enlightenment, to be able to engage with them on the basis of a common humanity and shared sensibilities. The alleged passivity of Indians in the face of famine was but one aspect of this alterity. In his account of Bengal in 1769–1770, the Dutch naval commander J. S. Stavorinus described other sights which to him were equally unintelligible, but which elided into his account of the famine itself—the case of a woman (a *sati*) immolating herself on her husband's funeral pyre and a Hindu holy man whose peculiar form of self-mortification (but also the reason why Hindus revered him) was having a brass ring through his penis with a heavy weight attached to it.[50] In such a sensationalized world of self-imposed suffering, it was hard for Stavorinus, as for many another European, to identify with Indians' suffering as if it were his own.

There is, indeed, a self-reflexive character to most European accounts of the famine, as if the Indians' experience is not only too painfully disturbing to contemplate (or even witness) but also beyond the realms of meaningful comprehension. These narratives tell us much more about what Europeans think, see, and feel about the assault on their sensibilities and "humanity" than they inform us about Indian experience and suffering. The anonymous account published in the *Annual Register* in 1771 provides some examples of this. The famine comes to him; he does not seek it out. His way of recounting the calamity is to refer to the numbers of dead and dying he can see from his bedroom window each morning. He even, uncharitably, sends his servant "to desire those who had strength to remove further off." Among other inconveniences caused to him and his fellow Europeans in Calcutta by the influx of the starving and dying, is that, with so many corpses being devoured by fish, birds, pigs, and other animals, their choice of diet is greatly restricted. Like the fish in the Hughli, "pork, ducks, and geese, also lived mostly on carnage; so that our only meat was mutton when we could get it, which was very dear, and from the dryness of the season so poor that a quarter would not weigh a pound and a half."[51]

Nor was this attitude confined to those besieged in Calcutta. Though some undoubtedly engaged in acts of charity at their own expense, Europeans up-country often found the importuning and suffering of the poor unbearable, an intolerable affront to their own sensibilities. Dutch merchants at Patna were so disturbed by the sight of "hundreds of Indians perish[ing] daily for want of food," that they "avoided going out of the[ir] lodge, in order not to behold the misery of these wretched inhabitants, who lay dying in crowds, along the streets and highways."[52] Becher at Murshidabad observed in June 1770 that the "scene of misery . . . shocks humanity too much to bear description," adding, as if to convey its ultimate horror, "Certain it is, that in several parts the living have fed on the dead." [53] Six weeks later he reported that with more than five hundred people dying daily in Murshidabad, he was pessimistic about the ability of a large portion of the population to survive until a new harvest could be gathered in. The great numbers he feared would perish, like those currently dying around him, "greatly affect my feelings and humanity as a man." [54] In not dissimilar fashion, in his report on the aftermath of the famine, Hastings sought to defend company officials from criticism on the grounds that it had been their "unhappy lot . . . to be witnesses and spectators of the suffering of their fellow-creatures." [55] It was as if the famine were only intelligible in terms of the suffering it imposed upon those unfortunate Europeans obliged to witness its horrors. The experience of the famine sufferers themselves was inaccessible.

Ultimately, it might be argued, that suffering did not go unheeded, for reports of the enormous mortality and needless misery in Bengal fueled criticism of the company's rapacious revenue collecting and the corruption, extortion, and monopolistic trading practices of its servants. To many it seemed the height of infamy that the company, even when the famine was at its height, showed more concern for its revenues than for the people's distress and actually exceeded its anticipated income, "owing," as Hastings tactlessly revealed, "to its being violently kept up to its former standard." [56] The outcry in England over the famine merged with more general criticism of the company's conduct and administration. In 1776 one anonymous but clearly well-informed writer decried the fact that, after extracting more than £10.5 million from Bengal over the previous ten years and driving thousands of people to despair, the court of directors had added insult to injury by stating that "every justifiable measure should be adopted for availing ourselves of all the advantages we had in prospect from our possession of the revenue." [57] He envisaged the haggard people of India presenting their indictment of the company before an imaginary court made up of all the civilized nations of the world and declaring that "famine, pestilence and the English have covered our land with horror and desolation. The two last have abated, but the English still remain to exact the same tribute from the sad survivors of all this misery." [58]

Events in Bengal, highlighted by the famine, revealed the ambiguous attitudes that surrounded the sudden acquisition of immense wealth and power in India and created concern that the growth of empire overseas might corrupt British morals, institutions, and "traditional liberties" nearer home. [59] In this sense, too, the understanding of developments in India was self-reflexive, unleashing fears more for the future of Britain than for the remote suffering of Bengal. The court of directors asked the council in Bengal to investigate charges circulating in Britain that, by monopolizing the grain market, company officials had helped cause or intensify the famine. The council protested its innocence, observing to the directors in March 1772: "Had any of your servants or others been guilty of such malpractices, we should have considered it our duty to have taken proper notice of it by the severest marks of our resentment." [60] Though no charges were ever brought against European officials in India, in Britain Parliament tightened its control of Indian affairs: the Regulating Act of 1773 and the impeachment of Warren Hastings were among the consequences. Ironically, the only individual formally put on trial for monopolizing grain during the famine was the Naib-Diwan, Muhammad Reza Khan, who, with Becher, had made the first accusations of malpractice against company officials and their Indian agents. Reza Khan was eventually acquitted in 1774, but that he was singled out in this way showed how criticism was deflected away from Europeans and the company and how Indians were increasingly deemed untrustworthy and unsuited for high office. [61] The famine of 1770 thus helped initiate a policy by which Indians were excluded from senior positions in the administration of their own country and confined to the subordinate ranks of the colonial bureaucracy.

"COMPLAINTS AND LAMENTATIONS"

The claim advanced by Abbé Raynal and others that Indians showed remarkable passivity and fatalism in the face of the calamity of drought and famine is substantially misleading. That there was little overt resistance is unsurprising. Over the previous fifteen years the rural population of Bengal and Bihar had been subject to a regime intent on exacting as much from them as possible by means of rents, taxes, trade monopolies, and "presents" and which commanded enough coercive strength to stifle any opposition. Lord Clive, himself one of the principal architects of the revolution in Bengal, declared in 1765 that in the last few years the province had witnessed "such a scene of anarchy, confusion, bribery, corruption, and extortion [as] was never seen or heard of in any [other] country . . . ; nor such and so many fortunes acquired in so unjust and rapacious a manner."[62] It was not to be wondered at that many among the population despaired of finding any redress for their suffering from such a grasping and exploitative regime. The years of rapacity had, moreover, left them with few material resources to endure the additional catastrophe of drought and famine.

Even so, a closer reading of the evidence suggests that, contrary to a European perception of passivity, vociferous protests were made to Indian and European officials in the early months of the crisis. The pressures these officials in turn were subject to, to maximize the revenues, made them unable, or unwilling, to heed the cries for help,[63] but the protests were evident to eyewitnesses all the same. In August 1769, when the effects of drought were first becoming apparent in Bihar, the resident at Patna reported that neither he nor Shitab Roy, the Naib-Diwan, "can stir out, but we are stopped by multitudes of the poor pressing to make known their distress."[64] Eight months later, Harwood in Rajmahal reported, more from annoyance than compassion, that on his tours of the district he met with "nothing but poverty and distress in every part. I cannot move from my house but I am obliged to listen to the sad tale of some reduced or ruined family."[65] A subcollector, Pratit Roy, wrote that thousands of peasants were "reduced to the necessity of offering me their plows and oxen as their all—and so clamorous are they in their complaints and lamentations that it is difficult for me to transact business in the cutcherry [office]."[66]

"Clamorous" does not equate with passivity and fatalism. Nor does the attempt by peasants to sell their oxen, plows, and whatever other possessions they had, nor their attempts to avert starvation by consuming precious seed corn. In the countryside of eighteenth-century India flight or "desertion" was a not uncommon response to agrarian hardship and oppression, and it was often actively encouraged by landholders on the lookout for peasants to clear and cultivate "waste" land. In a situation of drought and impending famine it was sensible for peasants who could no longer cultivate their own fields to seek work elsewhere, even as day laborers. Migration to Patna, Murshidabad, and Calcutta also made sense given the large quantities of grain stored in the cities and the greater prospect of finding relief there. These and other survival strategies, familiar from the famines of nineteenth-century India,[67] were not without positive effect. As far as their own means allowed, Indian landed elites yielded to traditional expectations and customary notions of charity by giving food to the needy; Indian officials, like Reza Khan, appear to have made considerable efforts to procure and distribute grain at their own expense.[68] The scale of the famine, however, dwarfed individual effort, while the company, ever jealous of its revenues, authorized only "painfully inadequate" relief operations and was unwilling even to grant remissions of revenue, or *takavi* loans, to aid the postfamine recovery of peasant agriculture.[69]

At a time of military insecurity along its borders, one of the company's foremost concerns was to protect the food supply of its troops, but raids by detachments of soldiers to seize whatever they needed from the depleted countryside met with some resistance. Attempts to import grain from the state of Awadh drew the wrath of inhabitants there. Merchants in Murshidabad and Calcutta grew anxious lest their stores or consignments of grain were seized by the poor, though, unlike in the 1784 famine in eastern Bengal, there were no reports in 1769–1770 of food riots and looting of grain shops.[70] Further demonstrations of popular anger took the form of arson attacks on *golas* in Bengal in April and May 1770. Incendiarism might seem a self-defeating act, but it must be understood as an expression of intense fury at the withholding of grain kept in private stores and granaries and not released to those who needed it most.[71] In the wake of the famine itself hungry peasants joined gangs of bandits in attacking those villages where food might still be found.[72] But, as in any famine where relief measures are wholly inadequate, intense suffering, hunger, and disease inexorably led to exhaustion and despair. Europeans like Stavorinus often saw only the last desperate acts—such as a woman drowning herself in the Ganges with two young children she could no longer feed—the closing scenes in a long-unfolding tragedy, not the weeks and months leading up to them, in which the poor had struggled in various ways to find the means of their survival.[73]

Moreover, as Stavorinus put it, the "evil" of famine did not come alone but was "augmented by another scourge, almost equally calamitous"—an epidemic of smallpox, which "attacked people of all ages, and brought many to the grave." [74] Famines in India, as elsewhere, often resulted in a far greater number of deaths from disease than from starvation. Throughout the nineteenth century cholera was one of the main causes of death in famine times, spread by contaminated food and water and exacerbated by physical debility and the effects of eating "surrogate foods." Cholera also killed with great rapidity, before hunger itself could become the actual cause of death. But though cholera became a leading source of famine-related mortality in the nineteenth century, it was not widely noted in Bengal before the epidemic of 1817, and it was to this that subsequent epidemics in India and across the world were generally traced. This may reflect the paucity of reliable medical observation in India before 1800, and there is some indication that epidemics of cholera did occur in Bengal in the 1780s and 1790s.[75] There is, however, no evidence that it was a major course of mortality in 1770, and a disease so horrifying in its manifestations, so swift and deadly, would surely have attracted contemporary notice. Equally, although malaria swelled mortality in many later famine episodes in India, it does not seem to have been widely prevalent in the crucial months of 1769–1770, when sources speak not of "fever" but of "contagion" or more specifically of smallpox.[76]

It is known from nineteenth-century sources that epidemics of smallpox occurred periodically in Bengal, especially during the early months of the year (it was accordingly known as *basanta-roga*, the "spring disease").

Until cholera and malaria assumed greater prominence in the famine mortality of the mid- and late nineteenth century, smallpox was one of the principal diseases associated with drought and famine. Fatalities in 1770 included the Nawab of Bengal and the head of the Dutch station at Chinsura, but smallpox claimed the bulk of its victims from the famine poor. It spread rapidly, with levels of mortality as high as 50 percent among the poor and malnourished, who flocked to the towns and cities in search of relief. As a readily communicable "crowd disease," passing rapidly among mobile, nonimmune populations, smallpox may have been exceptionally prevalent in eastern India in the second half of the eighteenth century as a result of repeated military campaigns, rural unrest, and disturbed social conditions. Smallpox would help to explain why so many people died so rapidly in the early months of 1770.[77]

The presence of smallpox enables us to go one stage further in trying to assess indigenous reactions to the crisis of 1769–1770, for Bengalis were by no means "passive" even in the face of this foul and often fatal disease. One practical response was the widespread use of variolation (smallpox inoculation) in late-eighteenth- and early-nineteenth-century Bengal. The recipient gained lifelong protection against the disease through the injection of live smallpox matter, usually into the upper arm, by specialist inoculators known as *tikadars*. Several European commentators, among them medical practitioners like J. Z. Holwell, saw variolation performed and testified to the care that was taken over this potentially hazardous operation, the high level of immunity conferred, and the controlled risks of contagion involved. Indeed, the *tikadars'* practice was presented as a model for the way in which Europeans (in the days before Jennerian vaccination) might protect themselves against the disease.[78] Nor was variolation the only response. Smallpox was also regarded as a manifestation of the Hindu goddess Sitala. If honored and propitiated in the right manner, through songs, prayers, and "cooling" offerings to assuage her "heating" wrath, Sitala could be persuaded to quit the individuals whose bodies she had feverishly seized possession of and to leave them with few disfiguring marks. Ralph Nicholas has argued that in the course of the eighteenth century Sitala rose from the status of a minor deity to become a major focus of worship, a goddess widely celebrated in Bengali devotional texts. He sees this spiritual and literary outpouring and the growth of the Sitala cult as a direct response to the "time of serious troubles" then afflicting Bengal, not least the drought, famine, and epidemic of 1769–1770.[79]

CONCLUSION

In the minds of many European commentators the Bengal famine of 1770 was a "natural disaster," but in more senses than are usually intended by that term. For those who served or defended the English East India Company, it was convenient to believe that the famine had been caused by natural phenomena—the shortage of rain and the exceptional "dryness of the season"—which in turn caused wholesale crop failures, food scarcity, and mass starvation. But perceptually the place of nature in the making of this catastrophe went far beyond its immediate causation. In a manner that starkly conveyed to contemporaries the horror of famine, scavenging birds and animals fell upon the dead and dying, and, in Shore's words, "riot[ed], unmolested, on their prey." After famine had abated, tigers, elephants, and impenetrable jungle took over the ruined and depopulated countryside from its former human inhabitants. Nature, malevolent or merely opportunistic, was a register of the precipitous decline from prosperity and order. The famine was also, in colonial retrospect, a measure of the greater vulnerability to the forces of nature of India under a "native" regime than under the "enlightened" rule and "modern civilization" that colonialism represented. The famine helped to transform European ideas of Bengal from a garden of seemingly inexhaustible tropical abundance into a land blighted by droughts, floods, and famines, ravaged by recurrent epidemics of smallpox, cholera, and malaria. And it helped shape ideas of Bengalis as passive and weak, subject to nature in a way their European rulers believed themselves no longer to be. The Bengal famine was perhaps the first Asian "disaster" in modern times to have an impact on Europe, but it did so by reinforcing an identification of Asia with nature rather than by emphasizing a common humanity.

While the famine of 1770 helped create or entrench European ideas about India, it did little to stimulate a more genuine understanding of the country and its people. Perhaps this has too often been the fate of "disasters" in Asia and Africa that have temporarily seized the attention of the Western world. The Bengal famine illustrated how, from the very outset of colonial rule, Europeans found so much about India strange, unintelligible, remote from their own experience and sensibilities. Even among those who attributed the famine to human greed and indifference rather than natural causes, it was the significance of the famine for the conduct of British commerce and empire overseas, or for the threatened contamination of British politics by the taint of Eastern corruption and Oriental despotism, that ultimately mattered more than the famine-struck millions of Bengal and Bihar.

NOTES

1   For a recent discussion of the Asiatic Society and the Orientalist project, see Thomas R. Trautmann, *Aryans and British India* (Berkeley and Los Angeles: University of California Press, 1997).

2   The conflict in Enlightenment thinking between a willingness to recognize other societies as equal, even in some respects superior, to Europe, and the creation of a hierarchy of societies with Europe at the top is discussed by John Gascoigne in *Joseph Banks and the English Enlightenment: Useful Knowledge and Polite Culture* (Cambridge: Cambridge University Press, 1994), chap. 4.

3   Lord Teignmouth, *Memoir of the Life and Correspondence of John Lord Teignmouth*, vol. I (London: Hatchard and Son, 1843), 25–26.

4   "Account of the Late Dreadful Famine in India," *Annual Register, 1771*, 4th ed. (London, 1786), 205–06.

5   Ibid., 206. This article had previously appeared in *The Gentleman's Magazine* but was reprinted "for the honour of our country and in the interests of humanity" because its damning account of merchants' greed and widespread suffering had "not yet been contradicted." Ibid., 205.

6   Narratives of the famine include W. W. Hunter, *Annals of Rural Bengal*, 5th ed. (London: Smith, Elder and Co., 1872), 19–37; Nani Gopal Chaudhuri, *Cartier: Governor of Bengal, 1769-1772* (Calcutta: Firma K. L. Mukhopadhyay, 1970), 31–46.

7   Charles Grant, "Observations on the State of Society among the Asiatic Subjects of Great Britain," in Ainslie Thomas Embree, *Charles Grant and British Rule in India* (London: George Allen and Unwin, 1962), 36.

8   Hunter, *Annals*, 30.

9   Cited in "Memoir by Mr George Campbell on the Famines which Affected Bengal in the Last Century," in J. C. Geddes, *Administrative Experience Recorded in Former Famines* (Calcutta: Bengal Secretariat Press, 1874), 420.

10   Shore, "Minute," 18 June 1789, in "The Fifth Report from the Select Committee on the Affairs of the East India Company," *Parliamentary Papers*, 1812, Appendix I: 182; see Teignmouth, *Memoir*, 46.

11   Hunter, *Annals*, Appendix B, "The Great Famine of 1770, Described by Eye-witnesses," 401.

12   Hunter, *Annals*, Appendix A, "Bengal in 1772, Portrayed by Warren Hastings," 381.

13   Hunter, *Annals*, 34.

14   Chaudhuri, *Cartier*, 71.

15   For the Lisbon earthquake and its impact, see Clarence J. Glacken, *Traces on the Rhodian Shore: Nature and Culture in Western Thought from Ancient Times to the End of the Eighteenth Century* (Berkeley and Los Angeles: University of California Press, 1967), 521–23.

16   Adam Smith, *An Inquiry into the Nature and Causes of the Wealth of Nations*, 5th ed. (London: Methuen, 1930). As the apostle of free trade, Smith believed that intervention in the grain trade by East India Company officials had helped cause the severity of the food shortages and argued that "famine has never arisen from any other cause but the violence of government attempting, by improper means, to remedy the inconvenience of dearth." Ibid., 27–28. Within thirty years Smith's economic ideas had become the gospel of British famine policy in India: S. Ambirajan, *Classical Political Economy and British Policy in India* (Cambridge: Cambridge University Press, 1978), chap. 3.

17   Hunter, *Annals*, 19.

18   Hemendra Prasad Ghose, *The Famine of 1770* (Calcutta: The Book Company, 1944), 7–9. For Bankim's treatment of the famine, see Bipin Chandra Pal, *The Spirit of Indian Nationalism* (London: The Hind Nationalist Agency, 1910), 37; Tapan Raychaudhuri, *Europe Reconsidered: Perceptions of the West in Nineteenth Century Bengal* (Delhi: Oxford University Press, 1988), 186–88.

19   For the nationalist complaint that the British had turned India into "a land of poverty and of famines," see Romesh Dutt, *The Economic History of India, I: Under Early British Rule* (London: Routledge and Kegan Paul, 1901), 51.

20   Ghose, *The Famine of 1770*, p. 18. For the 1943 famine, see Paul R. Greenough, *Prosperity and Misery in Modern Bengal: The Famine of 1943–44* (New York: Oxford University Press, 1982).

21   Much recent discussion of the famine has focused on its impact on the commerce and agrarian economy of early colonial Bengal: see, especially, Binay Bhushan Chaudhuri, "Agricultural Growth in Bengal and Bihar, 1770–1860: Growth of Cultivation since the Famine of 1770," *Bengal Past and Present* 95 (1976): 290–340; Rajat Datta, "Rural Bengal: Social Structure and Agrarian Economy in the Late Eighteenth Century," unpublished Ph.D. thesis, University of London, 1990.

22   Ideas of India and Asia generally in this period are discussed in P. J. Marshall and Glyndwr Williams, *The Great Map of Mankind: British Perceptions of the World in the Age of Enlightenment* (London: J. M. Dent and Sons, 1982), chap. 5.

23   Abbé Raynal, *A Philosophical and Political History of the Settlements and Trade of the Europeans in the East and West Indies*, vol. I, trans. J. Justamond, 3rd ed. (London: T. Cadell, 1777), 36–7.

24   François Bernier, *Travels in the Mogul Empire, A.D. 1656–1668* (1819 edition, reprinted Delhi: S. Chand, 1968). In 1769, on the eve of the famine, the Dutchman Stavorinus described Bengal as being "justly esteemed the most fruitful part of Asia." J. S. Stavorinus, *Voyages to the East Indies*, vol. I, trans. S. H. Wilcocks (first published 1798, reprinted London: Dawsons, 1969), 122.

25   Raynal, *History*, I: 471.

26   "Account," 206.

27   Hunter, *Annals*, 32, 34.

28   Shore, "Minute," 182.

29   William Hodges, *Travels in India during the Years 1780, 1781, 1782 and 1783* (London: n.p., 1793), 23–28, 37–38. Kate Teltscher in *India Inscribed: European and British Writings on India, 1600–1800* (Delhi: Oxford University Press, 1995), 127–28, sees this as deliberate propaganda on behalf of the company in the wake of the 1770 famine.

30   Thomas Babington Macaulay, "Lord Clive," in *Critical and Historical Essays*, vol. I (London: Dent, 1907), 502–03. Macaulay was drawing upon and embellishing the descriptions of earlier writers, notably Robert Orme, *A History of the Military Transactions of the British Nation in Indostan from the Year MDCCXLV*, vol. II (first published 1763,

new edition, London: F. Wingrave, 1803), 4, with its prefamine reference to Bengal as "the paradise of India." The description of eastern India as a garden was not uncommon in the late eighteenth century: Teltscher, *India Inscribed,* 175–76.

31   For the 1752 famine, see J. Z. Holwell, *India Tracts,* 2nd ed. (London: T. Becket and P. A. de Hondt, 1764), 165; for the later famines and epidemics, James Taylor, *A Sketch of the Topography and Statistics of Dacca* (Calcutta: G. H. Huttmann, 1840), 297–307, 322–35; and for the beginning of economic decline, Chaudhuri, *Cartier,* 76–77; and Taylor, *Dacca,* 307.

32   Sten Nilsson, *European Architecture in India, 1750–1850* (London: Faber and Faber, 1968), 98–99 and plate 24. The *gola* was, in fact, never used for its intended purpose.

33   Kyd to Board, Fort William, 15 April 1786, in Kalipada Biswas, *The Original Correspondence of Sir Joseph Banks Relating to the Foundation of the Royal Botanic Garden, Calcutta* (Calcutta: Royal Asiatic Society of Bengal, 1950), 3.

34   Ibid., 12.

35   Hunter, *Annals,* 50.

36   Ibid., 61–69.

37   "Account," 206.

38   Becher, 26 August 1769, Campbell's "Memoir," 412.

39   Council, Bengal, to Court of Directors, 20 November 1769; Campbell's "Memoir," 412.

40   Nobkishwur to Becher, n.d., Bengal Select Committee Consultations (hereafter SCC), 28 April 1770, Oriental and India Office Collections (OIOC), London.

41   Hunter, *Annals,* Appendix B: 406.

42   Raynal, *History,* I: 473–74. Significantly, Raynal's account of Indian "inactivity" in 1770 has been used to support similar claims for the 1943 famine: Greenough, *Prosperity,* 267–68.

43   Raynal, *History,* I: 474.

44   Ibid.

45   Alexander, 16 March 1770, SCC, 29 March 1770, OIOC.

46   Shore, "Minute," 185.

47   Hunter, *Annals,* 42.

48   Macaulay, "Clive," 503.

49 Macaulay, "Warren Hastings," *Essays*, I: 562–63. The idea of Bengali "effeminacy" can also be traced back to the historian Robert Orme in the 1760s.

50 Stavorinus, *Voyages*, I: 133–34, 447–50. Of the *sati*, Stavorinus wrote: "What most surprised me, at this horrid and barbarous rite, was the tranquility of the woman, and the joy expressed by her relations, and the spectators. The wretched victim, who beheld these preparations making for her cruel death, seemed to be much less affected by it, than we Europeans, who were present. She underwent every thing with the greatest intrepidity, and her countenance seemed, at times, to be animated with pleasure, even at the moment when she was ascending the fatal pile." Ibid., 447–48.

51 "Account," 206–07.

52 Stavorinus, *Voyages*, I: 151.

53 Becher, 2 June 1770, SCC; 9 June 1770, OIOC.

54 Becher, 12 July 1770, SCC; 19 July 1770, OIOC.

55 Hunter, *Annals*, Appendix A: 380.

56 Ibid., 381.

57 *A Short History of English Transactions in the East Indies* (Cambridge: J. Almon and E. and C. Dilly, 1776), 154.

58 Ibid., 176.

59 See Linda Colley, *Britons: Forging the Nation, 1707–1837* (London: Pimlico, 1994), 102–03.

60 Letter to Court of Directors, 9 March 1772, in *Fort William-India House Correspondence VI, Public, Select, and Secret, 1770–1772*, ed. Bisheshwar Prasad (Delhi: National Archives of India, 1960), 369.

61 Abdul Majed Khan, *The Transition in Bengal, 1756–1775: A Study of Saiyid Muhammad Reza Khan* (Cambridge: Cambridge University Press, 1969), chap. 9.

62 Cited in Stanley Wolpert, *A New History of India*, 2nd ed. (New York: Oxford University Press, 1982), 187.

63 Khan, *Transition*, 227.

64 Campbell's "Memoir," 411.

65 Harwood, 28 March 1770, SCC; 28 April 1770, OIOC.

66 SCC, 28 April 1770, OIOC.

67   David Arnold, "Famine in Peasant Consciousness and Peasant Action: Madras, 1876–8," in *Subaltern Studies III*, ed. Ranajit Guha (Delhi: Oxford University Press, 1984), 62–115. For the more general issue of the "passivity" of famine "victims," see David Arnold, *Famine: Social Crisis and Historical Change* (Oxford: Blackwell, 1988), chap. 3 and 4.

68   Khan, *Transition*, 218–22; David L. Curley, "Fair Grain Markets and Moghul Famine Policy in Late Eighteenth-Century Bengal," *Calcutta Historical Journal* 2 (1977); 1–26.

69   Hunter, *Annals*, 36.

70   James Alexander, Patna, 4 May 1770, SCC; 26 May 1770, OIOC; "Account," 206; Chaudhuri, *Cartier*, 42, 51–52; Taylor, *Dacca*, 300.

71   "Account," 205; Chaudhuri, *Cartier*, 38.

72   Hunter, *Annals*, 70–71.

73   Stavorinus, *Voyages*, I: 151–53.

74   Ibid., 153–54.

75   Taylor, *Sketch*, 334–35; C. Macnamara, *A History of Asiatic Cholera* (London: Macmillan, 1876), 34–36.

76   In addition to Stavorinus, see Robert Kyd, "Memorandum for Forming a Memoir or Report of the State of the Provinces Respecting Agriculture, Productions, Commerce, Population and Manufactures," Mss Eur. 95/1, 167–68, OIOC.

77   Ralph W. Nicholas, "The Goddess Sitala and Epidemic Smallpox in Bengal," *Journal of Asian Studies* 61 (1981): 33–34. For conditions affecting smallpox epidemics in India, see Leonard Rogers, *Smallpox and Climate in India: Forecasting of Epidemics* (London: His Majesty's Stationery Office, 1926).

78   Stavorinus, *Voyages*, I: 452; J. Z. Holwell, *An Account of the Manner of Inoculating for the Small Pox in the East Indies* (London: T. Becket and P. A. de Hondt, 1767); David Arnold, *Colonizing the Body: State Medicine and Epidemic Disease in Nineteenth-Century India* (Berkeley and Los Angeles: University of California Press, 1993), 121–33.

79   Nicholas, "Sitala," 32–33.

5

Shaking the Unstable Empire

The Lima, Quito, and Arequipa Earthquakes, 1746, 1783, and 1797[1]

CHARLES F. WALKER

The Andean region of South America has borne the brunt of more than its fair share of natural disasters. Analysis of an ice core from the southern Peruvian Andes has revealed, for example, that in the last 1,500 years, periods of drought and excessive rainfall have been just as common in the region as periods of "normal" precipitation. One-hundred-and-fifty-year cycles of drought have been followed, after brief periods of average rain, by cycles of high levels of rain that have often caused flooding. Most recently in this long cycle, in 1997–1998, El Niño ravaged the coast of Ecuador and Peru, killing hundreds and leaving thousands homeless. Earthquakes, however, are the most recurrent and feared natural disaster in the Andes. One scholar counted more than fifty "major earthquakes" in Chile alone from 1570 to 1985. Peru also suffers dozens of tremblors every century. One in particular stands out in recent history:[2] On 31 May 1970, an earthquake measuring 7.7 on the Richter scale struck north of Lima. While its epicenter was in the Pacific Ocean, it devastated the Huaylas Valley. During the quake a massive section of ice and rock came loose from a mountain peak that stood over the valley at

22,000 feet. As the avalanche gained velocity and size racing down the slope, it reached speeds of 200 miles an hour. A billion cubic feet of water, ice, rock, and mud buried the town of Yungay, killing 10,000 people, nearly everyone in the town except a lucky dozen who escaped to the top of the cemetery and a group who were on the outskirts of the town watching a circus. Today, all that can be seen of the former town are the very tops of two palm trees that used to stand over the central plaza. Combined, the earthquake and avalanche killed 75,000 people, injured 50,000, and left 800,000 homeless.[3]

The eighteenth century, as others in this collection have pointed out, was puncuated by disasters worldwide. The Andes region was no exception: it experienced droughts, epidemics, floods, famines, *and* earthquakes. This chapter examines three major earthquakes of that period: in Lima in 1746; Arequipa in 1783; and Quito in 1797.

Earthquakes and other disasters reveal aspects of society not usually visible to the curious observer; accounts describe, for example, the domestic sphere, discussing sleeping arrangements or spatial divisions, topics rarely mentioned in archival sources. They also open up cloistered areas such as monasteries, providing details on nuns' material and even spiritual life. Natural disasters do not just take us, however, into usually prohibited or obscure physical locations. They expose belief systems, as survivors grope for explanations, culprits, and heroes. The aftermath of a catastrophe also tests the structures of subjection; people question reigning ideologies and practices that become evident in the efforts of the state and the dominant classes to assist victims and rebuild from the ravages. Often, a dialectic between the return to traditional beliefs and forms of domination and the search for new meanings and structures emerges.

In the three earthquakes we will study here, we see ideological retrenchment, as the victims relied on conventional notions such as the understanding of an earthquake as punishment for sin, or the racialized view of colonial society that ultimately blamed the multicolored lower classes for the devastation. Following all three earthquakes, rumors abounded about messianic movements and uprisings, some of which can be discounted as the product of upper-class paranoia (in itself interesting and important). Yet at the same time, the earthquakes prompted people to question the social order—the ideologies as well as the forms of domination. There is no doubt that many people, particularly in the lower classes, aggressively challenged existing social and political norms. These two distinct currents collided in the aftermath of each of the three earthquakes.

Disasters do not simply reflect but also can radically change society. Social differences are, often quite literally, torn down. The architecture, clothing, and other aspects of material culture that once served to differentiate the rich from the poor suddenly cease to exist. In many cases, the exigencies of survival diminish differences along gender, class, or racial lines. Earthquakes and other disasters therefore both offer useful vantage points from which to view society and are themselves significant sources of change. This chapter analyzes such change as it examines official reactions to each earthquake. Two related issues loomed large in eighteenth-century Spanish America: concerns about controlling and exploiting the black, Indian, and multihued lower classes, and opposition encountered by colonial authorities from the upper classes, the church, and the middle ranks. Each earthquake accentuated these horizontal and vertical divisions in late-colonial Spanish America. In the case of Lima, authorities worried about containing the lower classes. In the two earthquakes in the Andes—in Quito, central Ecuador, and in Arequipa—officials endeavored to put the burden of rebuilding on the already weary backs of Indians. Disagreements, however, among elite groups—representatives of the state, the church, and the upper classes—impeded these efforts.

THE CITY OF KINGS

On 28 October 1746 at 10:30 P.M. a massive earthquake struck the central coast of the Peruvian viceroyalty. The majority of the population of Lima, its nearby port Callao, and inhabitants up and down the coast were asleep. A slight tremor that quickly turned into a massive, four-minute earthquake rudely awoke them. One account claimed that if "the most astute man attempted to create the perfect calamity, he could not have imagined the horrors inflicted on Lima and Callao."[4] The earthquake damaged all but twenty of Lima's three thousand houses and harmed most of the city's seventy-four churches and fourteen monasteries as well as the public buildings that adorned the Plaza de Armas. The death rate in Lima was surprisingly low, approximately 1,200 out of a population of 50,000: a fact declared a miracle. Callao fared much worse. A tsunami created by the quake killed almost all of that city's population and destroyed most of its buildings. In an anonymous report prepared for the viceroy and published in translation in London, the writer noted: "But of all [earthquakes] which have happened since their first Conquest, so far at least as hath come to our knowledge, we may with Truth affirm that none ever broke-out with such astonishing Violence, or hath been attended with so vast a Destruction as that which happened lately in this Capital."[5] In his long prologue, the English translator of this official account called the catastrophe "one of the most dreadful, perhaps, that ever befell this Earth since the general Deluge."[6]

Lima, the capital of the Peruvian viceroyalty, was the economic and political center of Spanish South America. Laid out in classic checkerboard fashion, Lima had at its center the Plaza de Armas, where the viceroy, the archbishop, and the city council ruled from imposing buildings. Most of the viceroyalty's commerce moved through the "City of the Kings"[7] and the port of Callao. Lima was a multiethnic city. A 1700 census divided the inhabitants into four categories: 56 percent white; 12 percent Indian; 10 percent mulatto; and 22 percent black, out of a total population of 34,724. A more vivid 1790 document divided the population into nine ethnic groups, calculating that Spaniards ("whites" in the 1700 census) made up 38 percent of the city's population, blacks 18 percent, mulattos 12 percent, mestizos 9 percent, Indians 8 percent, zambos, or people of Indian and black descent, 7 percent, and the other groups less than 5 percent each. It gave the population total as 49,443, a low estimate.[8]

Efforts dating from the sixteenth century to segregate Lima racially had softened by the late colonial period. While members of the colonial upper classes had their houses along the blocks surrounding the plaza, Indians, blacks, and other groups also resided there. Even those neighborhoods initially designed for specific racial groups were racially mixed by the eighteenth century. For example, in 1571, builders constructed a neighborhood to the east of the city center for Indians. It was given the name El Cercado, or the Walled District, due to the adobe wall that surrounded it. And to the north, across the Rimac River, the San Lázaro neighborhood was a primary residence for blacks. Yet by the 1750s, Indians made up less than half of the El Cercado population, while blacks only constituted a quarter of the population in San Lázaro.[9] The mixed ethnic map of Lima reflected the blurring of the boundaries between different ethnic groups. A single distinction between *gente decente*, or respectable people, and the plebs slowly replaced the complex chart of caste hierarchies. The upper classes differentiated themselves from the masses in both the private and public spheres. Their houses featured elaborate baroque facades and other social class markers.[10] Lima's different racial groups rubbed elbows on a daily basis, meeting in the Plaza de Armas or other public areas, though such contact did not imply social equality. In fact, many of the Indians and blacks living near the Plaza de Armas worked as servants for the elite.

The massive earthquake on 28 October 1746 obviously terrified *all* strata of Lima's diverse population equally. People ran madly through the streets, some leaving safe buildings to be struck by falling wood and bricks, others finding salvation in the open air. One person noted, "On this occasion the Destruction did not so much as give Time for Fright, for at one and the same Instant almost, the Noise, the Shock, and the Ruin were perceived together."[11] The marquis of Obando described how the rumbles of the aftershocks drowned out the shouts of help from people buried underneath debris. Father José Eusebio de Llano y Zapata, a Jesuit with scientific inclinations who wrote several accounts of the earthquake, described the hysteria the morning after as inhabitants mourned their losses: "What the men spoke was a type of language, only their faces expressed their thoughts; many with a simple sigh said a book of anguish. It was not life they were living but death that they were enduring."[12] Many others also noted how the catastrophe impeded the senses. The viceregal account commented that the destruction left people speechless. Panic continued as 220 aftershocks, many of them strong enough to tumble brittle buildings, frightened the Lima population for four days following the earthquake. Then for months afterward, tremors prompted people to head for the hills east of the city.

Lima's architecture kept the death tolls lower than could have been expected. Located on a coastal desert where it almost never rains, the city's buildings tended to be single-storied with light roofs. Thus, the majority of the population "happened to be preserved either in the hollow Places which the Ruins left, or on Top of the very Ruins themselves, without knowing how they got-up thither, as if Divine Providence had thus conducted them that they might not perish."[13] Lima's ornate churches and monasteries, however, fared poorly in the earthquake. In the most prominent example, the central cathedral's two towers toppled over, destroying much of the main hall.[14] Peruvian and Spanish commentators noted the destruction with disbelief. Viceroy José Antonio Manso de Velasco compared Lima to a battle scene, where "the enemy enters with blood and fire, converting the most beautiful buildings into piles of dirt and rock."[15] The official account reported that it was difficult to comprehend how so many lives had been saved yet how God provoked the destruction of his own temple.[16] The British translator of this report, who emphasized the church's wealth and priests' licentiousness, reported the destruction of Lima's numerous churches and monasteries with barely concealed satisfaction. He smugly pointed out that while the Spanish attributed the relatively low death rate to the "miraculous Protection of the blessed Virgin, who indeed was the Goddess worshipped there," the real cause had been the low buildings.[17]

The huge tsunami that devastated Callao, the port city 10 miles to the west of Lima, was preceded by the eerie sound of the sea drawing itself out before crashing down on shore. Some people were so terrified, first by the moving earth and then by the sound of the approaching sea, they could not unlock their doors. Many people on or near the harbor had rushed out to the anchored boats, but the wall of water tore these vessels to pieces. Some desperately grabbed on to pieces of floating wood only to be crushed and swept out to sea. Others attempted to escape by jumping the gates of the city and fleeing east. The water rushed 3 miles inland, trapping them as well.

Only two hundred of the five thousand inhabitants of Callao survived, among them two men and a woman who, the day after the catastrophe, washed ashore alive on the beach of Miraflores to the south of Lima, 12 miles from Callao. Twenty-two people clung to a piece of canvas from a painting on the city's walls; others came to shore on San Lorenzo Island, 5 miles off the coast. More miracles were reported. Witnesses claimed that the Augustine Church had been carried intact by the water to Callao Island, a distance of 4 miles. One survivor reported seeing a ship fly over the city. Yet despite these and other marvelous reports of preservation, bits of two gates and parts of the city's outer wall were all that remained of Callao a few months later.[18] Reports of the Callao tsunami terrified the Lima population; rumors circulated that the water would soon reach the capital.

The people of Lima responded to the catastrophe with processions and other public displays of faith. Authorities sent predicants and confessors to the different neighborhoods in order, in the words of Father Pedro Lozano, "to console all the desperate, and exhort them to take advantage of such terrible punishment to reconcile themselves with God through penitence."[19] Religious processions snaked their way through the rubble that littered Lima's streets, as clerics and lay people requested penance and aid in rebuilding. Many recited, "Lima, Lima, Your Sins Are Your Ruin."[20] One account, vividly entitled "The Desolation of the City of Lima and the Flood of the Port of Callao," described a world turned upside down: "Meat was eaten on Fridays, altars constructed everywhere, marriages consummated without Priests. Nuns were freed from the cloister, not only due to the lack of buildings and walls but . . . so they could search for life's basic needs."[21] The frequent aftershocks were not the only reminders of the catastrophe. The viceroy described birds feasting on cadavers, while sunstroke, tertian fever, bronchitis, dysentery, and gastrointestinal ailments took their toll for months.[22]

Not surprisingly, the "True and Particular Relation of the Dreadful Earthquake which Happen'd at Lima, the Capital of Peru, and the Neighbouring Port of Callao . . . Published at Lima by Command of the Viceroy," a text published in Spanish and English in several countries in numerous editions, lauded the efforts of Viceroy Manso de Velasco to remedy this dramatic situation. He reportedly "placed his own life in danger in Lima by touring the ruins on horseback the next day and trying to calm peoples' nerves," direct action uncharacteristic of high-ranking colonial officials.[23] (On the night of the earthquake the viceroy had been forced to sleep on an improvised cot.) He first sought to guarantee food and water for the city, ordering the aqueducts cleared and ovens fixed and demanding that wheat supplies be put on sale at standard prices and that butchers continue to slaughter meat. Commentators noted, nonetheless, the scarcity and thus high price of bread.[24] The viceroy's efforts soon involved more than emergency measures to assure sustenance. Social control was required both to contain crime and to restrain the popular imagination.

SOCIAL CONTROL AND "THOSE LESS INCLINED TO BLUSH"

The danger of mass looting and even social unrest terrified the Lima population. People besieged Callao in pursuit of unprotected riches, digging for gold, silver, and other valuables, and stripping rings and other jewelry from cadavers. Others lined the beaches to gather the goods washed up after the tidal wave. In Lima, thieves took advantage of the smoke and chaos to ransack the tottering homes of the affluent.

Discussions of crime in colonial Peru inevitably entailed race, and the 1746 earthquake was no exception. Llano y Zapata commented that thieves and looters abounded "above all in Peru in which the difference in nations has made a miscellany of colors; and those less inclined to blush are more inclined to larceny and insults such as these damn rebels."[25] Every first-person account referred to the lower classes' propensity to theft and the slaves' penchant for fleeing their owners. A three-hundred-page memorandum about the controversies in rebuilding the city included several passages about the ransacking of wood from destroyed or damaged homes. The houses of the noble class surrounding the Plaza de Armas had initially fared better than most because of their wooden frames and arches. Nonetheless, these and other buildings fell prey to looters who sold wood for high prices. The report claimed that the "licentious and uncontrollable" plebs stole all of the wood that had withstood the earthquake. Because almost all of the city's population—"nobles and plebs, large and small families"—needed wood to build temporary shelter in the form of huts, thieves carried off pieces of wood from debris and tore boards from standing houses. Nothing could be done to stop the trade in this valuable lumber.[26]

Viceroy Manso de Velasco took vigorous measures to prevent crime, restore order, and rebuild the city, and in recognition of his efforts, in 1756 the Spanish Crown granted him the title of Count Superunda, "Over the Waves." The viceroy formed three patrols "to repress the insolence of the people, principally that of the blacks and slaves."[27] He set up gallows in Lima and Callao, sent out soldiers to patrol the two cities, ordered that the royal armory and royal mint be guarded carefully, and threatened that thieves would be hanged immediately.[28] In his memoirs, he described naming neighborhood judges and granting them broad powers in order to slow "the crime wave [*latrocinio*] taken up by blacks, mulattos, and other vulgar people."[29] The viceroy was vigilant in not only the material but also the spiritual protection of the population. He ordered that women, "in any state, class, or condition," wear clothing that cover them to their feet and their wrists, even when they were riding a mule. They were instructed to make sure that their servants did likewise.[30] The marquis of Obando had noted the "ridiculous clothing" worn in the aftermath of the destruction of their homes.[31]

Descriptions of the earthquake emphasized that only determined measures taken by Viceroy Manso de Velasco prevented the complete breakdown of social control. The "Desolation of the City of Lima" depicted "Blacks and the slaves dedicating themselves to looting deserted ruins" and the "increasingly confident plebs" stealing unprotected goods.[32] Supposed prophecies of Lima's seventeenth-century saint, Santa Rosa—about the destruction of Lima by a flood reaching the Plaza de Armas and thus saving the Indian neighborhoods to the east—circulated during the 1746 panic. According to Alberto Flores Galindo, the revival of Santa Rosa's prophecy was linked to the millenarian belief that Indians would retake the city of Lima. In his words, "the fear of some is the hope of others."[33] In the 1740s, before and after the earthquake, the Spanish state faced an uprising in the central jungle east of Lima, led by Juan Santos Atahualpa. The Spaniards' difficulties in defeating Santos Atahualpa in a region not too distant from Lima heightened their apprehension after the earthquake. Concern over a mass uprising shaped the policies and language of the colonial state. Not only did Viceroy Manso de Velasco enact harsh measures to ensure social control but also authors accentuated the danger of social chaos while portraying the lower classes as opportunists seizing on the chance to steal. If no author invoked the threat of an uprising, it nonetheless remained an issue on their minds.[34]

The viceroy had to expend considerable effort convincing people to return from the foothills outside of Lima. The continual aftershocks and the horrendous news from Callao petrified the city's population. Furthermore, on 30 November, panic set in throughout Lima as rumors that the ocean was about to flood Lima crisscrossed the city. Thousands of people again fled the city to the east. The marquis of Obando described "the wails of children, the sobs and howls of women, the sighs of men, and the moans of the old."[35] He contended that a group of blacks spread the rumor in order to take advantage of the panic and the depopulation of Lima to loot at their will. He bitterly noted that "the utterly crude plebs robbed many, and although our Viceroy punished some, he did not manage to intimidate them, with the best houses abandoned, and their owners dazed."[36] When the marquis tried to convince a group of people to return to the city, one woman grabbed a stone and aimed it at him, declaring that she preferred to die there than be threatened by such "terrible fears."[37] At least one person died in the stampede out of the capital on 30 November.

REBUILDING THE CITY

After the initial measures taken to ensure supplies of food and water and to reimpose social control, Viceroy Manso de Velasco and other authorities turned to the question of how to rebuild Lima. They discussed the possibility of moving the city, surveying the valleys to the south.[38] Proponents emphasized that the present site would never be free of the danger of an earthquake, recalling especially the devastating temblor of 1687. They cited the case of Palermo, which in the wake of a massive earthquake in 1692 had been rebuilt with wider streets and plazas.[39] The viceroy rejected this plan, however, primarily because of its expense. He calculated that rebuilding elsewhere would cost at least 300 million pesos, an enormous sum. Building a new cathedral alone would demand at least 7.5 million pesos, while repairing it would only come to 1.1 million. He also mentioned the high cost of building protective walls around the city and a presidio.[40] As would occur in Lisbon ten years later, authorities turned down a proposal to move the damaged city because of the high cost.[41]

The city council presented other arguments against a move. They began with the legalistic or formal point that the viceroy did not have the king's permission and thus could not even begin to make a decision. They then emphasized the population's opposition to the move. First among many disadvantages, the authors stressed, were the empty fields and buildings of the abandoned city that would become a haven for thieves and vagrants. They worried that giving runaways such a prime place to relocate would further swell the ranks of "maroons," thus weakening the institution of slavery. Urban policy could never disregard concerns about social unrest. Further, they pointed out that the move would invalidate the array of obligations and loans, or *censos*, between religious orders and property owners. Not only would this ruin the orders economically but it would also be the "seed of endless conflicts and lawsuits."[42] By early 1747, authorities no longer considered moving Lima.

Instead, the viceregal regime created an elaborate plan to rebuild the city in such a way as to minimize future damage from earthquakes. Under the leadership of the French astronomer, mathematician, and architect

Louis Godin, a commission recommended widening streets, limiting the height of buildings, prohibiting arched towers, replacing stone structures with wattle and daub, or *quincha*, and ensuring adequate plazas and public space to serve as refuge in case of disasters.[43] The plan prohibited tall, heavy structures and sought to ensure ample space in the streets even if buildings fell. These reforms were strikingly similar to the measures taken in Europe after the earthquake in Sicily in 1692–1693 and in Lisbon in 1755, when urban reformers sought to widen streets and plazas in order to ensure escape routes, hinder looting, and provide camping space. In general, the disasters in Europe served as pretext to implement the Renaissance ideal of wide, straight streets, in sharp contrast to the medieval pattern of narrow, twisted streets.[44] The debates in Lima, which counted on a strict grid layout, resembled those of Lisbon a decade later.

Concerns over social control, particularly rebellious slaves and the licentious plebs, shaped these plans. To justify his measures, Godin reiterated the threat of slaves fleeing and taking over abandoned homes. In a supporting document, Viceroy Manso de Velasco described the challenges he faced in the aftermath of the earthquake as slaves in and around Lima "disobeyed their masters, . . . even attempting to keep their belongings," while the "plebs" robbed at will.[45] He blamed Lima's architecture and contended that he had to take these extraordinary measures because "property-owners lost their own houses." Several times in this lengthy document, Godin, the viceroy, or representatives of the Cabildo, the city council, justified the drastic changes in building codes in the name of preventing opportunities for slaves to free themselves or for the lower classes to steal. In order to accomplish this, Godin and his commission called for shorter, sturdier buildings, ones that would not have to be abandoned in an earthquake. Because of Peru's shaky social order, unstable buildings were unacceptable.

Godin's first recommendation, to replace stone and brick structures with *quincha*, prompted little controversy. Members of the Cabildo did express concern that if the walls were too thin, then thieves could burrow in. Therefore, the commission permitted lower walls of adobe or brick.

Some worried about the prospect of outsiders digging into Lima's numerous convents, an issue that ultimately was not pursued.

Godin's second reccomendation, to prohibit buildings higher than 5 *varas*, or about 5 meters, did however, prompt a controversy, that lasted for several years and left a voluminous paper trail in the archives. Property owners resisted efforts to restrict structures to 5 *varas* high. On this question, the property-owning elite of Lima confronted the Bourbon state and ultimately stymied their efforts at urban reform. Upper-class property owners defended their right to have elaborate facades and two-story buildings by presenting a series of technical arguments: that taller buildings were actually safer; that rebuilding was prohibitively expensive; that the earthquake had bankrupted many of the property owners; that the king and the city council did not have the right to demolish buildings; and that insufficient room remained within the city walls to build more single-story buildings. Yet in their lengthy campaign, they ultimately relied on a social defense: that they, the "rational people," *el pueblo racional,* had suffered the most in the earthquake, had more important houses, and knew what was best for the city. They recognized that the majority of the population wanted the second stories torn down but contended that these opinions should not be taken into consideration because they were from the lowly plebs. Contrasting the generous Spaniards and their elegant homes to the pusillanimous Indians and their wretched huts, the defenders of the upper classes turned this struggle into a defense of rational and decent people versus the vulgar masses.[46]

The city council responded by countering the technical issues of security, cost, and prerogatives. The council members pointed out that even after three months, people had not returned to sleep in the second stories because of their well-founded fear. These people knew, according to the council response, that these structures posed a danger. The council's anonymous representative then returned to the essence of the viceroy's arguments, also invoking a social argument: that Lima architecture could not withstand the region's periodic earthquakes and that the destruction not only took many lives and destroyed property but also prompted social chaos. If the building methods were not changed, the misery, looting, and turmoil that had engulfed Lima would recur. At this point, the writer left the usual level of abstraction and descended rhetorically to the streets. He described vile living quarters and rampant diseases so horrifying that many survivors envied those who had perished in the earthquake.[47]

Viceroy Manso de Velasco relented. In November 1747 he ordered a house-by-house inspection to verify which upper floors could be preserved. While all of those made of adobe had to be torn down, those of wattle and daub that appeared sturdy could remain. It seems that most property owners were able to convince the commission that their houses were stable.[48] In a confrontation between counts, marquises, and other nobles and a lowly group of masons in charge of the inspection, the aristocrats would normally have their way.

This was not the only, or even the greatest, controversy surrounding Viceroy Manso de Velasco's efforts. He battled with the church hierarchy for more than a decade over the loans and liens owed on destroyed or damaged property. The colonial state was caught between destitute landowners, who claimed that they could not pay back the sums owed for damaged or even destroyed property, and the bereft church, which had also lost considerable property and needed money to rebuild churches, monasteries, and convents and to fund its various activities. One twentieth-century chronicler of Lima, José Gálvez, colorfully described the "secularization" of property after the earthquake: "While preachers commanded sinners to pray and repent, many of these sinners rubbed their hands with glee and occasionally pounded their chests, thinking about the prospects of easy acquisitions."[49] This conflict earned Manso de Velasco the enduring hatred of Archbishop Don Pedro Berroeta. When Manso de Velasco, by then Count Superunda, prepared to leave Lima in 1755, Berroeta and his supporters denounced him. Among their many accusations, they claimed that the viceroy and his backers had profited tremendously by collecting all the accumulated gold, silver, and jewels that washed up on the shore in the days following the earthquake. The viceroy's lawyer refuted this by wryly pointing out that most of these treasures had sunk to the ocean floor. Conflicts about the nature of rebuilding Lima thus did not only involve the state and the upper and lower classes; the church played a prominent role as well.[50]

The controversies over regaining control in and rebuilding Lima demonstrate the fractures in colonial domination. While a horizontal division between the upper classes (the self-proclaimed rational or decent people) and the lower classes strengthened in the eighteenth century, the upper classes, the church, and the different levels of the state feuded. Lima's upper class—the most powerful group in Spanish South America—chafed at the Bourbons' various reforms. The fear of and disdain for the lower classes, a highly racialized sentiment that became almost a reflex action in colonial (and postcolonial) Peru, brought the state and the upper classes together, but only temporarily. The property owners' efforts against the viceregal urban reforms, as well as the conflict with the church briefly summarized here, demonstrate the obstacles faced by the Bourbons, who could not easily impose their vision of a modernized Lima. The earthquake brought to light and accentuated the tensions that would mark the viceroyalty until independence in the 1820s.

THE EARTHQUAKE'S AFTERMATH: WHO PAYS AND WHO REBUILDS?

On 13 May 1784, an earthquake rocked the Arequipa region of southern Peru. It killed at least fifty people in the city of Arequipa, which had a population of twenty thousand, and claimed an untold number in the surrounding areas.[51] Authorities reported that only 72 of the city's 2,609 houses remained habitable days after the disaster. A more destructive earthquake struck the Central Highlands to the south of Quito in Ecuador on 4 February 1797. The five-minute catastrophe killed more than twelve thousand people and devastated the agricultural and textile economy.[52] In both cases, disaster sparked bitter debates about how the towns and cities were to be reconstructed—who was to do the work and who was to pay for it? Officials sought to make Indians bear the brunt of the reconstruction work. These discussions highlighted elite notions about

Indians and their role in the colonial society. They also demonstrated divisions within colonial power groups, divisions that would come to the fore in the movement for independence in the early nineteenth century.

In Arequipa, the Intendant Don Baltasar de Sematnat took immediate measures to guarantee sufficient food for the city, ordering that priority be given to fixing ovens and bakeries. Solicitor General López del Castillo noted that with winter soon to arrive, the Arequipa population faced further misfortune: "If in abundant times (the poor) suffer shortages, how gravely will they suffer in the fatal state in which they now find themselves?"[53] He then made a shrewd case for the colonial state to grant Arequipa inexpensive, semicoerced Indian labor through a forced draft called the *mita*. He calculated that the city had suffered damages totaling thirty million pesos. This represented an astronomical figure, particularly for the Spanish Crown, which at this point was investing minimally in its American colonies and instead extracting as much revenue as possible to pay for its costly wars in Europe. Knowing that the Bourbon rulers would balk at spending such a sum, López del Castillo presented a solution. He argued that the city should be granted six thousand Indian workers from the four "Indian provinces with many towns" that surrounded Arequipa. López del Castillo calculated that this workforce would suffice to rebuild the city. He justified this request on a number of counts.

He emphasized the importance of Arequipa in manning the armies that repressed a number of revolts, including the massive Tupac Amaru Rebellion of 1780–1781 that spread throughout much of the Andean region. He noted that Arequipa battalions had fought from Upper Peru (present-day Bolivia) to Cusco.[54] He then cited the Toledan Reforms from the late sixteenth century, the guiding text of much colonial policy, which set wages at below two reales a day.[55] López del Castillo implied that the Indians would earn near this standard in Arequipa and that they earned less than this throughout the Andes, except in the mines. He contended that the workers would eat better in Arequipa and return to their homes after their work duty with money to buy essential items. Finally, López del Castillo lauded the sovereign, "who, with his paternal love and tenderness grieves for the calamities of his people," had generously opened the coffers of the royal treasury to aid the town of Messina, devastated by an earthquake in 1783.

Authorities like López del Castillo wanted to rebuild Arequipa on the backs of the Indian population living in surrounding areas. This type of exploitative reliance on the Indians had become almost a reflex in colonial Peru,[56] where Indian communities were forced to send one-seventh of their adult male population for one year of work, usually in the harsh mines. Because of its high Indian population and the labor demands of the nearby Potosí silver mine in Upper Peru, southern Andean communities in Peru had for centuries provided an inordinate share of the *mita* workers; the institution endured in this region longer than any other. Demographic decline forced many communities to send more than one-seventh of their male population since the dead were not taken off the lists. Indigenous community authorities, *kurakas*, were forced to rustle up the workforce or pay large fines or face jail sentences.

The earthquake in central Ecuador struck the districts of Ambato, Riobamba, and, to a lesser degree, Latacunga. People died not only when houses and other buildings collapsed but also as landslides plummeted down the steep Andean hillsides, burying inhabitants, blocking rivers, and causing floods. The disaster damaged irrigation ditches, estates, and textile mills, particularly the massive San Ildefonso mill, hampering agricultural and textile production. The extensive flooding forced authorities to relocate the town of Riobamba.[57] The response to the massive earthquake followed the pattern of Lima and Arequipa. First, authorities secured food and water supplies. Governor Luis Muñoz de Guzmán y Montero de Espinoso ordered the village magistrates, or *alcaldes ordinarios*, to obtain "in any way possible" supplies for the affected rural areas to assist the wounded and save the season's harvests. He promised that those who donated supplies would be repaid, in part from the valuables found in the ruins. Noting that "greed can tempt human fragility," he forbade any food to be hidden or sold at a higher price than the ordinary. People burnt manure and kindling to rid the air of "corrupted miasma" and thus to prevent a plague.[58]

Yet authorities had more to worry about than ensuring food supplies and cleaning the air. In the days after the earthquake, rumors reached Quito, the capital of the *audiencia*, that Indians were going to take advantage of the turmoil and rebel. The *corregidor*, or magistrate, of Latacunga, 50 miles to the south of Quito, expressed great concern about an Indian uprising. He added, quite correctly, that the Indians had rebelled on "many occasions." The Andes were the site of dozens of revolts in the eighteenth century, the most notable that of Tupac Amaru and Tupac Katari in Peru and Upper Peru, from 1780 to 1783. In Ecuador, rebels had controlled the city of Quito for months in 1765 and at least ten uprisings had struck the highlands between 1730 and 1805.[59] A later letter claimed that rebels, intending to kill the town's priest and *kuraka*, had taken control of the town. The rumor proved false. Nonetheless, looting and other disturbances lasted for weeks.[60]

Authorities treated reports of a potential Indian uprising differently than those of rebelliousness by blacks and slaves. For the latter, they deemed severe repression adequate. Governmental authorities and elite group interpreted the looting and other criminal activities reported in the wake of the Lima earthquake as manifestations of the lower classes', particularly blacks', dishonest spirit and the temporary breakdown of social control. They believed that severe measures would suffice to prevent further crimes. In regard to relations between the state and Indians, elite (i.e., non-Indian) notions in the eighteenth century combined a seemingly contradictory mix of benevolence and coercion. The official from Latacunga who reported the rumors of an uprising pointed out that Indians can usually be reduced with "gentleness and ingenuity."[61] He was relieved to report "all returned to normal with the whipping of three Indians, one man and two women." One employee in the High Court wondered if this punishment had even been necessary.

The combination of punishment and restraint can be explained in part as a tactical response to rebellion. While authorities wanted to punish transgressors, often in gruesome and public fashion, they also sought to avoid provoking another uprising or straining already bad relations. Thus in the Cusco area following the Tupac Amaru Rebellion, while the leaders were publicly tortured and executed and their limbs exhibited throughout the region, Indians had surprising "success" negotiating with the state in subsequent decades.[62] Yet the explanation of this seemingly contradictory reaction to rumors of an Indian uprising goes beyond mere strategy. It reflected late colonial discourse and practice on the "nature" of the Indian population, particularly the central question of how best to "incorporate" them into the colonial social and economic body.

Overlapping and conflicting notions of the role of the state vis-à-vis the Indian collided in the eighteenth century. All of these are present in the wake of the Quito earthquake. On the one hand, the state was still understood as the "protector" of the indigenous population, the arbiter between the native population and external groups. For example, the "Protector of Indians" still represented an important office. In fact, as seen below, this authority challenged the more exploitative practices against the Indian population contemplated by authorities after the 1797 earthquake. Documents regarding the earthquake acknowledged this paternalistic role of the state. Yet for many, the state had to protect the Indians from themselves. Justifications of exploitative policies like the *mita*, forcing Indians to work, the *repartimiento de bienes*, to buy overpriced goods, and the *tributo*, to pay special taxes, emphasized that without them, Indians would lapse back into a pagan, unproductive subsistence economy. According to this pervasive view, without the prodding of the state, Indians would not benefit from colonial civilization, particularly material culture. Non-Indian analysts of Andean society in the eighteenth and later centuries stressed that the Indians were content with their "miserable" huts, woven clothing, food, and so forth. Therefore, by forcing Indians to work, consume, and pay taxes, the state protected and enriched them. A distinction can be seen between those who saw the role of the state as protecting the Indians from external exploiters and those who saw it as protecting the Indians from themselves.[63]

A third perspective gained ground in the eighteenth century, one that did not see the state as the protector of the Indian population. Instead, the Indians were understood and treated as deceitful savages who needed to be controlled. The series of rebellions that had shaken Bourbon control of the Andes heightened the anti-Indian fury. Even the sternest calls for repression, however, were tempered by calls for restraint. All of these views came to the fore in the debates about how to rebuild from the devastation of the Quito earthquake.

The marquis of Miraflores, a distinguished resident of Latacunga and owner of numerous estates, had a seemingly benevolent solution to the exorbitant cost of rebuilding Quito: he called for the Indians to be exonerated from the head tax. This proposal sparked great controversy that lasted for years. Not only was the Indian head tax the key source of governmental income but also its collection and enforcement undergirded labor practices, local power struggles, and relations between the church and the state. In his long justification of such a measure, the marquis of Miraflores did not attempt to conceal his motives. He argued that the exoneration "would stop the Indians from being eaten alive [*descarnarse*] from the demand of the prompt payment of tribute, and with this money they could attend the urgent necessities that they face in rebuilding their homes, barns, irrigation ditches, textile mills, and other necessary implements for the subsistence and development of haciendas [large estates] and textile mills." [64] His plan sought to lower estate owners' labor costs, as wages could be decreased if Indian workers did not have to pay the head tax. The marquis argued that the haciendas would pay the Indians, including those who worked under debt servitude ("It is necessary to get them into debt in order to concentrate, conserve, and maintain them in the haciendas and textile mills"), but less because of the workers' diminished tax burden. It is not clear whether the marquis favored exempting village Indians who did not work on estates. What is clear is that the marquis sought above all to favor estate owners.

A royal decree dated 22 August 1797 exonerated Indians from the affected areas from the head tax for a year. This prompted immediate controversy and confusion. The bishop of Quito noted that while the destruction of churches was the worst effect of the earthquake ("God, Our Lord, is now forced to live in huts poorer than that of Bethlehem"), he had not requested subsidies for reconstructing, as secular authorities had. Referring to the tax exemption, he labeled it an insignificant amount for each beneficiary, not enough to improve their fortune or to build a "decent house" for God. The bishop then presented the key justification of the tribute: it was a small sum that exonerated Indians from more burdensome taxes and kept them working. With the payment of four or five pesos a year, the male Indian

> is freed from other taxes, even the ecclesiastical; I guarantee that any other subject would gladly fulfill this obligation to his great advantage; and the Indian exempted from it for a year is not assured of benefit in not paying it, nor when paying it does he suffer in earthly goods; instead the tax is the best measure for the government to force these people to work, to prevent slothfulness, to take away their funds for drunkenness and to erase the memory of their Incas. . . . The annual sum of this tribute, calculated at 100,000 pesos per year, could be invested in factories, temples, and even civil buildings such as jails and hospitals.

The bishop correctly pointed out that the payment of the head tax exonerated Indians from the sales tax and other fiscal demands.[65] The bishop presumably also worried that priests would not receive the small portion of the tribute revenues normally allotted to them. He concluded by noting that the Indians, with their unfurnished, unadorned huts, "suffered less than everyone else in the earthquake and instead of enduring losses they abandoned themselves to looting, with many of them benefiting from it."[66]

Authorities disagreed about what to do with the tribute the Indians had paid before the earthquake. The decree by the Royal Court apparently called for the return of this money to the Indians, a plan supported by the protector of the Indians, certain judges, and *kurakas*. The marquis of Miraflores and the bishop of Quito, on the other hand, favored the High Court's efforts to use the money to relieve non-Indians, especially the elite.

The president of the High Court called for a tax exemption for estate and textile mill owners instead of for Indians. He argued that, if returned, the three or four pesos per person would slip through the Indians' fingers and not improve the "common good." He echoed the bishop's views, contending that "despite their natural misery," the Indians suffered less than others in the disaster. Their houses, mere hovels in his eyes, had resisted while the solid buildings of Spaniards and other non-Indians had collapsed. An authority from Ambato, to the south of Quito, argued that the Indians were actually better off with the earthquake thanks to the ample opportunities for theft. He called for the restoration of the head tax, emphasizing its importance in guaranteeing a labor supply. He claimed that the corn the Indians grew satisfied their dietary demands and that they only worked in order to pay tribute. The protector countered this view, arguing that the earthquake killed thousands of Indians and devastated their fields and livestock.

Controversy also ensued over whether Indians were exempted from the entire tribute amount or whether they had to pay the approximately 25 percent that funded the bureaucracy and subsidized the church. Authorities contended that the Indians in the affected area paid 112,533 pesos a year, with 78,990 reaching the viceregal coffers. Many insisted that even with the exoneration, Indians still had to pay the 33,442 pesos destined for the administration and the church, an argument that the protector of Indians disputed. In a note to the general accountant in Quito, the *corregidor* of Latacunga accused the protector of Indians of writing a letter stating that the king had exonerated Indians from the entire head tax. Some *kurakas*, the local Indian authorities, had received the letter. The *corregidor* claimed that if the letter had been circulated among the Indians, the consequences would have been "fatal," particularly for anyone trying to collect the tax. He called the protector's actions "a crime," asserting that, in light of the Indians' inclination to "riot and mutiny," the rumors could have provoked an uprising. The *corregidor* noted that priests, governors, sacristans, and "many others" relied on the tax for their subsistence. The protector of Indians and several *kurakas* were brought to trial. In their defense, they denied that Indians had taken advantage of the earthquake to steal, insisting instead that the Indians had lost the most. The outcome of this trial as well as the general debate about the head tax are not found in the archival sources. The controversy was not an obscure discussion about fiscal policy and society, restricted to the upper realms of Ecuador's political and religious circles. Taxes constituted a linchpin of Indian-state relations and any change threatened local and regional political hierarchies. A chain of authorities depended on the collection of the head tax, and they reacted to the vague new policies.

In contrast to many modern regimes, authorities succeeded in all three cases in providing the population with food, water, and shelter. The concern and abilities of the colonial absolutist state in caring for basic needs should not be underestimated. Yet the postcalamity efforts rapidly moved beyond ensuring basic necessities and into the questions of what type of cities and towns should rise from the ruins, and who should pay for and provide the labor for such efforts. In Lima, tensions escalated over the criminal activities and even subversive capacity of the dark-skinned lower classes. These concerns shaped the rebuilding of Lima, taming the Bourbons' efforts to create what they deemed a more rational, controllable city. Yet a bitter controversy between the colonial state and the Lima elite also emerged, as the latter sought to maintain their architectural privileges, crucial in denoting social superiority. In the two Andean cases of Arequipa and central Ecuador, discussions and policies focused on how best to ensure Indian labor, and money to rebuild, thus creating a collision between divergent notions of Indians' nature and their relation to the state. Heightened labor and fiscal demands on Indians in the context of multiple tensions between the colonial state and the upper classes characterized the Andean region until they materialized into wars of independence.

INTERNATIONAL FASCINATION

The earthquakes that beset Lima, Arequipa, and Quito were not isolated events whose impact was limited to the affected area and a few concerned colonial bureaucrats. The squabbles over who was to pay for the earthquakes provoked paper wars that left thousands of pages of primary material for historians.[67] Each earthquake was widely publicized at the time and written about for years. Other Peruvian earthquakes gained great international attention as well. The *True and Particular Relation of the Dreadful Earthquake which Happen'd at Lima*, "published at Lima by command of the Viceroy," was translated and published in London in 1748. It included a detailed translator's preface; introductory chapters that described Lima and Callao and presented theories about the causes of earthquakes; the translation itself; chapters on the population of Peru, taken largely from Frézier's account; and finally an appendix with a brief account of a severe earthquake in Jamaica in 1692.[68] Besides its two editions in London, the book was also published in Mexico, Portugal, and Boston, and in Philadelphia by Benjamin Franklin and D. Hall.[69] Numerous other accounts of the catastrophe came forth in the following years in Lima, Callao, Madrid, and Belgium.[70]

The unusually high number of publications on the Lima catastrophe reflected the web of controversies that arose in its aftermath, as different groups vied to put their views and necessities in writing. Moreover, the Lima disaster coincided with an international fascination with earthquakes that had been heightened by the Lisbon earthquake in 1755 and by various intercontinental debates about disasters and society. In Peru, Viceroy Manso de Velasco supported the publication of an account that chronicled his efforts. Subsequently, the church, landowners, and prominent observers with scientific interests such as Llano y Zapata also edited their observations. One Lima account pointed out, "It seems that one cannot treat such notable phenomenon [earthquakes] without natural curiosity inducing you to look into their causes."[71] Similarly in Arequipa, city authorities, ever vigilant of events in the capital, also sought to leave a published account "so in the future the level of damage of the earthquake would be known."[72] Yet the number of publications inside and outside of Peru indicates that the explanation transcended the desire to register accomplishments or publicize demands.

In the eighteenth century, debates about the causes of earthquakes raged. In New England, John Winthrop and Reverend Thomas Prince posed the debate as a struggle between natural philosophy and theology. Others focused on more scientific grounds. In the early eighteenth century, explanations for the causes of earthquakes centered on subterranean fires, vapors, and water. Amedée Frézier had used his travels along the Pacific coast of South America to support theories that contended that water weakened the earth's surfaces and led the land to collapse. The English translator of the Lima account countered this view and argued that earthquakes are explosions that lift the surface of the earth, rocking it greatly.[73] In the latter part of the century, scientists focused more on air currents and electricity. While most of the key scientists of the era were Europeans, not only did many of them travel to the American continent—for example, the La Condamine expedition that began in 1735—but also they shared their work with American scientific societies.

The Lisbon earthquake on All Saints' Day in 1755 provoked a great number of publications: more than twenty accounts of the disaster were published in London within six weeks, while the writing of Voltaire and others turned the catastrophe into a major moment in European letters. The accounts of Lisbon also questioned the causes of earthquakes and initiated debates that revealed international disagreements about science and domination. While some Dutch saw Lisbon as "wrath against Roman idolatry," others debated whether it constituted an act of God or was the result of natural causes.[74]

English observers of the Lima catastrophe used it to highlight Spanish decadence. These accounts of the Lima earthquake indicated the heightened tensions between the British and Spanish. The preface to the London translation of the "Brief Account . . ." epitomized the English view of Spanish colonial decadence, the Black Legend. The author emphasized the opulent churches and seemingly pious population. He pointed out the licentious behavior of the Lima inhabitants—their blasé attitude toward marriage, for example—and detailed the profligate activities of priests. He also noted the wealth of Peru, particularly the abundance of gold and silver, which he claimed could be found on or near the surface of the ground. The anonymous author, the translator of the Peruvian account, was not simply Spain-bashing; he held clear imperial designs. He presented the disruption of the earthquake as an excellent opportunity for England to conquer Peru: "[I]t was always judged, even in their most prosperous Condition, that this was practicable: For the Troops of these Countries were never other than an undisciplin'd Militia, without order, and immers'd in Luxury and Effeminacy." [75] The great social divisions between Indians and Spaniards as well as the purported misbehavior of the priests would aid British efforts in Peru; he recognized that his representation of the society could promote a British invasion of Peru.

As this English author understood, earthquakes literally open up society, revealing a great deal about communities and social divisions. In Lima, Arequipa, and central Ecuador, authorities responded effectively to the immediate needs of the population. Their attention then turned to preventing social protest and to rebuilding. Racialized notions of order, hierarchy, and the economy drove these efforts. The colonial state, the upper classes, and the occasional member of the lower classes discussed who should bear the brunt of the cost of rebuilding. In doing so, they discussed who suffered because of the catastrophe and how to prevent further disasters. The three earthquakes reflected intriguing differences in views about Andean Indians and the multicolored urban plebs of Lima and highlighted the multiple divisions between and within the colonial state, the church, and the upper classes, groups that agreed on the need to control and exploit the lower classes, but disagreed on how to achieve this. Furthermore, the three earthquakes illuminated, even accentuated, tensions that persisted until and beyond the wars of independence of the 1820s.

NOTES

1   I would like to thank Carlos Aguirre, A. J. Bauer, Marcos Cueto, Barbara Hickman, Alessa Johns, Matt Mulcahy, Brendan O'Malley, Adam Warren, and David Sweet for their help in preparing this essay.

2   L. G. Thompson, E. Mosley Thompson, J. F. Bolzan, and B.R. Koci, "A 1500-Year Record of Tropical Precipitation in Ice Cores from the Quelccaya Ice Cap, Peru," *Science* (6 September 1985): 971–73; Anne-Marie Hocquenghem, Luc Orltieb, "Eventos el niño y lluvias anormales en la costa del Perú: Siglos XVI-XIX," *Boletín del Instituto Francés de Estudios Andinos* 21, no. 1 (1992); James H. Shirley, "Temporal Patterns in Historic Major Earthquakes," *West Georgia College, Studies in the Social Sciences*, special issue, "Investigating Natural Hazards in Latin American History" XXV (1986).

3   For a gripping account of this tragedy and its aftermath, see Barbara Bode, *No Bells to Toll* (New York: Paragon House, 1989). Anthony Oliver-Smith has also researched on this tragedy; see esp. *The Martyred City: Death and Rebirth in the Peruvian Andes* (Albuquerque: University of New Mexico Press, 1986).

4   *Desolación de la ciudad de Lima, y dilubio del Puerto del Callao* (Lima, 1746), 1.

5   *A True and Particular Relation of the Dreadful Earthquake, which Happen'd at Lima, the Capital of Peru, and the Neighbouring Port of Callao, on the 28th of October, 1746*, 2d ed. (London, 1748) , 132.

6   Ibid., iii.

7   Founded in January 1535, Lima was originally named La Ciudad de los Reyes in honor of the Epiphany.

8   María Pilar Pérez Cantó, *Lima en el siglo xviii. Estudio socioeconómico* (Madrid: Universidad Autónoma de Madrid, 1985), 49–52.

9   On social geography, see among others Alberto Flores Galindo, *Aristocracia y plebe: Lima 1760-1830* (Lima: Mosca Azul, 1984); Juan Günther Doering and Guillermo Lohmann Villena, *Lima* (Madrid: MAPFRE, 1992); Lyn Lowry, "Forging an Indian Nation: Urban Indians under Spanish Colonial Control (Lima, Peru, 1535–1765)," Ph.D. diss., Dept. of Anthropology, University of California, Berkeley, 1991; Aldo Panfichi, "Urbanización temprana de Lima, 1535–1900," in *Mundos interiores: Lima 1850–1950*, ed. Aldo Panfichi and Felipe Portocarrero (Lima: Universidad El Pacífico, 1995).

10   On changing social divisions in eighteenth-century Spanish America, see Richard Morse, "Urban Development," in *Colonial Spanish America*, ed. Leslie Bethell (Cambridge: Cambridge University Press 1987); Jorge Basadre, *La multitud, la ciudad y el campo en la historia del Perú* (Lima: Ediciones Treintaitrés and Mosca Azul, 1980); Patricia Seed, "Social Dimensions of Race: Mexico City, 1753," *Hispanic American Historical Review* 62 (1983): 559–606.

11   *A True and Particular*, 134.

12   "Carta o diario que escribió D. José Eusebio de Llano y Zapata a su más venerado amigo y docto corresponsal el Dr. D. Ignacio Chirivoga y Daza, Canónigo de la Santa

Iglesia de Quito," in Manuel D. Odriozola, *Terremotos. Colección de las relaciones de los más notables que ha sufrideo esta capital y que la han arruinado* (Lima: A. Alforo, 1863), 70–108, quote from 72.

13   *A True and Particular*, 135.

14   Jorge Bernales Ballesteros, *Edificación de la Iglesia Catedral de Lima (Notas para su historia)* (Sevilla, Universidad de Sevilla, 1969), 78–87.

15   *A True and Particular*, 135.

16   *A True and Particular*, 144–45; see also Padre Pedro Lozano, "Relación del Terremoto que arruinó a Lima e inundó al Callao el 28 de Octubre de 1746," in Odriozola, *Terremotos*, 37–38.

17   *A True and Particular*, intro., vii–xii.

18   *A True and Particular*; Lozano, "Relación," 41–44; Llano y Zapata, "Carta o diario," 98–102.

19   Lozano, "Relación," 43.

20   Basadre, *La multitud*, 94.

21   *Desolación*, 6.

22   Conde de Superunda, *Relación de gobierno, Perú (1745–1761)*, ed. and intro. by Alfredo Moreno (Madrid: CSIC, 1983), 259; Archivo General de Indias (hereafter AGI), Lima, Legajo 984, "Expedientes e instancias de partes, 1749–1752." See also David Cahill, "Financing Health Care in the Viceroyalty of Peru: The Hospitals of Lima in the Late Colonial Period," *The Americas* 52, no. 2 (1995).

23   *A True and Particular*, 156.

24   Llano y Zapata, "Carta o diario," 76.

25   Ibid., 77–78.

26   AGI, Audiencia de Lima, Legajo 509, "Expediente sobre la oportunidad de rebajar los capitales…" While condemning the lower classes, the author emphasized how the catastrophe had cut social differences, or at least made living conditions more equitable. Because wood was an expensive commodity, builders used it sparingly in Lima, primarily to frame doorways and openings and for choice doors.

27   Lozano, "Relación," 45.

28   Superunda, *Relación*, 260–63. For a good summary of his efforts, see E. W. Middendorf, *Perú: Observaciones y estudios del país y sus habitantes durante una permanencia de 25 años* (Lima: Universidad San Marcos, 1973), tomo 1, 106.

29   Superunda, *Relación*, 261.

30   Llano y Zapata, "Carta o diario," 92.

31   Marqués de Obando, "Carta que escribió el Marqués de Obando a un amigo suyo," in Odriozola, *Terremotos*, 47–48.

32   *Desolación*, 7–8.

33   Alberto Flores Galindo, *Buscando un Inca*, 4th ed. (Lima: Editorial Horizonte, 1987), 198–99. The art historian and leading authority on Santa Rosa, Ramón Mujica, has not found indications of ideas circulating about this prophecy after the earthquake. Personal communication.

34   On Juan Santos, see Stefano Varese, *La Sal de los cerros* (Lima: Inide, 1973); Steve J. Stern, "The Age of Andean Insurrection, 1742–1782: A Reappraisal," in *Resistance, Rebellion, and Consciousness in the Andean Peasant World, 18th to 20th Centurie,* ed. Steve J. Stern (Madison: University of Wisconsin Press, 1987), 34–93.

35   Llano y Zapata, "Carta o diario," 73.

36   Obando, "Carta que escribió," 47–48.

37   Ibid., 55–56.

38   They discussed moving it toward Lurigancho to the north and farther to the south, to San Bartolo. AGI, Audiencia de Lima, Legajo 511, "Reedificación de Lima tras el Terremoto de 1746, 1748–1751."

39   Doering and Villena, *Lima*, 130.

40   AGI, Leg. 511, 27b.

41   For the comparisons I have relied on Stephen Tobriner, "Earthquakes and Planning in the 17th and 18th Centuries," *Journal of Architectural Education* XXXIII, no. 4 (1980): 11–15, and his "La Casa Baraccata: Earthquake-resistant Construction in Eighteenth-Century Calabria," *Society of Architectural Historians* XLII, no. 2 (1983): 131–38. On Lisbon, I have also used C. R. Boxer, "Some Contemporary Reactions to the Lisbon Earthquake of 1755," *Revista de Facultade de Letras* (Universidade de Lisboa) XXII, 2a serie, 2 (1956): 113–29; C. R. Boxer, "Pombal's Dictatorship and the Great Lisbon Earthquake, 1755," *History Today* (1955): 729–36; T. D. Kendrick, *The Lisbon Earthquake* (Philadelphia: J. B. Lippincott Co., 1955).

42   AGI, Leg. 511, 32–37. On the earthquake and *censos*, see Susana Aldana Rivera, "¿Ocurrencias del Tiempo? Fenómenos naturales y sociedad en el Perú colonial," in *Historia y desastres en América Latina*, vol. 1, ed. Virginia García Acosta (Bogota: La Red/Ciesas, 1996), 167–94.

43   Godin, a member of the Paris Academy of the Sciences, led a scientific expedition to Peru in 1735. In 1744, he took the chair in mathematics at San Marcos University in Lima. He died in Cádiz in 1760, the director of the Armada's Coast Guard Academy. Antonio Lafuente and Antonio Mazuecos, *Los caballeros del punto fijo. Ciencia, política y aventura en la expedición geodésica hispanofrancesa al virreinato del Perú en el siglo XVIII* (Madrid: SERBAL/CSIC, 1987), esp. 142–46 and, for a portrait, 61.

44   Tobriner, "Earthquakes and Planning" and "La Casa Baraccata."

45   AGI, Leg. 511, 244b.

46   Ibid., esp. 67–90a.

47   AGI, Leg. 511.

48   I have inferred this because only a few references in primary and secondary sources discuss second stories being torn down.

49   José Gálvez, *Las calles de Lima* (Lima: IPC, 1943), 115.

50   This controversy left a long paper trail. See among many sources AGI, Audiencia de Lima, Legajo 787, "Autos de Residencia del Virrey."

51   On Arequipa in this period, see Kendall W. Brown, *Bourbons and Brandy: Imperial Reform in Eighteenth-Century Arequipa* (Albuquerque: University of New Mexico Press, 1986); Sarah Chambers, "The Many Shades of the White City: Urban Culture and Society in Arequipa, 1780–1854," Ph.D. diss., Dept. of History, University of Wisconsin, Madison, 1992; Alberto Flores Galindo, *Arequipa y el sur andino, siglos xviii–xx* (Lima: Editorial Horizonte, 1977).

52   One graph tabulates 12,553 dead; AGI, Leg. 403. On the fatalities of the earthquake and general demographic trends in eighteenth- and nineteenth-century Ecuador, see Rosemary D. F. Bromley, "Urban-Rural Demographic Contrasts in Highland Ecuador: Town Recession in a Period of Catastrophe 1778–1841," *Journal of Historical Geography* 5, no. 3 (1979): esp. 291–94; Bromley, "Disasters and Population Change in Central Highland Ecuador, 1778–1825," in *Social Fabric and Spatial Structure in Colonial Latin America,* ed. David J. Robinson (Syracuse: Syracuse University Press, 1979), 85–115.

53   "Relación del terremoto del 13 de mayo de 1784," in Fr. Victor M. Barriga, *Los Terremotos en Arequipa* (Arequipa, 1951), 302. See also Jorge Bernales Ballesteros, "Informes de los daños sufridos en la ciudad de Arequipa con el terremoto de 1784," *Anuario de Estudios Americanos* XXIX (1972): 295–314.

54   "Relación del terremoto del 13 de mayo," 302–04.

55   The peso was made up of eight reales—thus the expression "two bits" means a quarter.

56   On the *mita*, see among many studies Enrique Tandeter, *Coercion and Market: Silver Mining in Colonial Potosí, 1692–1826* (Albuquerque: University of New Mexico Press, 1993).

57   See Bromley, "Urban-Rural Demographic Contrasts," 292–93.

58   My analysis of the Ecuador earthquake initially relied on the archival notes generously provided to me by Arnold Bauer. AGI, Audiencia de Quito, Leg. 403.

59   See Segundo Moreno Yañez, *Sublevaciones indígenas en la audiencia de Quito, Desde comienzos del siglo XVIII hasta finales de la colonia* (Quito: Universidad Católica del Ecuador, 1985); Kenneth J. Andrien, *The Kingdom of Quito, 1690–1830: The State and Regional Development* (Cambridge: Cambridge University Press, 1995); Anthony McFarlane, "The 'Rebellion of the Barrios': Urban Insurrection in Bourbon Quito, 1765," *Hispanic American Historical Review* 69, no. 2 (1989): 283–330; Martin Minchom, *The People of Quito, 1690–1810: Change and Unrest in the Underclass* (Boulder: Westview, 1994).

60   Suzanne Austin Alchon, *Native Society and Disease in Colonial Ecuador* (Cambridge: Cambridge University Press, 1991), 123.

61   AGI, Audiencia de Quito, Leg. 403, letter dated 25 February 1797.

62   I develop this argument in Charles F. Walker, *Smoldering Ashes: Cuzco and the Creation of Republican Peru, 1780–1840* (Durham: Duke University Press, 1999). The colonial state's reliance on the Indian head tax increased its need to negotiate.

63   Ibid.

64   AGI, Audiencia of Quito, Leg. 403. It is fascinating how the marquis weaves together Indians' necessities and those of textile and estate owners.

65   In fact, Indians sometimes fought to pay the tax. See Núria Sala i Vila, *Y se armó el tole-tole: tributo indígena y movimientos sociales en el virreinato del Perú, 1784-1814* (Lima: IER José María Arguedas, 1996), chap. 6.

66   AGI, Audiencia of Quito, Leg. 403, letter from 21 April 1799. In Arequipa, the church and the state collided in the aftermath of the earthquake over even a more fundamental issue than that of the head tax. The governor-intendant and the bishop of Arequipa fought over who was to conduct the inventory of the damage. The conflict lasted for months and although the governor-intendant was put in charge, both provided detailed reports of the havoc caused by the Arequipa earthquake.

67   For example, debates about debts and the grave situation of the city's religious buildings prompted representatives of the church to publish a twenty-four-page account of its sorrowful situation: *Representación Jurídica, Allegato Reverente, Que se Haze por parte de*

las Religiones de esta Noble Capital. Al Excmo. Señor Don Joseph Manso de Velasco (Lima, 1747); In the name of Lima's property owners, Don Miguel de Valdivieso y Torrejón answered with his own pamphlet: *Allegación Jurídica por parte de los Vezinos Dueños de Casa de Esta Capital, Sobre la Rebaja de Los Censos, Por la Ruina que Padecieron con el Terremoto de 28 de Octubre de 1746* (Lima, 1748).

68   *True and Particular Relation of the Dreadful Earthquake which Happen'd at Lima the Capital of Peru* . . . (Philadelphia, reprinted and sold by B. Franklin and D. Hall at the New Printing Office, near the Market, 1749); ibid. (Boston, [1755?]). This last date is given on the microfilm copy from Lilly Library, Indiana University.

69   *Individual y verdadera* . . . (Mexico, 1746); London, 1748 and 1748; Lisbon, 1748; Philadelphia, 1749; Boston, n.d. On these editions, see Toribio Medina, *La Imprenta en Lima* (Santiago, 1904), 430–33.

70   For a thorough analysis of these publications, see Medina, *La Imprenta.*

71   Biblioteca Nacional de Madrid, Manuscript #1438, "Descripción de la Ciudad de Lima, capital del Reino del Perú . . . (Lima, [1774?]).

72   Bernales Ballesteros, "Informe de los daños," 298.

73   John Gates Taylor, "Eighteenth-Century Earthquake Theories: A Case-History Investigation into the Character of the Study of the Earth in the Enlightenment," Ph.D. diss., Dept of History, University of Oklahoma, 1975, chapter 3.

74   Boxer, "Some Contemporary"; Kendrick, *The Lisbon Earthquake.*

75   *A True and Particular Relation,* xi.

"The Hungry Year"

1789 on the Northern Border of Revolutionary America

ALAN TAYLOR

*I*n the spring and early summer of 1789 hunger became widespread on the northern borderland shared by Canada and the United States. Within the United States, the suffering was greatest in the newly settled upland districts in northeastern Pennsylvania, upstate New York, and western Vermont. In Canada, the hunger extended from Niagara on the west through the Province of Quebec and into the Maritimes. Although occasionally noted in local histories, the extent and significance of the dearth of 1789 has escaped the attention of national historians in the United States; no previous work has drawn together the many local episodes to reconstruct its sweep. Indeed, American historians are wont to deny even the possibility of such an episode of widespread hunger in their nation's past.

The contemporary sources often, yet vaguely, refer to deaths from starvation, but they never specify names and numbers. Usually the sources locate the purported deaths just over the horizon in some other locale. Because the hunger prevailed primarily in places without comprehensive vital records, the demographic consequences of the dearth remain murky. My best guess is that, although the suffering was widespread and severe, deaths were few. Consequently, the hunger is best called a "dearth" rather than a "famine" (which is characterized by a severely enhanced level of mortality; see, for example, the Bengal famine of 1770, assessed by David Arnold in this collection). However, this is a distinction of contemporary social science that was not available to the sufferers of 1789, who often referred to their plight as a "famine."

In addition to documenting the extent and intensity of the dearth of 1789, this chapter seeks its causes. Our commonplace view of "disasters" takes for granted the human presence in harm's way and characterizes disasters as "natural," as simply the uncontrollable, albeit lamentable, consequence of extreme swings in geophysical processes: storms, earthquakes, floods, and volcanoes. However, recent revisionist scholarship on contemporary disasters argues, in the words of Anthony Oliver-Smith, "that human groups and institutions play a far more active role in the creation of destructive agents and circumstances than is usually imagined or portrayed." Societies tend to place certain people, usually the poorest and powerless, in dangerous circumstances; blaming "nature" for the consequent "disaster" serves to absolve the social order, reaffirming its claims to justice—especially if the rulers can provide palliatives to the victims. Following the lead of this revisionist scholarship, I will argue that the causes for the dearth of 1789 were a complex medley where social and cultural considerations loomed larger than the intervention of what we call "nature."[1]

Nature did contribute to the dearth in two related forms: a wheat parasite, the Hessian fly, curtailed the wheat harvest of 1788 in parts of the borderland; and an unusually cold spring in 1789 was psychologically devastating. Both forms derived largely from a global cooling effected by volcanic dust in the upper atmosphere. But three social aspects intensified and extended the localized natural problems into a geographically broad crisis. First, market incentives drained provisions from the borderland at the worst possible time—in the fall and winter of 1788–1789. Second, during the following spring, poor and poorly informed settlers emigrated into the suffering districts, compounding the shortage of food (especially in northern Pennsylvania, upstate New York, and western Vermont). Third, belated but alarmist reporting of the crisis by the press in June extended the alarm, raising grain prices and provoking speculative hoarding, where there had previously been a "natural" surplus (primarily in southern and eastern New England).

As is often the case with dearths and famines, the crisis was primarily one of maldistribution of supply, rather than an absolute shortfall in production. Only the inroads of the Hessian fly reduced farm production, and this was limited to one grain—wheat—and geographically to parts of Canada and New England. From that core region, the crisis became widespread through a process of magnification by the other four causes. Although "natural" in origin, the cold spring did not so much reduce food supply as spread panic. By arousing fears that the crisis would be prolonged, the long, cold spring discouraged people with grain from parting with it, hindering the movement of food that might have alleviated suffering in the few places with an absolute shortfall. The combined effects of external market, internal migration, and alarmist reporting did not reduce food production, but instead exported a surplus and then concentrated especially vulnerable people into the vacuum.

Because disasters are conjunctions between the social and the natural, they offer richly documented occasions for assessing the social structures and norms of afflicted communities. During the dearth of 1789 inequalities of market power enabled people with the best information and a surplus of grain to reap windfall profits, at the expense of the impoverished in grain and the laggards in information. Fundamentally, disasters both reveal and heighten a society's inequalities.

The dearth of 1789 is also politically telling because the suffering region was bisected by a newly established boundary between the American republic and the Canadian provinces of the British Empire. The contrasting responses, north and south, to the dearth reveal the differing public cultures established by the American Revolution and demarcated by the new border. Although both British North America and the United States were market-based societies, the larger public sector and more paternalistic ethos of the British Empire contrasted with the virtual absence of state action and public resources in the American republic. Indeed, the differing responses to the dearth furthered the cultural process by which the British colonial elite defined their identity against their understanding of the Americans as excessively commercial and socially callous.

EXTENT

In the spring and early summer of 1789 hunger reigned in the Indian villages and the many new settlements of the northeastern United States and in their counterparts across the border in British-held Canada. Throughout that vast northern borderland, settlers and visitors described a severe and occasionally deadly dearth of food for people and their livestock. In April 1789 land speculator and developer William Cooper returned to Cooperstown, his new settlement in central New York. He found that "there remained not one pound of salt meat nor a single biscuit. . . . Judge of my feelings at this epoch, with two hundred families about me, and not a morsel of bread." [2]

To Cooper's immediate south, hunger prevailed in the new settlements along the Susquehanna valley of New York and northeastern Pennsylvania. Armed, hungry, and penniless settlers halted and plundered several boats transporting flour up and down the river. One merchant lost twenty bushels of flour. His friend reported, "The people . . . collected about him in arms & told him they would not starve, that they had not money to pay him but must have flour & would pay him when they were able." In normal times, the settlers obeyed the laws protecting private property. But during an emergency they claimed the right to seize food, promising eventual payment at predearth prices. Apparently, such bread rioting was confined to the upper Susquehanna because there the settlers were especially desperate and there they had access to cargoes of external grain moving up and down the river. Most other hungry settlers lived too far from shipments of grain for rioting to have any effect. [3]

In mid-July, Samuel Preston led a party of surveyors up the

Susquehanna to lay out a road along the New York–Pennsylvania border. Hungry settlers gathered and followed along, begging for food. On 18 July Preston assured them that he could not afford to part with his scant supplies. "But all these arguments had no effect . . . and I was obliged to dribble them out a little at a time, lest they should rise and take it all by violence, which considering the starving condition of the people, for very few of them had any kind of bread, I apprehended there was danger of." During the next three days, he encountered twenty more families "all in a starving condition for provision, many . . . weakened with starving, even past ability to labor or tend their corn." On 31 July he recorded in his journal, "The people's distress for provisions increased. Their importuning me increased also . . . I fully expected them to raise [up] and take all I had." Whenever Preston did spare them a little food, he observed, "I believe they were really very hungry by the way they eat."⁴

Conditions were even worse further north and west in the Genesee country of western New York. Indeed, many Genesee settlers fled eastward to the comparative plenty of the Susquehanna valley. In June 1789, Benjamin Young reported from Loyalsock Creek on the upper Susquehanna:

> The people of the Genesee and Niagara Country are crouding in upon us every day, owing to the great scarsity of provisions, the most of them who have gone there lately are starving to *death* and it is shocking to humanity to hear of the number of families that are dying daily for want of sustenance. . . . The wild roots and herbs that the country affords, boiled & without salt, constitute the whole food of most of the unhappy people who have been decoyed there thro' the flattering account of the quality of the land.

During the summer eastern newspapers printed and reprinted Young's letter as a warning to prospective settlers to stay home.⁵

Hunger also prevailed among the Indian villages of central and western New York. In February the Onondaga sachem Kaightoten reported "that his nation were in great want of provisions." Bearing that news to New

York's governor in Albany, the Onondaga emissary had to kill his horse for provisions en route. On 1–3 June the Oneida tribe assembled at Fort Schuyler, on the upper Mohawk River, in hope of obtaining food from the visiting New York Commissioners of Indian Affairs. The sachem Good Peter explained, "We are so faint that we cannot speak to you, and our Women and Children are come likewise to see you and are very hungry and have no provisions at home." But the commissioners had little food to spare. Further west, at Canandaigua, in mid-July the land speculator Oliver Phelps had to feed hundreds of starving Cayuga, Onondaga, and Seneca Indians. His agent Judah Colt recalled:

> They came & went away hungry, notwithstanding upwards of 100 heads of Cattle was killed for them. Flour was not plenty. It was reported during the Treaty & I think [it] not unlikely that the flour of one barrel made up into bread sold for 100 Dollars worth in silver plates of various kind of Indian ornaments. Many horses died distempered during the Treaty. The Indians fed on them freely & also the blood and entrails of all the Beef slaughtered.[6]

In the spring and summer of 1789, the Reverend Samuel Kirkland, a missionary among the Oneida Indians, recorded the hunger's grim inroads on his people and himself. In March, Kirkland reported that "the uncommon scarcity of provisions" prevailed "universally through the territory of the Six Nations, and down the Mohawk-River till we reach Albany." In late April, as the Indians exhausted their supply of corn, he noted, "Their pressing, importunate applications to me for relief are too much for the feelings of humanity to remain unmoved, even to the injury of one's property. They come with their intreaties and apply to me as their Father and only friend, who will compassionate them in their distresses; and I cannot turn a deaf ear to their cries." On 25 June an Indian father with five children pleaded to Kirkland, "We are very hungry and almost starved. . . . My family have not tasted any bread, or meat for many days; nothing but herbs and sometimes small fish. I am so weak I can't hoe any corn. I have been travelling all day among white people, but they can't give me any thing." Kirkland's own supplies ran low and he reduced himself to two and sometimes only one meal a day. In early July he became bedridden with fatigue and dysentery for "want of suitable food."[7]

Hunger also prevailed eastward among the new towns in the hill country of the upper Hudson valley and the New England interior. On 13 May 1789 Dr. Alexander Coventry went to the gristmill near Claverack, New York, for grain, but he could get only a single bushel of rye, "there being only two bushels in the mill." On the other side of the Massachusetts border in Lanesborough, a town in Berkshire County, Captain Daniel Brown gave away three hundred bushels of grain "and a very large quantity of potatoes" to the "poor families in the vicinity . . . and thereby saved them from distress, and perhaps death." Further north, on the New York shore of Lake Champlain, in early May a correspondent reported, "It is almost impossible to describe the extreme distress surrounding the people here. No bread or provision of any kind. The scene is truly painful. . . . Some have died, and many are sick. I was without bread fourteen days, and obliged to live on my seed potatoes."[8]

The hunger was also severe and widespread in the new settlements among the Green Mountains of Vermont. In May the Reverend Nathan Perkins, a visiting missionary, grimly reported, "The year 1789 will be remembered by Vermont as a day of calamity and famine—dearness of truck & want of bread in all their dwellings. It is supposed by the most judicious & knowing that more than 1/4 part of the people will have neither bread nor meat for 8 weeks—and that some will starve." He noted, "Several women I saw had lived four or five days without any food, and had eight or ten Children starving around them—crying for bread & the poor women had wept till they looked like Ghosts."[9]

Similar reports of hunger extended from Nova Scotia in the Maritimes westward through the old French villages and towns along the St. Lawrence River to the newer settlements founded by Loyalist refugees around Lake Ontario. In June from Digby in Nova Scotia, William Clark reported, "The Dearness of Provisions & Scarcity of many things, not to be had for money, the Poverty of the People, and apprehensions of an approaching famine, have induced Some Gentlemen to put forward a petition to his Majesty, praying [for] some immediate Relief, or Numbers of the people must actually Starve." [10]

Conditions were equally harsh in the Province of Quebec, especially in the rural villages near Montreal. In early June the executive council of Quebec collected grim testimony about the hunger. Witnesses calculated that the wheat harvest of 1788 was less than half that of the preceding year. William Grant testified "that there is not one bushel of wheat for sale within twenty miles" of his residence at Trois Rivières. After touring the rural parishes in the District of Montreal, John Blackwood reported in early June:

> The distresses of the generality of the Inhabitants was inconceivable, numbers leaving their habitations and were begging about the Country to avoid starving. . . . Many of the Inhabitants even eat the carcasses of every Dead animal they found, and that several had even killed their Horses for the sustenance of their families, and that many had little else to give their Children than broth of boiled peas [and] straw.

The merchant Alexander Cairns could not obtain a single bushel of wheat from his habitant debtors, in a district where he had previously collected six thousand bushels annually. [11]

In response to the worsening shortage of grain, the magistrates of Quebec and Montreal, the province's leading towns, steadily raised "the assize of bread," the regulated price for loaves of white and brown bread. Examined over time, the shifting assize reveals the pace and severity of the dearth. In Montreal during July 1788, before the dearth began, the prevailing four-pound loaf of white bread cost six pence, as did the six-pound loaf of brown (such a loaf was considered sufficient to feed most families for a day). That price rose during the fall as merchants and consumers recognized the short harvest. By December the white loaf cost nine pence and the brown cost ten pence. During the winter and spring of 1789 the price soared as consumption exhausted the previous fall's grain crops. In July 1789 the price peaked at fourteen pence for white and sixteen pence for brown—more than twice the costs of the year before (see Tables 1 and 2 at the end of this chapter). As a consequence, most of the town's inhabitants could no longer afford their daily bread. During April and May 1789 in Montreal a charitable subscription provided rations of bread, beef, and peas to "about Fourteen Hundred Persons daily." On 1 June Alexander Fraser of Montreal warned that the charitable fund "is nearly consumed and God only knows what those poor families will suffer when that is finished."[12]

The hunger also prevailed in the Loyalist settlements along the upper St. Lawrence and around Kingston, on the eastern end of Lake Ontario, and Niagara on the west. In March, a Niagara settler insisted that "cats, &c. have been substituted for beef." He was "doubtful how he and his neighbours will be able to spin out life until next harvest." At the end of May, the merchant John Richardson ascended the St. Lawrence from Montreal to Kingston. Writing to a correspondent in New York's Mohawk valley, Richardson reported, "The people in the new settlements are starving for provisions, and pouring in crowds to your quarter for a supply." In early June, Philip Stedman traveled to Quebec to testify before the provincial council that only twenty of the six hundred settler families at Niagara had eaten bread during the preceding three months. For want of grain and meat, most were reduced to boiling and eating basswood bark. In passing east from Niagara bound for Quebec, Stedman found similar suffering in the settlements along the upper St. Lawrence. At the end of June, Captain Joseph Bunbury of Kingston reported that most of the inhabitants had "not for many weeks past tasted any kind of meat, bread or biscuit."[13]

Causes

The contemporary sources say remarkably little about the causes of the apparently short harvest of 1788. It seems that only in Canada, and perhaps in pockets of northern New England and upstate New York, was there an absolute decline in the harvest. In 1804 the agricultural reformer Lord Selkirk visited Canada and investigated the dearth of 1789. He concluded, "The cause of the failure is not well understood. It was called a

Blight—from not knowing what else to call it. Some ascribe it to remarkably heavy rains just before harvest." More particular was the Montreal merchant John William Woolsey, who testified in June 1789: "The cause of the scarcity, as he understood [it], was the wet season of the last year and the destruction by the insect called the Hessian Fly." This explanation fits the December 1788 observation by Lord Dorchester, the governor general of British North America: "The last harvest of wheat appears to have been more defective than was at first apprehended, many of the ears being found empty at the thrashing." The tiny Hessian fly penetrates the wheat stalk to lay its eggs; the hatched larvae feed upon and consume the ear as it matures, leaving a hollow kernel. The damp, cool weather of the summer of 1788 favored the inroads of the Hessian fly on the growing wheat.[14]

But even in Canada, where the crop shortfall was greatest, the inroads of the Hessian fly were more than "natural" because farmers had pursued a market-oriented strategy that gambled their life's bread on the wheat crop that was the Hessian fly's special delight. Instead of pursuing a subsistence-first strategy of diversified grain crops that included barley and rye (which were more resistant to the Hessian fly), Canadian farmers dedicated most of their tillage to wheat. They did so, first, because the export market offered especially high prices for Canadian wheat in 1787 and 1788 and, second, because they did not anticipate the spread of the Hessian fly, a newly arrived European parasite that migrated northward from Long Island over the course of the 1780s. During the winter and spring of 1788 Canadian farmers had sold most of the previous fall's wheat harvest to merchants for export to England. During the summer of 1788 Quebec's merchants exported 200,358 bushels of wheat and 9,886 barrels of flour: food that would be sorely missed in a few months. Farmers and merchants felt secure in the exports, counting upon the promising harvest of 1788 to restock the granaries. Consequently, the devastation wrought by the Hessian fly on the 1788 wheat crop came as a very painful surprise. The damage only became manifest when the farmers began to thresh the September 1788 wheat harvest. Lord Dorchester later explained, "The number of sheaves gathered having promised . . . three times the quantity of grain [that] they were found actually to contain at the thrashing . . . so that the real state of the country was unknown till the stock was nearly exhausted." With perfect hindsight, in September 1789 Captain Freeman of Quebec blamed the spring and early summer hunger on the governor general for "inconsiderately permitting, last autumn, too general an exportation." Had Canadians been less wedded to the export market and, consequently, less dedicated to wheat, the impact of the Hessian fly would have been less life-threatening.[15]

The especially cold and damp summer of 1788, which facilitated the Hessian fly's proliferation, derived from the relatively cold global climate and abnormal wind circulation patterns of the 1780s. Climate historians attribute the unusual global pattern to major volcanic explosions in Iceland and Japan in the spring and summer of 1783. The eruptions blew millions of tons of particulates into the upper atmosphere, reducing the warming sunlight that could reach the earth's surface. Because it took years for the dust to dissipate, the eruptions lowered global temperatures, curtailed growing seasons, disrupted regional wind patterns, and dislocated precipitation for the rest of the decade. The suffering was especially intense in Japan, where as many as a million peasants may have died from the volcano-induced famine of 1783–1784. The disruption of "normal" precipitation patterns also curtailed the 1785 grain harvest in the uplands of Mexico, producing famine conditions there in 1786.[16]

Both northeastern America and northwestern Europe felt the greatest impact of the cold regime in 1788 and early 1789. Ordinarily relatively dry in summer, New England and Canada experienced cold and heavy rains during the summer of 1788. Ordinarily cool and wet, England and France suffered through a hot and prolonged drought in the summer of 1788. Because farmers and grain merchants in both northeastern North America and northwestern Europe had made their crop choices in anticipation of normal conditions, both sets suffered grievous disappointments in the abnormal conditions of 1788.

During the summer of 1788 England and especially France experienced an untimely inflow and unusual stagnation of torrid air from the Sahara to the south; hailstorms followed in July, when the Atlantic provided a cold, damp front that collided with the "anti-cyclone from the Sahara." According to the climate historian H. H. Lamb, 1788 was the driest year in 250 years of English record keeping. The summer drought withered, and then the hailstones battered, the standing grain plants, producing a fall shortage of flour, an escalating price for bread, and widespread rural anxiety. The winter of 1788–1789 proved unusually cold, and the spring of 1789 was especially late, delaying planting and arousing fears that the dearth would endure through the year. Because northeastern North America and northwestern Europe were linked by the trans-Atlantic market, the greater harvest failure in the latter led to increased demands on the former, extending and deepening the hunger there.[17]

Political intervention, especially in France, magnified the market incentives for American merchants to export grain to Europe. Recognizing the crisis, on 23 November 1788 the French king and the Council of State offered unusual incentives for American imports: premiums of thirty sous per quintal of wheat and forty sous per quintal of flour imported between 15 February and 30 June 1789. In addition, the French exempted American vessels bearing wheat or flour from the usual freight duties. In April 1789 the French doubled the bounties and extended them and the exemption on duties through August. In April, the British Parliament passed a bill permitting the importation of grain and flour from the United States—previously prohibited by law. Mercantile correspondence and newspaper reports carried the profitable news of the European demand and incentives to American seaport merchants, who scrambled to assemble cargoes of wheat for export. During 1789 France imported from the United States an unprecedented 140,959 barrels of flour; 3,664,176 bushels of wheat; 558,891 bushels of rye; and 520,262 bushels of barley. In May 1789 the Quebec merchant John William Woolsey traveled to New York City, hoping to purchase grain for importation into Canada. Finding little, he was "informed by the merchants there, that the country had been lately drained by great exportations."[18]

The urban merchant's windfall was the frontier settler's despair. Export of American grain from the older towns with surpluses deprived the frontier settlements of a reserve at the worst moment. In effect, frontier settlers in new communities with a grain shortfall found themselves losing out in the bidding for the grain surpluses in older farm districts. For example, during the 1780s the newer settlements in the uplands of central New York relied upon the wheat raised in the nearby but older farms in the warmer and more fertile Mohawk valley. William Cooper of Cooperstown (in upland Otsego County) recalled, "In the winter preceding the summer of 1789, grain rose in Albany to a price before unknown. The demand swept the whole granaries of the Mohawk country. The number of beginners who depended upon it for their bread greatly aggravated the evil, and a famine ensued." Frontier settlers had not escaped into self-sufficient independence from a market society. On the contrary, the dearth of 1789 revealed the power and reach of the trans-Atlantic market, and it demonstrated the dependence of frontier settlers on external food reserves.[19]

During 1788 and early 1789 a surge in settler migration to frontier communities in the uplands of New York, Vermont, and Pennsylvania concentrated poor families at the worst time in the worst places, when and where food was scarcest. Bringing too little food with them, the migrants mistakenly counted upon obtaining provisions from nearby farmers. To the settlers' dismay, in the late spring of 1789 they belatedly discovered that the farmers had already sold their surplus to merchants and were hard-pressed to feed themselves. The mid- to late 1780s was a period of explosive frontier settlement as the return of peace unleashed the demand for new farms, a demand pent up during the long years of revolutionary war. For example, according to annual tax lists, in New York's Otsego country the number of families tripled from 64 in 1787 to 170 a year later. In April 1788 John Tunnecliff assured William Cooper, "Our Cunterey Grose Very fast. The Rode to the Butternutes is thro your Estate as thick setteled as Great Briton is in general. At the W[es]t side of Lake Otseager is still fuller." The prospects for further growth were promising because, "several of your Tenance has Larg family of children which I Pray God to

Bless With Helth and Sucksess." However, all those young, hungry mouths proved a liability a year later when the settlers ran out of food and even more newcomers arrived without sufficient provisions. At Cooperstown on 7 May 1789 William Cooper explained to his friend (and fellow land speculator) Henry Drinker, "The Vast Multitudes of People that Come Dayly to this Country have Causd a Scarcity of Provitions allmost to Famine and in the Genesee quite so. . . . (Henry I have had 30 in a Day Seaking Lands of me but [who] Could not Look out much in the woods for want of Something to Subsist upon)."[20]

Just as the new settlers recognized their plight, the climate threatened an even bleaker future. In 1789 in northern North America the global cold regime produced a particularly long and cold winter. In some locales the especially severe and snowy winter depleted the deer herds, to the detriment of human hunters. The deep snows hid the deer's usual sources of ground feed and encumbered their movements, rendering them an easier prey to wolves. A Canadian settler at the Bay of Quinte recalled the dispiriting consequences for human hunters: "The snow was unusually deep, so that the Deer fell an easy prey to their rapacious enemies, the wolves, who fattened on their destruction, whilst men were perishing from want. Nothing could be had in the woods."[21]

The prolonged winter cold delayed the spring, postponing the date when farmers could pasture their livestock and plant their grains. On 30 April 1789 Dr. Alexander Coventry of Claverack, Columbia County, New York, recorded in his diary, "Cold, cloudy, pretty calm; Blue Mountains covered with snow. This [is] a very backward season; wheat . . . does not seem to have grown any this spring. . . . Hoar frost yesterday morning, and cold for season." In early June a Vermont newspaper observed:

> The great want of that necessary article BREAD, it is feared, . . . will be more severely felt the next season than it is the present, occasioned by the warm enlivening beams of the sun being witheld from us—for we can assure the public, that on ascending Mount Ayscutney, the 3d instant the snow was found from 12 to 25 inches in depth; and on the night of the 4th instant the frost was so

severe in this place, as to congeal the water in a bucket to ice of a considerable thickness.

Similarly, on 4 June 1789 a correspondent from the Susquehanna valley of northern Pennsylvania reported, "The weather continues remarkably cold, and the season backward—the buds of many hickory trees not all expanded—frosts the three last nights—this morning ice as thick as window glass in the watering-trough in my yard."[22]

The late spring imperiled the settlers' cattle, who had exhausted their supply of winter hay and desperately needed new grass in their pastures. Many farmers were forced to slaughter cattle that they had counted upon as breeding and working stock. Livestock deaths deprived many north country families of the dairy cow that provided their milk and of the oxen needed to plow their fields to plant a new crop. By debilitating (or killing) livestock and by delaying planting, the sustained spring frosts threatened to postpone the harvest of 1789. Given the short northern growing season in upland districts, the late planting raised the specter that the grain crops might not mature before the killing frosts of September. Consequently, the late spring and dying cattle took a psychological toll on settler morale. Already anxious over the short or overexported crop of 1788, many Americans and Canadians dreaded that the cold and late spring meant that worse was to come. The consequent public alarm drove up prices and encouraged speculative hoarding, especially in June, when eastern newspapers spread the combined news of frontier hunger and the bleak prospects for the next harvest.[23]

Those news reports proved counterproductive, helping to extend the dearth's reach into the older, lower, and more eastern towns, which had not suffered from any significant shortfall in agricultural production. In southern New England prosperous farmers and merchants began to hoard grain in anticipation of rising prices that would net them windfall profits. By reporting frontier hardships, editors had meant to help by discouraging further migration to the frontier and by encouraging relief efforts. Instead, the news widened the hunger as cupidity proved more compelling than empathy. In June in Vermont a newspaper writer bitterly complained that "many persons of distinguished rank in life" had proved "the most officious and instrumental, in raising the price of grain to such an unreasonable height, as to render it utterly impossible for the sons of affliction to purchase, pleading in excuse '*That there is no way to determine the value of a bushel of wheat, only by what it will bring*.'" Although Stamford, Connecticut, was an old, coastal community far from the northern and upland origins of the dearth, by June that town's poorer inhabitants were suffering from hunger. On 28 June 1789 Ebenezer Dibble reported, "I never knew so great a cry for bread, and want of means to procure it." [24]

Some editors belatedly recognized their role in spreading the panic that extended the dearth. As the publisher and editor of the *Worcester Spy*, Isaiah Thomas had played a key role in reporting the hunger. On 18 June he tried a different tack:

> The accounts lately published and circulated, respecting the scarcity of grain, appear to be greatly exaggerated. That there was not a sufficient supply in the British settlements is without a doubt true; and in consequence large quantities have been sold to the British subjects in America by the inhabitants of these States. A great handle we are assured has been made of this, by speculators and avaricious holders of grain, to enhance the price, but as the crops now look promising—the probability is that in a short time grain will be much more plenty and cheaper than at present, and these canker worms to society [will] be disappointed in acquiring unjust gain.

In ensuing weeks, other newspapers from Portsmouth, New Hampshire, to Philadelphia, Pennsylvania, reprinted Isaiah Thomas's attempt to deflate the speculative bubble. [25]

Forsaking their earlier alarmism, during July and August the northeastern newspapers sought to soothe public anxiety with reassuring reports that the new crops appeared especially promising, despite the late spring. A Vermont newspaper insisted (and other newspapers reprinted), "The gloom is dispelled from the countenance of the industrious peasant, and the pleasing anticipation of plentiful harvests relieves the mind amidst the present scarcity." On 9 July the *New-Hampshire Gazette* asserted, "The probability is, that within a short time, bread corn will be more plenty and cheaper than it has been the year past; and that the avaricious, oppressive monopolizers and holders of this stuff of life, will be obliged to eat it themselves, or sell it at a less price than they gave." [26]

In sum, in its full extent and at its deepest intensity in June and early July of 1789, the dearth derived from the interplay of natural deviations from norms of temperature and precipation with the social consequences of the trans-Atlantic market. Even in Canada, social arrangements—primarily the export market that led merchants to demand payment in wheat from their farmer-creditors—compounded nature's assault on the expected harvest. Moreover, the dearth's southern and eastern extension into the new settlements of upstate New York, northern Pennsylvania, and western New England owed much to nature's unusual cold late into the spring of 1789. But that southern and eastern expansion primarily depended on the untimely and simultaneous escalations in grain exports to Europe and in human imports into frontier settlements. Finally, the third extension of the dearth, into the older, lower towns of eastern New England, derived principally from the alarm and hoarding inspired by newspaper coverage.

RELIEF

During the spring and summer of 1789 the starving settlers of the northern borderland had a three-fold problem: they did not have enough to eat; they had little or no money to buy food; and there was little or no food to be bought in their vicinity. For immediate relief, the settlers had to hunt for and eat small animals and wild plants that they had previously disdained as distasteful or paltry. Although unpleasant and laborious, this recourse to gathering had the advantages of being immediate and proximate: several wild plants produced edible fruits, nuts, or roots in June or July, well before the slower-growing domesticated plants cultivated by the settlers in their new clearings. In May 1789 a resident of northern New

York reported, "The common sustenance of the women and children has been tadpoles boiled in water, and pea straw which they swallowed till they began to swell in the glands of the throat." Niagara's settlers told a visitor that they survived by eating "strawberry leaves, beech leaves, flax seed dried, and ground in a coffee mill—catched the blood of a little pig—bled the almost famished cow and oxen. . . . The children leaped for joy at one robin being caught, out of which a whole pot of broth was made. They eat mustard, potato tops, sassafras root, and made tea of the tops. The relation was deeply affecting." Ironically, although their ultimate goal as settlers was to replace the diverse array of wild plants and animals with a narrower range of domesticated grasses, grains, and livestock, in the crisis of 1789 the settlers had to depend on the natural flora and fauna for their immediate survival.[27]

Wild leeks were an especially important emergency food because they matured early and abounded in the low, moist, shady grounds by creeks and hollows. In flush times settlers disdained its strong taste, but when dearth reigned, starvers could not be choosers. In central New York, William Cooper recalled:

> Many were reduced to such distress, as to live upon the roots of wild leeks; some more fortunate lived upon milk, whilst others supported nature by drinking a syrup made of maple sugar and water. The quantity of [wild] leeks they eat had such an effect upon their breath, that they could be smelled at many paces distance, and when they came together, it was like cattle that had pastured in a garlic field. A man of the name of Beets mistaking some poisonous herb for a leek, eat it, and died in consequence.

In search of the wild leek, some hungry settlers made hasty, fatal mistakes. Poisonous "muskrat root" (or "water hemlock") grew along stream banks and bore a dangerous resemblance to the edible wild leek. The root occasionally claimed the lives of unwary settlers after a few hours of intense torment. It may be that in 1789 more settlers died from eating poison plants than from starvation. In the vicinity of Niagara the settlers learned to find edible and to avoid poisonous plants by following their rooting pigs into and through the woods.[28]

The annual spring run upstream by migratory fish species—alewife, shad, salmon, and herring—proved especially timely in 1789 for frontier settlers and Indians throughout the afflicted districts. In June, Lord Dorchester had no food to spare for the starving Indians dwelling at Buffalo Creek and Grand River, both near Niagara. Instead, he directed the local commander to loan two seine nets so that the Indians could more readily catch fish. In central New York, William Cooper's settlers wove twigs into a crude seine net to capture thousands of herring ascending the Susquehanna River. In the following decades, millers would destroy these fish runs by damming the rivers for water power, but in 1789 most of the frontier rivers flowed untrammeled, providing essential relief to the starving settlers.[29]

Caught between the exhausted harvest of 1788 and the delayed crops of 1789, the suffering settlers and Indians watched their slowly maturing grain plants with desperate impatience. In late July and early August many hastened the harvest by cutting some of their immature wheat for artificial ripening by drying in the sun or over a fire. After shelling the husks, they boiled the wheat to make an edible mush. On the upper Susquehanna in early August, Samuel Preston reported that, as a result of their first substantial meal in the weeks, "the distress and pain was very great, so when they came to eat boiled wheat it . . . [made] them exceedingly sick and raise[d] a high fever."[30]

Ultimate relief came at summer's end as hot weather combined with abundant rains to prosper the harvest. In August Nathaniel Gorham reported, "A prospect of great crops of every kind—plenty of rain & a very hot season has brought forward the Indian Corn in a most surprising manner. The English harvest [i.e., rye and wheat] was very abundant." Despite their late start in the spring, the borderland farmers harvested good crops of grain in August and September. In October 1789 Captain Freeman of Quebec reported that "the abundant crops of this Season makes our Province the land of plenty." Farmers reaped a still better crop a year later. In July 1790 William Cooper celebrated his relief: "The Crops here away are much Better than hath been Ever known. My Settelment will have thousands of Bushells." In September 1790 the bread price in Montreal fell to six pence—the same price that had prevailed two years before, prior to the dearth (see Tables 1 and 3). In 1791 the traveler Patrick Campbell reported that the Canadian merchants complained of a glut of grain on hand.[31]

The good harvests of 1789 and 1790 indicate that the volcanic dust in the upper atmosphere had dissipated, permitting global temperatures, wind currents, and rainfall patterns to revert to normal. Complaints about the Hessian fly diminished. Because long and frigid winters inhibit or destroy the fly's larvae, the very late spring of 1789 may have been an unanticipated boon to the farmers. Although the spring frosts delayed the 1789 crop, they may have ultimately saved it. After 1789 some northern frontier districts occasionally suffered for want of food, but there was not another general dearth in the northern borderland until 1816, when another especially powerful volcanic eruption produced the notorious "year without a summer."[32]

THE STATE

On the American side of the border most settlers and Indians muddled through with little help from the state, but Canadian natives and newcomers benefited from a larger and more paternalistic government. On both sides of the border, the first recourse of governments was to impose an embargo on the export of grains. The authorities hoped to husband local supplies of grain and alleviate public panic. Vermont acted first. On 7 March the governor and council banned, for one month, the export of food produced within the state. On 17 April Lord Dorchester suspended all grain and flour exports from the Province of Quebec for a year. On 28 May and 10 June Connecticut and Rhode Island adopted temporary embargoes on grain raised within their states. On 18 July Nova Scotia's lieutenant governor and executive council struck a blow against Canadian solidarity by forbidding the reexport to Quebec of any grains obtained from the United States. Given that there was precious little grain and very high prices for it in the suffering regions, the embargoes were, at best, mere palliatives to public anxiety. At worst, the embargoes were counter-productive, adding to the panic that induced those with surpluses to hoard rather than to sell.[33]

At the same time that British colonial officials imposed an embargo on domestic grains, they also threw open their ports to foodstuffs imported from the United States. Previously the British Empire's mercantile regulations had banned such imports in order to protect and promote grain cultivation in Canada. But the failed harvest of 1788 compelled the governor general to suspend the restriction on American imports. By proclamations issued in January, April, and June, Lord Dorchester gradually widened the opening, initially limited to the Lake Champlain corridor, to include the Maritimes and the entire St. Lawrence valley. Clinging to mercantile principle, Dorchester continued to restrict the provision trade to boats and ships owned and navigated by British subjects. But on the provincial periphery, subordinate officers wisely tolerated food imports in American boats. An officer at Kingston explained that enforcing the restriction to British boats would have brought "fatal consequences to the distressed Inhabitants of Upper Canada."[34]

The opening to American imports provided far more relief than did the hollow embargo on the nonexistent domestic grains. Although foodstuffs were equally scarce in the border country of New York and Vermont, grains and flour abounded in the warmer climes farther south, especially in Virginia and Maryland, where the harvest of 1788 had been good. In the mid-Atlantic states during the summer of 1789, merchants assembled cargoes of grain and flour for shipment to the northern frontier and Canada in 1789. On 20 July in northern New York a correspondent reported, "The number of waggons, laden with Indian corn, which, for about two months past, have passed Stillwater and Saratoga, for the [Great] Lakes and Canada, is almost incredible." He counted about one hundred wagons per day in late July. Even more American grain moved by ship to the port of Quebec on the St. Lawrence, where by 30 July the merchants had procured

2,092 barrels of American flour, compared to only 8 barrels imported from Great Britain. On 28 July the Quebec merchant Thomas Aston Coffin reported that the importation "has afforded great relief & dissipated the gloom—a further considerable quantity is daily expected." During the following week, another 3,169 barrels of American flour reached the port of Quebec. As a consequence of the American imports, the Montreal assize of white bread fell from fourteen pence per loaf in July to nine pence per loaf in August (see Table 2).[35]

In addition to adopting regulations to preclude food exports and to attract food imports, governments might have expended funds directly to purchase and deliver provisions to the hungry. In the United States the new and feeble federal government could do nothing, and only one state—New York—provided public relief. Large parts of Pennsylvania, Vermont, Connecticut, Massachusetts, Rhode Island, and New Hampshire suffered from hunger, but their governments expended no funds for food relief.

Two special circumstances catalyzed New York's allocation of food aid. Of the northeastern states, New York had both the largest stock of public lands for sale *and* the largest population of Indians. In the short run, keeping the peace with the natives was essential to the state's long-run ambitions to sell, settle, and develop its immense interior. During the 1780s New York's leaders worked zealously to render the Indians dependent upon modest annuities delivered in cash, food, and clothing in payment for title to most of their lands. The dearth of 1789 presented the state with at once an unanticipated crisis and a new opportunity. On the one hand, a failure to feed the Indians would undermine New York's power over them. The Indians were quick to remind the state's Indian commissioners that they had a responsibility to live up to their paternalistic pretenses. On 3 June when the commissioners neglected to provide anticipated food relief, the Oneida sachem Good Peter complained, "This is very strange and we are not accustomed to such treatment." On 30 June the Oneida sachems objected, "If hunger should kill us while so near our American Brothers, it would be a lamentable story indeed." On the other hand, by rescuing the Indians from the dearth, the state subsequently could claim an obligation from the Indians to make further land concessions.[36]

Moreover, as the northeastern state with the largest public domain for sale and settlement, New York especially needed to preserve the good reputation of its frontier lands. If settlers starved and fled, they would blacken that reputation, imperiling New York's ambitions to develop rapidly its hinterland and to rely quickly upon land sales, rather than taxes, for public revenue. In a 6 July speech to the state legislature, Governor George Clinton urged an appropriation to relieve the "distresses experienced by the failure of the last year's crops, particularly in the exterior settlements, and by the poorer class of people." On 14 July the New York state legislature appropriated £ 600 to buy corn in southern counties for distribution to the settlers and Indians in the state's four northern frontier counties. [37]

Given the extent of the crisis, the aid allocated by New York was late and paltry. The state sent 350 bushels to feed six Indian tribes who numbered at least 2,000. Given an average annual minimum consumption of 6 bushels per person, the food aid—if evenly distributed—would have sustained the total Indian population for just eleven days. The appropriation probably purchased another 1,650 bushels for distribution among a settler population of about 45,000 in the four afflicted counties—the equivalent of three days' rations per person. Ostensibly the Indians received the aid as a gift, "as," in the words of Governor Clinton, "a testimony of our Friendship for you." Of course, they would pay dearly for it in future land concessions. The food advanced to the settlers was deemed a loan rather than a gift; recipients were supposed to pay for their share by 1 January 1790. The belated, small, and stingy nature of this aid attests to the limited scope of the state in the American republic—and the pervasive belief that problems should be coped with by individuals and locales.[38]

More New York Indians and settlers obtained relief by striking private deals with external merchants. Tired of waiting on the state legislature, the Mohican Indians of New Stockbridge (in central New York) sent emissaries to the merchants of Schenectady and Albany to contract for 150 bushels of Indian corn. Lacking cash, the Mohicans promised payment in

October in ginseng root. During the 1780s ginseng was a wild plant that abounded in the forests of central New York, and it was in great mercantile demand for profitable export to the Chinese market. The settlers in the hinterland of Whitestown, New York, sent a delegation to Fort Plain in the Mohawk valley to plead with Isaac Paris, a merchant and miller, for relief. In return for promised ginseng, he diverted to them flour and meal that he could have exported via New York City to Europe. To honor their saving bargain with the merchant, the settlers named their town "Paris" in his honor. This attests to the cultural, social, and political power of the entrepreneur in the early American republic.[39]

In contrast to the United States, the public sector played a larger role in relieving hunger in Canada, especially in the settlements near the British army posts around the Great Lakes. Because the posts had stockpiled provisions for their garrisons, the commanders could loan food to starving settlers. In theory (and in normal years), the nearby Loyalist settlers were supposed to supply the British garrisons, but in 1789 the army had to feed the starving farmers of Upper Canada. The need and relief were both greatest at Niagara, where Lt. Col. Peter Hunter advanced barrels of pork, peas, and rice to the needy settlers as a loan to be repaid in their more prosperous future. In mid-June the visiting merchant John Richardson reported, "The distresses of this settlement for provisions have been great, and had it not been for the humane assistance of Col. Hunter, and the uncommon plenty of fish, half the people must literally have starved." The Loyalist settlers around Kingston and Detroit (then occupied by the British) obtained similar, but smaller, loans, from their local garrisons. Because neither the American state governments nor their new and impecunious federal government possessed any military posts on the northern frontier, American settlers could not turn to them for relief.[40]

Still greater public relief came to the Canadians in emergency cargoes of wheat, flour, and peas shipped to Quebec from England by the home government. The relief shipment reached Quebec during the early fall. By the end of November the shipments totaled 1,000 tons of flour, 23,000 bushels of wheat, and 24,000 bushels of peas. This publicly funded relief effort by the British dwarfed the paltry American response, which was limited to a single state. Although Quebec's population was less than half that of New York State, the former received about twenty-five times as much public relief thanks to the largesse of the British government.[41]

Although abundant, the aid was belated, arriving in Quebec in October and November, after the new harvest and American imports had abated the hunger. In late October Judge Adam Mabane of Quebec observed:

> Several Vessels have arrived from England laden with Provisions as it seems the Ministry had been alarmed with the accounts of the Scarcity which prevailed here last May and June. The measure was certainly benevolent, but the Evil had ceased by the Supplies which had arrived from the American States and by the new Crop which has been very good and abundant.

In Montreal the official price for a loaf of white bread had already fallen from fourteen pence in July to nine pence in August. The October arrival of the public relief had a more modest impact, lowering the white bread price to seven pence. However, by swelling food stocks and appeasing public anxiety, the public relief maintained bread prices at modest levels through the subsequent winter and spring (see Tables 2 and 3).[42]

BORDERS

After 1763 and until the American Revolution, Canada and the Atlantic colonies had belonged to the same British Empire. At the end of the American Revolutionary War, the peace treaty of 1783 established an artificial border between the new American republic and the British provinces of Canada. British leaders tried to give significance to the northern border by settling thousands of Loyalist refugees as frontier farmers and by imposing mercantile restrictions on the flow of commerce. The imperial officials hoped to strengthen the border defenses with a population alienated from the new American republic and capable of transforming the forest into productive farms that could feed the frontier's garrisons. The

British government subsidized the Loyalist settlers with free land grants, two years of rations, winter wheat seed, farm tools, and the construction of public grist mills. Imperial officials also hoped to boost Canadian agricultural development by prohibiting the importation of grains, flour, and livestock from the United States. The officials anticipated that, in the short run, Canada would become self-sufficient in foodstuffs and that, in the longer run, Canada could replace the American republic as the primary provisioner of the British colonies in the West Indies.[43]

The dearth of 1789 threatened the British neomercantilist effort to distinguish and develop Canada. To save his starving settlers, the governor general had to rescind for a year the ban on American food imports that he had helped to design earlier in the decade. The influx of American grain and flour eased the hunger in Canada but underlined the agricultural superiority of the more temperate United States, discouraging British ambitions to develop Canada as the empire's bread basket.

On the other hand, the dearth of 1789 presented an opportunity for the British to demonstrate that they were committed to the well-being of their Canadian subjects and that their rule was preferable to that of the American republic. During the 1780s British authorities in Canada chronically worried that the loyalty of the people, both Francophone and Anglophone, was weak and needed bolstering. It seemed clear that most of the French habitants were dangerously unreconciled to the British conquest and occupation of Quebec. And, despite their wartime sacrifices and sufferings, the Loyalists remained suspect because, as Americans, they seemed susceptible to the seditious contagion of republicanism. By delivering abundant food relief with a paternalistic flair, the British hoped to strengthen their weak hold over Canadian hearts and minds. In October 1789, Lord Grenville, the British secretary of state, explained to Lord Dorchester that the aid was supposed to have "the effect of impressing the minds of His Majesty's Subjects under your Lordship's Government with a just sense of His Majesty's paternal regard for the welfare of all his People." Grenville understood that imperial authority required occasional, conspicuous displays of paternalism.[44]

In 1791 the British rulers canceled the Canadians' debts for the food relief with a flourish intended to contrast the paternalism of their regime with the commercialism of the neighboring American republic. In 1791 Prince Edward toured Canada and announced, "My father is not a merchant to deal in bread and ask payment for food granted for the relief of his loyal subjects." The contrast with the commercialized American republic could not have been more pointed. In republican America the bread merchants ruled (and the towns bore their names).[45]

By employing food relief as a performance of imperial theater, the British compensated for the dearth's economic demonstration that Canada was agriculturally marginal and recurrently dependent on American foodstuffs. In early 1789 the British had to suspend their mercantile regulations to enable their subjects to survive by trading with the Americans, undermining the British claims that their imperial framework was essential to Canadian prosperity. The renewed demonstration of the empire's economic vulnerability in North America rendered British authorities uneasy and helped to drive their rhetoric that posited a sharp boundary in political culture between their own subjects and the American republicans to the south. Persistent economic interdependence obliged the British to invent a border primarily in the realm of political culture.[46]

During the 1790s and the early nineteenth century, the northern border gradually came to demarcate significantly different national identities and political values as the British Canadian elite dialectically defined themselves against their understanding of the United States as a greedy commercial republic that flattered the common folk but ignored or exploited the poor among them. The British colonists gave cultural meaning to the border as they constructed a paternalistic counteridentity to the crass identity they constructed of the United States. Initially, the dearth of 1789 threatened to unravel the construction of an effective northern border, but the contrast of American and Canadian responses to the hunger was one important, early step in the postrevolutionary partition of North America.[47]

The legacy of that partition endures in the contrasting historical memory (or amnesia) regarding the dearth of 1789 in Canada and the United States. Unknown in American historiography, the dearth does appear conspicuously in Canadian tradition and history, where "the hungry year" represents a great national ordeal successfully endured. In part, Canadians remember and Americans forget the dearth because it affected almost everyone in Canada but menaced a smaller proportion of the larger and more extended population of the United States. But American historians also have not seen the dearth of 1789 because it so poorly fits our nation's master narrative of sustained growth, frontier opportunity, and widespread prosperity. Denial in historical memory echoes the denial of public assistance to most of the American hungry in 1789. In contrast, the dearth of 1789 better suits the Canadian pride in their patient and stoical endurance of a harsh climate.[48]

TABLE 1: THE MONTREAL ASSIZE OF BREAD, 1788, IN PENCE

Month	4 Lb. White Loaf	6 Lb. Brown Loaf
May 1788	5.5	5.5
June 1788	6.0	6.0
July 1788	6.0	6.0
Aug. 1788	6.0	6.0
Sept. 1788	6.5	6.5
Oct. 1788	8.0	8.0
Nov. 1788	8.0	8.0
Dec. 1788	9.0	9.0

Sources: *Quebec Gazette*, 15 May, 12 June, 10 July, 7 Aug., 4 Sept., 9 Oct., and 4 Dec. 1788; *Montreal Gazette*, 6 Nov. and 4 Dec. 1788.

TABLE 2: THE MONTREAL ASSIZE OF BREAD, 1789, IN PENCE		
Month	4 Lb. White Loaf	6 Lb. Brown Loaf
Jan. 1789	9.0	10.0
Feb. 1789	9.0	10.0
Mar. 1789	10.0	11.0
Apr. 1789	12.5	14.0
May 1789	13.0	15.0
June 1789	13.0	15.0
July 1789	14.0	16.0
Aug. 1789	9.0	10.0
Sept. 1789	9.0	10.5
Oct. 1789	7.0	7.5
Nov. 1789	7.5	8.5
Dec. 1789	7.5	8.5

Sources: *Montreal Gazette*, 4 Jan., 5 Feb., 5 Mar., 9 Apr., 7 May, 4 June, 9 July, 4 Aug., 7 Sept., 8 Oct., 12 Nov., and 10 Dec. 1789.

TABLE 3: THE MONTREAL ASSIZE OF BREAD, 1790, IN PENCE		
Month	*4 Lb. White Loaf*	*6 Lb. Brown Loaf*
Jan. 1790	7.5	8.5
Feb. 1790	7.0	8.0
Mar. 1790	7.0	8.0
Apr. 1790	7.0	8.0
May 1790	7.0	8.0
June 1790	7.0	8.0
July 1790	6.5	7.5
Aug. 1790	6.5	7.5
Sept. 1790	6.0	6.0

Sources: *Montreal Gazette*, 7 Jan., 4 Feb., 4 Mar., 8 Apr., 6 May, 10 June, 8 July, 5 Aug., and 8 Sept. 1790.

NOTES

I am indebted to Jenny Franchot, Carla Hesse, Alessa Johns, Elizabeth Mancke, Ted Steinberg, and Chuck Walker for comments that helped me to improve this chapter. I am also grateful to Alessa for her vision, humor, persistence, and leadership, in organizing the initial conference on eighteenth-century disasters and in shepherding diverse essays through to publication. This chapter also benefited from the questions and suggestions posed by audiences at the University of California at Davis Institute of Governmental Affairs, the Agricultural History Center at U.C. Davis, the Organization of American Historians, the early American history seminar of the University of Minnesota, and the Library Company of Philadelphia.

1   Anthony Oliver-Smith, "Introduction: Disaster Context and Causation: An Overview of Changing Perspectives in Disaster Research," in *Natural Disasters and Cultural*

Responses, ed. Oliver-Smith, Publication 36 of *Studies in Third World Societies* (1986), 1–34, quotation 8; Kenneth Hewitt, "The Idea of Calamity in a Technocratic Age," in *Interpretations of Calamity from the Viewpoint of Human Ecology*, ed. K Hewitt (Boston: Allen & Unwin, Inc., 1983), 3–32.

2   William Cooper, *A Guide in the Wilderness; Or, the History of the First Settlements in the Western Counties of New York, with Useful Instructions to Future Settlers* (Cooperstown: New York State Historical Association, 1986, repr. of Dublin, 1810), 15–16; James Fenimore Cooper, *The Pioneers, or the Sources of the Susquehanna: A Descriptive Tale* (Albany: State University of New York Press, 1980, crit. ed. of New York, 1823), 234; Levi Beardsley, *Reminiscences; Personal and Other Incidents; Early Settlement of Otsego County* (New York: Charles Vinten, 1852), 19–20.

3   Samuel Wallis quoted in Peter Mancall, *Valley of Opportunity: Economic Culture along the Upper Susquehanna, 1700–1800* (Ithaca, N.Y.: Cornell University Press, 1991), 172; Benjamin Young to Benjamin Rush, 2 June 1789, Benjamin Rush Papers, Library Company of Philadelphia.

4   Samuel Preston, "Journey to Harmony," in *Samuel Preston, 1789-1989: From Buckingham to Buckingham*, ed. Patricia H. Christian (Equinunk, Penn.: Equinunk Historical Society, 1989), 78, 96, 103–07.

5   Benjamin Young to Benjamin Rush, 2 June 1789, Benjamin Rush Papers, vol. 32, 87, Library Company of Philadelphia. To discourage further migration to the frontier, Rush shared the letter with the newspapers; it reappeared in *Vermont Journal* (Windsor), 12 Aug. 1789, and the *Royal Gazette* (Halifax), 25 Aug. 1789.

6   Franklin B. Hough, ed., *Proceedings of the Commissioners of Indian Affairs Appointed by Law for the Extinguishment of Indian Titles in the State of New York*, 2 vols. (Albany: J. Munsell, 1861), 2, 313, 317–18; Oliver Phelps to Nathaniel Gorham, 14 July 1789, Phelps & Gorham Papers, Box 2, New York State Library, Albany; Judah Colt, "Diary [*sic*]," Ontario County Historical Society, Canandaigua, New York.

7   Walter Pilkington, ed., *The Journals of Samuel Kirkland: Eighteenth-Century Missionary to the Iroquois, Government Agent, Father of Hamilton College* (Clinton, NY: Hamilton College Press, 1980), 160–68; Pomroy Jones, *Annals and Recollections of Oneida County* (Rome, NY: by the author, 1851), 176–77.

8   Alexander Coventry, *Memoirs of an Emigrant: The Journal of Alexander Coventry, M.D.*, 2 vols. (Albany: Albany Institute of History and Art, 1978), 2: 213; "Boston, June 22," *Independent Gazetteer* (Philadelphia), 1 July 1789 (Captain Brown); "Extract of a Letter from a Gentleman living on Lake Champlain . . . May 9," *New Hampshire Gazette* (Portsmouth), 2 July 1789. The latter also appeared in *New-York Journal*, 1 July 1789; *Independent Gazetteer* (Philadelphia), 19 July 1789. See also "Albany, June 15," *New-Jersey Journal*, 17 June 1789.

9   Nathan Perkins, *A Narrative of a Tour Through the State of Vermont from April 27 to June 12, 1789* (Woodstock, Vt.: Woodstock Press, 1920), 21; Abby Maria Hemenway, ed., *The Vermont Historical Gazetteer: A Magazine Embracing A History of Each Town, Civil, Ecclesiastical, Biographical and Military*, 5 vols. (Burlington, Vt.: State of Vermont, 1867), 1: 52, 313.

10   Nova Scotia Executive Council Minutes, 25 May 1789, Reel 95289, Public Archives of Nova Scotia, Halifax (PANS hereafter); William Clark to Rev. Samuel Peters, 23 June 1789, MG 1 (Rev. Samuel Peters Papers), Reel 10958, PANS.

11   Testimony of John Blackwell, William Grant, Thomas Coffin, William Cleghorn, David Barclay, Alexander Cairns, John Painter, Matthew Lymburner, John Lees, Isaac Todd, Robert Lester, John Young, George Alsopp, Joseph Crette, John Pagan, and George Miller, in Quebec Executive Council Minutes, 1–3 June 1789, MG 11, Colonial Office 42, vol. 66, Public Archives of Canada, Ottawa (PAC hereafter).

12   For the assize of bread see the *Quebec Gazette*, 8, 15 May, 12 June, 10 July, 7 Aug., 4 Sept., 9 Oct., 6 Nov, and 4 Dec. 1788; 8 Jan., 5 Mar., 9 Apr., 4 June, and 9 July 1789; *Montreal Gazette*, 6 Nov., 4 Dec. 1788, 4 Jan., 5 Feb., 5 Mar., 9 Apr., 7 May, 4 June, and 9 July 1789. For the charitable relief see *Montreal Gazette*, 11 June 1789; Alexander Fraser testimony, Quebec Executive Council Minutes, 1 June 1789, MG 11, Colonial Office 42, vol. 66, PAC.

13   "A Loyalist," *Montreal Gazette*, 5 Mar. 1789; "Quebec, March 23," *Quebec Herald*, 13 April 1789 ("cats"); Alfred Leroy Burt, *The Old Province of Quebec* (Toronto: Ryerson Press, 1933), 378–81; John Richardson to John Porteous, 31 May 1789, in, "The John Richardson Letters," ed. E. A. Cruikshank, Ontario Historical Society, *Papers and Records*, VI (Toronto: Champlain Society, 1905), 23; Philip Stedman testimony, 3 June 1789, Quebec Executive Council Minutes, MG 11, Colonial Office 42, vol. 66, PAC; Captain Joseph Bunbury to Captain Le Maistre, June 30, 1789, in *Kingston Before the War of 1812: A Collection of Documents*, ed. Richard Preston (Toronto: University of Toronto Press, 1959), 144. See also Joseph Forsyth to John Porteous, 1 July 1789, Rev. John Stuart to the Bishop of Nova Scotia, 19 July 1789, and Stuart to Rev. William White, 9 Oct. 1789, in *Kingston Before the War*, 145, 146, 151; Edwin C. Guillet, *Early Life in Upper Canada* (Toronto, 1963), 209–11.

14   Patrick C. T. White, ed., *Lord Selkirk's Diary, 1803–1804: A Journal of His Travels in British North America and the Northeastern United States* (Toronto: Champlain Society, 1958), 179; John William Woolsey testimony, in Quebec Executive Council Report, 5 June 1789, enclosed in Lord Dorchester to Lord Sydney, 6 June 1789, MG 11, Colonial Office 42, Vol. 64, PAC; Dorchester to Sydney, 8 Dec. 1788, MG 11, Colonial Office 42, Vol. 63, PAC. For the Hessian fly see Timothy Dwight, *Travels in New England and New York*, 4 vols. (Cambridge, Mass.: Harvard University Press, 1969, reprint of New Haven, 1821), 3: 210–11; Percy W. Bidwell and John I. Falconer, *History of Agriculture in the*

Northern United States, 1620–1860 (Washington, D.C.: The Carnegie Institute of Washington, 1925), 95–96; Louis B. Wright and Marion Tinling, eds., *Quebec to Carolina in 1785–1786: Being the Travel Diary and Observations of Robert Hunter, Jr., a Young Merchant of London* (San Marino, Cal.: The Huntington Library, 1943), 150.

15   "Exports from the Province of Quebec in 1788," Miscellaneous Documents for 1788, MG 11, Colonial Office 42, vol. 66, PAC; Lord Dorchester to Lord Grenville, 30 Sept. 1789, MG 11, Colonial Office 42, vol. 65, PAC; Captain Freeman to Sir Frederick Haldimand, 24 Oct. 1789, MG 21, Haldimand Papers, Reel A-670, PAC.

16   H. H. Lamb, *Climate, History, and the Modern World* (London: Methuen, 1982), 237; Anne Walthall, *Social Protest and Popular Culture in Eighteenth-Century Japan* (Tucson, Az.: University of Arizona Press, 1986), 126–34, 155–56; Conrad Totman, *Early Modern Japan* (Berkeley: University of California, 1993), 238–240; Arij Ouweneel, "Silent Drama in the Milpas: Changes in the Agro-Ecosystem of Anahuac During the 1780s and 1790s," in *Le Nouveau Monde/Mondes Nouveaux: L'Experience Americaine,* ed. Serge Gruzinski and Nathan Wachtel (Paris: Éditions Recherche Sur les Civilisations: Éditions de l'École des hautes études en sciences sociales, 1996), 115–35. I am grateful to my colleague Arnold Bauer for alerting me to Ouweneel's essay.

17   H. H. Lamb, *Climate, History,* 238–39; Emmanuel Le Roy Ladurie, *Times of Feast, Times of Famine: A History of Climate Since the Year 1000,* trans. Barbara Bray (London: Allen & Unwin, 1972), 72–75. For the operation of the wheat market see Joyce O. Appleby, "The Changing Prospect of the Family Farm in the Early National Period," in *Working Papers from the Regional Economic History Research Center* (Wilmington: Hagley-Eleuthera Foundation, 1980), 1–25.

18   Thomas Jefferson to John Jay, 29 Nov. 1788, in *The Papers of Thomas Jefferson,* ed. Julian P. Boyd (Princeton: Princeton University Press, 1958), 14: 304–06; Jefferson, "Grain and Flour Imported from the United States of America into the Ports of France, in the Year 1789, from an Official Statement," in *Papers of Thomas Jefferson,* 19: 232; "Extract of a Letter dated Paris, 29 Nov. 1788, from the Honorable Mr. Jefferson to Mr. Jay," *New-York Journal,* 19 Feb. 1789; *New-Jersey Journal* (Elizabeth Town), 25 Feb. 1789; "London, April 22," *Cumberland Gazette* (Portland, Me.), 10 July 1789; testimony of John William Woolsey, in Quebec Executive Council Report, 5 June 1789, MG 11, Colonial Office 42, vol. 64, PAC.

19   William Cooper to Henry Drinker, 7 May 1789, Henry Drinker Papers, Correspondence Box 1741–1792, Historical Society of Pennsylvania (HSP hereafter), Philadelphia; Cooper, *A Guide in the Wilderness,* 15 (quotation); Moses De Witt, Journal, 1 June 1789, De Witt Family Papers, Box 6, Syracuse University Library Special Collections, Syracuse, NY.

20   Josiah Priest, *Stories of Early Settlers in the Wilderness; Embracing the Life of Mrs.*

Priest, Late of Otsego County, N.Y. (Albany: J. Munsell, 1837), 28; Tax Lists for Old England District (Otsego), Montgomery County, 1787, in New York State Treasurer's Records, Assessment Lists (1722–1788), box 2, folder 62, New York State Archives, Albany; Tax List for Old England District, Montgomery County, 1788, in Gerrit Y. Lansing Papers, box 1, folder 12, New York State Library, Albany; John Tunnecliff to William Cooper, 14 April 1788, William Cooper Papers, Hartwick College Archives; William Cooper to Henry Drinker, 7 May 1789, Henry Drinker Papers, Correspondence Box 1741–1792, HSP. For the postwar surge of frontier settlement see Douglas S. Robertson, ed., *An Englishman in America, 1785, Being the Diary of Joseph Hadfield* (Toronto: Hunter-Rose Co., 1973), 26–27; Alan Taylor, *William Cooper's Town: Power and Persuasion on the Frontier of the Early American Republic* (New York: Alfred A. Knopf, 1995), 90–92.

21 Henry Ruttan, "Reminiscences," in *Loyalist Narratives from Upper Canada*, ed. James J. Talman (Toronto: Champlain Society, 1946), 300.

22 Coventry, *Memoirs*, I: 213; "Windsor," *Vermont Journal* (Windsor), 8 June 1789; "New-York, June 15" *Independent Gazetteer* (Philadelphia), 17 June 1789. See also "Extract of a Letter from Quebec, date May 5," *New-Jersey Journal* (Elizabeth Town), 17 June 1789.

23 *Vermont Gazette* (Bennington), 8 June,1789; "Keene," *New-Hampshire Gazette* (Portsmouth), 11 June 1789; "Windsor," *Vermont Journal* (Windsor), 8 June 1789. For the loss of cattle in Upper Canada see Patrick Campbell, *Travels in the Interior Inhabited Parts of North America in the Years 1791 and 1792*, ed. H. H. Langton (Toronto: Champlain Society, 1937), 155.

24 *Vermont Gazette* (Bennington), 8 June 1789; *Vermont Journal* (Windsor), 29 June 1789; *New-Jersey Journal* (Elizabeth Town), 17 June 1789; "Albany, June 15," *New-Hampshire Gazette* (Portsmouth), 9 July 1789; Ebenezer Dibble to Rev. Samuel Peters, 28 June 1789, Peters Papers, Reel 10958, PANS.

25 *Worcester Spy*, 18 June 1789; *New-Hampshire Gazette* (Portsmouth), 25 June 1789; *Independent Gazetteer* (Philadelphia), 26 June 1789.

26 *New-York Journal*, 25 June 1789; "Bennington," *Vermont Gazette* (Bennington), 6 July 1789; "Bennington, June 29," *Independent Gazetteer*, 27 July 1789; *New-Hampshire Gazette* (Portsmouth), 9 July 1789; *Connecticut Courant* (Hartford), 17 Aug. 1789.

27 "Extract of a Letter from a Gentleman living on Lake Champlain . . . May 9," *New-Hampshire Gazette*, 2 July 1789; Jacob Lindley quoted in Robert Leslie Jones, *History of Agriculture in Ontario, 1613–1880* (Toronto: University of Toronto Press, 1946), 17–18; Guillet, *Early Life in Upper Canada*, 210; Rev. Amos D. Gridley, *History of the Town of Kirkland, New York* (New York: Hurd & Houghton, 1874), 32.

28 Gridley, *History of Kirkland*, 32; Cooper, *Guide in the Wilderness*, 16; *Otsego Herald*, 12 May 1796, 20 July 1815; Guillet, *Early Life in Upper Canada*, 210, 213.

29   Lord Dorchester to Sir John Johnson, 22 June 1789, RG 10, Indian Affairs, Reel C-1224, xv: 363, PAC; Hemenway, *Vermont Historical Gazetteer*, I: 52; Gridley, *History of Kirkland*, 32; Thompson, *Thorold Township*, 27; Cooper, *Guide in the Wilderness*, 16.

30   Hemenway, *Vermont Historical Gazetteer*, I: 52; Guillet, *Early Life in Upper Canada*, 211; Thompson, *Thorold Township*, 28; Preston, "Journey to Harmony," 107–10.

31   Nathaniel Gorham to Oliver Phelps, 15 Aug. 1789, Phelps & Gorham Papers, Box 17, New York State Library (Albany); Captain Freeman to Sir Frederick Haldimand, 24 Oct. 1789, MG 21, Haldimand Papers, Reel A-670, PAC; Preston, "Journey to Harmony," 107–10; William Cooper to Henry Drinker, 21 July 1790 and 20 Sept. 1791, Henry Drinker Papers, Correspondence Box 1741–1792, HSP; *Montreal Gazette*, 8 Sept. 1790; Jones, *History of Agriculture in Ontario*, 25.

32   The settlements in Maine suffered more severely from hunger in 1790 than in 1789. See Alan Taylor, *Liberty Men and Great Proprietors: The Revolutionary Settlement on the Maine Frontier, 1760–1820* (Chapel Hill: University of North Carolina Press, 1990), 70. For the crisis of 1816 see Post, *The Last Great Subsistence Crisis*.

33   Eliakim P. Walton, ed., *Records of the Governor and Council of the State of Vermont*, 8 vols. (Montpelier, VT: State of Vermont,1873–80), 3: 181–82; "An Ordinance," *Vermont Journal* (Windsor), 16 Mar. 1789; "An Ordinance, Chap. IX," *Montreal Gazette*, 27 May 1790; *New-Hampshire Gazette* (Portsmouth), 4 and 8, June 1789; *Independent Gazetteer* (Philadelphia), 16 July 1789; Samuel Huntington, *A Proclamation . . .* (Hartford, Conn.: State of Connecticut, 1789, Evans #45457); Nova Scotia Executive Council Minutes, 18 July 1789, RG 1, reel 15289, vol. 190, PANS.

34   Gerald S. Graham, *British Policy and Canada, 1774–1791: A Study in Eighteenth-Century Trade Policy* (Westport, Conn.: Greenwood Press, 1974, reprint of London, 1930), 63–65, 70–71; "Quebec, January 29," *Montreal Gazette*, 5 Feb. 1789; "Proclamation," *Montreal Gazette*, 9 April 1789; *Royal Gazette* (Halifax), 26 May 1789; "Secretary's Office—Quebec, 6th June 1789," *Montreal Gazette*, 18 June 1789; Captain Joseph Bunbury to Captain Le Maistre, 30 June 1789, in *Kingston Before the War of 1812*, 144–45. For lax enforcement on Lake Ontario see also John Richardson to John Porteous, 14 June 1789, "John Richardson Letters," 24.

35   "Albany, July 20," *New-Jersey Journal* (Elizabeth Town), 29 July 1789; "Quebec, August 6," *New-York Journal*, 27 Aug. 1789; Thomas Aston Coffin to Mrs. Coffin, 28 July 1789, Coffin Papers, vol. 3, Massachusetts Historical Society. Apparently the Quebec customs house records no longer survive for the period 1786–1792. See Gilles Paquet and Jean-Pierre Wallot, "International Circumstances of Lower Canada, 1786–1810: Prolegomenon," *Canadian Historical Review* 53 (1972): 384.

36   Good Peter's speech, 3 June, and the Oneida letter to the commissioners, 30 June 1789, in *Proceedings of the Commissioners*, 2: 317, 328. For New York's land and Indian

policies see Barbara Graymont, *The Iroquois in the American Revolution* (Syracuse, NY: Syracuse University Press, 1972), 259–91; Anthony F. C. Wallace, *The Death and Rebirth of the Seneca* (New York: Alfred A. Knopf, 1970), 150–83; Alfred F. Young, *The Democratic Republicans of New York: The Origins, 1763–1797* (Chapel Hill: University of North Carolina Press, 1967), 232–43, 267–70.

37   New York (State), *Journal of the Assembly . . . Thirteenth Session* (New York, 1790: State of New York, Evans #22009), 4 (Clinton speech), 19–20 (legislation); Gov. Clinton to the Oneida Indians, 14 July 1789, in *Proceedings of the Commissioners*, 2: 333.

38   New York (State), *Journal of the Assembly . . . Thirteenth Session*, 19–20; Gov. Clinton to the Oneida Indians, 14 July 1789, and Meeting of the Commissioners, 15 July 1789, in *Proceedings of the Commissioners*, 2: 333. At the 1789 price in Albany of six shillings per bushel, £600 would have procured two thousand bushels of corn. For the price of corn in 1789, see [William Cooper], "Extract of a Letter from Cooper's Town (Otsego Lake), dated 7 May 1789," *New-York Journal*, 2 July 1789. For thirty bushels a year as the subsistence level for a family of five see Bettye Hobbs Pruitt, "Self-Sufficiency and the Agricultural Economy of Eighteenth-Century Massachusetts," *William and Mary Quarterly*, 3d. ser., vol. 41 (summer 1984): 344–46.

39   Certificate by the Sachems and Councillors of the Muhheaconnuk Nation, 1 July 1989, Ayer Manuscript #836, Newberry Library (Chicago). I am grateful to Karim Tiro for alerting me to this document. Henry C. Rogers, *History of the Town of Paris and the Valley of the Sauquoit* (Utica, N.Y.: Utica Printing Co., 1881), 21.

40   Lt. Col. Peter Hunter to James Farquharson, 12 Feb. 1789, Wolford Simcoe Transcripts, MG 23 H I 1, Series 3, vol. 1, 260, PAC; John Richardson to John Porteous, 14 June 1789, in "Richardson Letters," 24; John Smith et al. petition, in *The Correspondence of Lieut. Governor John Graves Simcoe, with Allied Documents Relating to His Administration of the Government of Upper Canada*, ed. E. A. Cruikshank, 5 vols. (Toronto: Ontario Historical Society, 1923–31), 4: 359; W. H. Siebert, "The Loyalists and the Six Nation Indians in the Niagara Peninsular," Royal Society of Canada, *Transactions*, 3d. ser., vol. 9 (1915–16), 102.

41   Burt, *Old Province of Quebec*, 381; Thompson, *Thorold Township*, 28–29; *Quebec Herald*, 5 Oct. 1789.

42   Burt, *Old Province of Quebec*, 381; Thompson, *Thorold Township*, 28–29; *Quebec Herald*, 5 Oct. 1789; "Memorial and Petition," *Montreal Gazette*, 19 Nov. 1789; Adam Mabane to Sir Frederick Haldimand, MG 21, Haldimand Papers, Reel A-670, PAC. For the monthly assize of bread see *Montreal Gazette*, 9 July, 4 Aug., 7 Sept., 8 Oct., 12 Nov., 10 Dec. 1789; 7 Jan., 4 Feb., 4 Mar., 8 Apr., 6 May, 10 June 1790.

43   Jones, *History of Agriculture in Ontario*, 17–24; Graham, *British Policy and Canada*, 56–71; Harlow, *Founding of the Second British Empire*, II: 609–15; John E.

Crowley, *The Privileges of Independence* (Baltimore: Johns Hopkins University Press, 1993), 73–74.

44   Lord Grenville to Lord Dorchester, 20 Oct. 1789, MG 11, Colonial Office 42, vol. 65, PAC.

45   Prince Edward quoted in Guillet, *Early Life in Upper Canada*, 213.

46   This paragraph is indebted to helpful comments by Carla Hesse on an earlier version of this essay delivered as a paper in January 1998 at the annual meeting of the Organization of American Historians.

47   For the dialectical creation of meaningful borders see Peter Sahlins, *Boundaries: The Making of France and Spain in the Pyrenees* (Berkeley: University of California Press, 1989), 267–78.

48   For the Canadian tradition see Burt, *Old Province of Quebec*, 377–81; Guillet, *Early Life in Upper Canada*, 209–13; Jones, *History of Agriculture in Ontario*, 17. For American historians who minimize the existence of hunger in eighteenth-century America, see Jack P. Greene, *Pursuits of Happiness: The Social Development of Early Modern British Colonies and the Formation of American Culture* (Chapel Hill: University of North Carolina Press, 1988), 72–74, 91–92, 136–37; Jackson Turner Main, *Society and Economy in Colonial Connecticut* (Princeton: Princeton University Press, 1985), 149–51, 377–78; G. B. Warden, "Inequality and Instability in Eighteenth-Century Boston: A Reappraisal," *Journal of Interdisciplinary History*, 6 (1975–1976): 585–620; Gordon S. Wood, *The Radicalism of the American Revolution* (New York: Alfred A. Knopf, 1992), 122. Wood insists, "Although by the mid-eighteenth century the numbers of poor were increasing in the urban ports of Boston, New York, and Philadelphia, there was not, Americans realized, 'the least danger of starving amongst us.'"

Afterword

Carla Hesse

*E*arthquakes along the southeastern tip of Sicily in 1693 and the Pacific coast of South America in 1746, 1783, and 1797; famines in Bengal in 1770 and along the eastern borderlands between America and Canada in 1789; plagues in London in 1665 and Marseilles in 1720—the conjunction of these disasters, spanning three continents and more than a century, would not have seemed at all odd to the eighteenth-century mind. All three, in fact, would have appeared to emanate from the same source, bad air: too hot, too wet, too dry, too cold, or coming from the wrong direction. For the Europeans, bad air, or miasma, precipitated a radical imbalance between inner and outer states of being in humans and in other life forms, from animals to seeds of grain. It caused rotting, putrefaction, shriveling, decay, desiccation, and morbidity. In Quito in 1797, manure and kindling were burnt following the earthquake "to rid the air of corrupting miasma" in the hope of preventing plague.

The article on the plague in the great *Encyclopédie* of Diderot and d'Alembert (1750) linked all of these forms of disaster—earthquake, famine, disease, and especially plague—to one single cause, atmospheric imbalance. Righting matters, in the secular scientific sense, meant working to restore the proper ecological balance between inner and outer states of things. And this gave eighteenth-century Europeans plenty to do! Enlightened public administrators throughout the world busied themselves cleaning up putrid cesspools, creating new cemeteries, draining marshes, and improving air circulation in cities by widening roads and constructing public squares. Through public planning and an intensive pedagogy of public hygiene, diet, and even food distribution, city, state, and imperial officials fought a mighty battle around the globe to restore atmospheric balance. One of the stories this collection tells has to do with the rise of a new group of authorities, the agents of the modern European administrative state, who became, during the eighteenth century, a ubiquitous global presence—except perhaps in the wilds of republican North America, where an ethos of rugged individualism abandoned people to their own fates.

The essays gathered in this volume offer new reasons and new methods for studying natural disasters as historical subjects and, specifically, for focusing on the disasters of the eighteenth century. There are significant implications in the direction they are taking for contemporary historical writing as a whole. The disasters of the eighteenth century—and especially the Lisbon earthquake of 1755, which so shook Voltaire—have been of interest principally to historians of Enlightenment epistemology. "Natural" disasters struck at the very foundations of the new optimistic faith in the lawful regularity of nature. The unpredictability of natural cataclysms drove many post-Newtonian philosophers away from their comforting belief in mechanistic deism and toward the darker Humean skepticism of the later eighteenth century, with its probabilistic mentality of calculated risk. We see little of these epistemological stakes at play in this volume.

Similarly, we read little here about the physical effects or causes of the disasters examined. There is no attention to the demographic questions that played so central a role in the account of the rise of modernity given by the last generation of social historians of the eighteenth century—the advent of a more hospitable global climate (a global warming perhaps due to the disappearance of sunspots), which may explain the extraordinary shift in the rate of global population growth, or the "microbic unification" of the world through the intensification of global travel and mass migrations. We have no mention of the war between black and brown rats, a struggle that perhaps accounts for the remission of the plague on the European continent. These essays are not concerned with the natural causes or consequences of disasters (though they do not deny that such consequences ensued) but rather with the changes in perceptions that disasters precipitated.

Natural disasters produce dramatic ruptures in social consciousness. Daniel Defoe, like Thucydides before him, was fascinated by the way that disasters strip human beings of their social trappings and reveal their true moral nature. And disasters require a remaking of the social world in their wake. In the words of Charles Walker, they are "themselves significant sources of change." The rebuilding of the cities of southeastern Sicily in the aftermath of the earthquake of 1693 offers an example of social disorganization and reorganization—in which urban planners struggled against traditional patterns of social segregation and interaction. The response to the 1720 plague in Marseilles pitted proud city fathers against the mighty power of royal authority. It led on the one side to a renewal of Machiavellian civic humanism (a tragic view of a virtuous city-state struck by *Fortuna*), and on the other to a massive show of the military power to quarantine. In Lima, a mestizo architectural style emerged from the rubble, blending the most advanced European theories of fortification with indigenous Amerindian building materials and urban design. The famine in Bengal precipitated nothing less than a revolution in British perceptions of India. Once touted as a lush and beneficent garden of Eden, the brutal extremity of the 1770 famine led to a loss of innocence in the colonial gaze. India became, in the eyes of British travelers, a backward world; no longer a natural utopia, it now seemed a wild, primitive, and unpredictable land in need of European governance and civilization. In North America too, the differing responses to famine on the two sides of the political border resulted in the production of new social and moral identities: the Canadian social welfare state and American laissez-faire individualism. All of the essays in this volume offer examples of responses of public authorities to events that put the social order into grave jeopardy. And each shows how these disasters created occasions for the reinvention of public order.

Disaster was especially favorable to those who stood to profit from it: tradesmen and men of commerce. Eighteenth-century disasters created auspicious circumstances for the convergence of the commercial interests of the increasingly powerful merchant classes with the objectives of traditional political elites. We see this in the stories Defoe tells of the merchants profiting from disasters that befell London. We see it in the architectural strategies adopted in the rebuilding of Lima after the earthquake of 1746. We see it in the revival of civic humanism among the merchants of Marseilles during the plague of 1720. It is there, too, in the accusations of profiteering in the Bengali famine, when British traders exploited rather than alleviated suffering. And we see it in the story of the grain trading practices of the Americans and Canadians in the famine of 1789. Every disaster brought possibilities for change in its wake.

Global commerce found opportunities to remake the world in its image wherever disaster struck. In these essays we discover a new cultural history of catastrophe, one that does not limit itself to effects of unpredictability on the philosophical project of the Enlightenment. These histories extend their compass beyond the realm of formal philosophy in order to explore the reshaping of collective meanings and of social norms.

It is no small contribution of this volume that it offers a global perspective on eighteenth-century disaster. So much of contemporary historical writing (about all parts of the globe) still remains trapped in the nationalist paradigms we have inherited from the struggles and conflicts of the nineteenth century. But the eighteenth century was far less preoccupied with the shoring up of cultural and political differences. In both its mental outlook and its patterns of livelihood, the eighteenth century was in many respects the first global century. It was eighteenth-century Europe that inaugurated the idea of the universality of natural man—born free and equal and the bearer of fundamental rights, regardless of race, religion, or nationality. The eighteenth century was also a global century in the literal sense that commerce and economic life took on truly global dimensions. As Daniel Defoe recognized, the same moment that saw the first awakenings of modern national identities also witnessed the emergence of a new class of global citizens. "The tradesman," Defoe wrote, "can live in any part of the world."

Disasters, too, were truly global events, with consequences far beyond the immediate communities of the afflicted. Accounts of the Lima disaster in 1746 were published in at least a half dozen countries and as many languages. The Lisbon earthquake, through the writings of Voltaire and of many lesser talents, took on the dimensions of a world historical event. Harvest failure in northern Europe could send North Americans in search of food. And we discover in this book that the Bengal famine shook world trade and redrew the European cultural map of the world. It marked a turning point in European consciousness about other societies. The response of the Spanish imperial authorities to the series of disastrous earthquakes in South America became an occasion for the British to criticize what they perceived to be the backwardness of their Catholic competitors in the New World. And the urban planning of Sicilian architects was studied throughout the European and Europeanized world.

Traditionally, disasters have entered into global history as episodes used to illustrate the triumphal response of enlightened modernizing Europeans, armed with technical know-how that ultimately trumped the superstitions of religious authorities within Europe and around the world. The global victory of technology over superstition, we learn in these essays, was less clear-cut than earlier historians have suggested. First of all, the line between religion and science was more porous than later crusaders of secularization have suggested. Daniel Defoe could comfortably hold a belief in disasters as signs of particular Providences—that is, messages from God to the wicked—and at the same time believe that men could grasp the secondary causes of natural cataclysms and respond to them rationally in order to alleviate physical as well as spiritual suffering. Disasters, we discover, were as likely to reinforce superstitions as to create occasions for dispelling them. Triumph over the hunger of North America in 1789 could be an indication not only of resourcefulness but also of godly election. The earthquakes in Peru and Ecuador were occasions for God to work miracles—such as the fantastic survivals—as well as opportunities for the advance of secular public works.

Enlightened public administrators may have been an active presence wherever catastrophe struck upon the globe, but there is also considerable evidence of social resistance to technical progress. In Sicily urban planners moved the sites of cities, but citizens refused to move; or they moved, but not to where they were told. And they resisted newer and safer building practices, preferring narrow, winding streets to the rationalizing grid of public hygiene. Aristocrats in Lima insisted on maintaining the social markers of their higher status: the second-story balcony. In Marseilles the plague struck in the first place because local merchants evaded the royal regulations about ship quarantine in the port. And once the plague struck, it took 20,000 royal troops to ensure that the quarantine of the region was respected. Local elites saw in these progressive measures nothing less than the hand of royal tyranny, intent upon robbing the province and the city of its traditional liberties. Histories of the Marseilles plague became testimonies of civic resistance to despotic force. Thus the stories these essays tell is less one of the triumph of technology than of the socialization of loss and the remaking of both social and moral identity.

On the ethics of loss and survivorship, Defoe was profound. George Starr's chapter shows us how the translation of disaster into fiction permitted Defoe to create a narrative observer whose reactions to the social consequences of disaster offer the reader an ethical model of survivorship. Through his lens the commercial exploitation of loss is exposed as a moral evil; the story of the disaster heals; through the telling the suffering becomes survivable. Putting particular disasters into a global context thus makes it possible for this book to call into question colonialist polarities between a commercialized Europe and a survivalist Asia, between a prosperous North America and a famine-ridden Bengal, between the moral agency of secular modernity and the superstitions of non-Europeans.

Apart from intellectual historians interested narrowly in the history of skepticism, disaster had been written out of the history of the eighteenth century and especially out of the history of emergent Western democracies. Among American historians the "hungry year," 1789, had been all but forgotten in the rush to celebrate America as the land of opportunity and plenty. The moral negligence of the British in Bengal disappeared as the suffering of the Bengalis was naturalized into an eternal feature of the landscape. The recovery of these stories, even now, in this much less innocent era, is shocking and powerful. To absorb fully the lessons that these histories teach us requires not simply an expansion but a remaking of our own sense of our trajectory in time. Having read the chapters in this volume, we can only conclude that Europeans have both wrought disaster and suffered its consequences. The triumph of secular progress—be it through public planning or commercial expansion—appears at once more tenuous and more morally complex than older narratives have suggested. This book rightfully restores the darker side of human experience to its central place in the history of that "happiest of centuries." In so doing, it effects a shift in the deeper script of the rise of modernity; the comforting teleology of Western progress is here rewritten as a story of shared global survivorship and of the persistent moral dilemmas of a disenchanted liberal faith.

Contributors

David Arnold is Professor of South Asian History at the School of Oriental and African Studies, University of London. His published work includes *Famine: Social Crisis and Historical Change* (Oxford: Blackwell, 1988), *Colonizing the Body: State Medicine and Epidemic Disease in Nineteenth-Century India* (Berkeley and Los Angeles: University of California Press, 1993), and *The Problem of Nature: Environment, Culture and European Expansion* (Oxford: Blackwell, 1996). He is currently working on a study of science, technology, and medicine in colonial India.

Daniel Gordon is Associate Professor of History at the University of Massachusetts at Amherst. He has written *Citizens Without Sovereignty* (Princeton: Princeton University Press, 1994) and is the editor and translator of the Bedford St. Martin's edition of Voltaire's *Candide* (1999).

Carla Hesse is Professor of European History at the University of California at Berkeley. Her books include *Publishing and Cultural Politics in Revolutionary Paris (1789–1810)* (Berkeley and Los Angeles: University of California Press, 1991), and, with R. Howard Bloch, *Future Libraries* (Berkeley and Los Angeles: University of California Press, 1994). She is also cochair of the editorial board of *Representations*, a journal of cultural studies.

Alessa Johns is Assistant Professor of English at the University of California at Davis. Her interest in eighteenth-century cultural studies led her to organize a conference entitled *Disaster in the Eighteenth Century*, out of which this volume emerged. She has published articles on British women writers and, having researched German female authors in Munich thanks to a Fulbright grant, is currently completing a book, *Women's Utopianism in Europe, 1690–1800*.

G. A. Starr has taught English at The University of California at Berkeley since 1962; his publications include two books on Defoe, an edition of *Moll Flanders*, critical studies of several eighteenth-century literary topics, and an essay on "Art and Architecture in the Hungarian Reformed Church," appearing in a new volume, *Calvinism and the Visual Arts*.

Alan Taylor teaches the history of early America and the American West at the University of California at Davis. He is the author of *Liberty Men and Great Proprietors: The Revolutionary Settlement on the Main Frontier, 1760–1820* (Chapel Hill: University of North Carolina Press, 1990) and *William Cooper's Town: Power and Persuasion on the Frontier of the Early American Republic* (New York: Knopf, 1995), which was awarded the New York State Historical Association Manuscript Award, the Bancroft Prize, and the Pulitzer Prize in United States History.

Stephen Tobriner is a Professor of Architectural History in the Department of Architecture at the University of California at Berkeley. He is the author of *The Genesis of Noto, an Eighteenth-Century Sicilian City* as well as numerous articles on seventeenth- and eighteenth-century architecture and urbanism, the history of earthquakes, and seismically resistant architecture.

Charles F. Walker is the author of *Smoldering Ashes: Cuzco and the Creation of Republican Peru, 1780–1840* (Durham: Duke University Press, 1999). He has edited volumes in Spanish on intellectual history and social movements in the Andes during the eighteenth century and, with Carlos Aguirre, on social crime. An Assistant Professor of History at the University of California at Davis, he is currently writing a history of the 1746 earthquake in Lima.

Index

A Journal of the Plague Year (Defoe), 32, 35, 37–40, 45–47
Abbé Raynal, 89–90, 95–96; on East Indian Company, 90
Adorno, Theodor W., xv
agriculture, 153–55, 159, 163–64
Albany, 150, 157
Ambato (Ecuador), 129
American Revolution, 147, 169
Amil of Bishnupur, 94
Anaxagoras, xvi
Anaximander, xvi
Anaximenes, xvi
Andes, 113–14, 115, 135; and revolt, 130
antiseismic architecture, 50–73, 124; artificial caves in, 60; inventions in, 64–67, 69, 72, 124; and Renaissance architects, 50; Roman authors on, 53
Arequipa (Peru), 136; earthquakes in, xiv; (1783) 114, 115, 127–29, 135, 183
Aristotle, xvi, 16, 52–53, 66–67; *Meterologica*, 50
arson, 102
Artaud, Antonin, 14–15
Asiatic Society of Bengal, 81, 106 n.1
Athenian Mercury (Dunton), 37
avalanches, xii, 113–14
Avola, 49, 56, 58–59; relocation of, 55
Avola Vecchia, 55, 71

bad air. *See* miasma
Bankipur, 92
baraccata, 65–67, 69, 72
basanta-roga. *See* smallpox
Becher, Richard, 85, 86, 94, 98–99, 100
Belsunce, Bishop, 14
Bengal (India), 188; famine in (1770), xi, xii, xiii, xv, xviii, 81–111, 183, 185, 186, 187; (1784) 102; (1943) 87; perceived wealth of, 89–91; and religion, 94–95; colonial measures in, 92–93; European accounts of, 82–83, 86–87, 89–92, 94–95, 97–98, 185
Bernier, François, 90
Berroeta, Don Pedro, 126

Bertrand, Jean-Baptiste, 18–20, 22
Bihar (India): drought in, 84–85, 101; famine in, 86, 94, 106; flood in (1768), 83
Black Plague (1348), xxiv n.14
Blackwood, John, 152
Blanchot, Maurice, 3
boarders, 117, 147–48, 169–72
Bourbons, 51, 65, 67, 72, 127–28, 135; and taxation, 131–35; resistance to, 128, 130–31, *See also* imperialism
British Empire. *See* imperialism, British
British Government, 96–97; *see also* imperialism, British
British Parliament, 100
Brown, Captain Daniel, 151
bubonic plague, 4, 6; in London (1665), 32, 34
Bulwer-Lytton, 44
Bunbury, Captain Joseph, 153
Burdwan fever. *See* malaria
Bureau of Indian Affairs, British, 82; in New York, 150

Cairns, Alexander, 152
Calabria (Italy), xi, 49, 51, 56; earthquake (1783), 52, 57, 60, 65–73
Calcutta, 84; and famine (1770), 83–85, 90, 91, 94, 98, 102; and drought (1770), 94
Callao Port, 115, 116, 122; tsunami of, 118–20
Campbell, Patrick, 164
Canada, 147–48, 153–54, 159, 161, 164–66, 168–72; *see also* Quebec
Canandaigua, 150
cancer: as modern plague, 3
Candide (Voltaire), 24, 63, 184, 187
Canguilhem, Georges, 16
cannibalism, 40, 45, 84
Catania, 49, 55, 56, 58, 63, 71, 72
catastrophe. *See* disasters
Chattopadhyay, Bankim Chandra, 87
Chaudhuri, Nani Gopal, 86
Chile, 113
Chive, Lord, 101
cholera, 92, 103–4, 105